Antonin Artaud

Titles in the series *Critical Lives* present the work of leading cultural figures of the modern period. Each book explores the life of the artist, writer, philosopher or architect in question and relates it to their major works.

In the same series

Antonin Artaud

David A. Shafer

REAKTION BOOKS

For Selma Selmanagić

Published by Reaktion Books Ltd
Unit 32, Waterside
44–48 Wharf Road
London N1 7UX, UK
www.reaktionbooks.co.uk

First published 2016
Copyright © David A. Shafer 2016

Printed and bound in Great Britain by
Bell & Bain, Glasgow

A catalogue record for this book is available from the British Library

ISBN 978 1 78023 570 7

Contents

Antonin Artaud photographed in 1920, in the
consulting room of his psychiatrist Dr Toulouse.

Introduction

In an interview from 1996, the French cultural theorist Jean Baudrillard averred, 'Everyone should have a singular, personal relation to Artaud. With him, we are always on a very inhuman level. He has become an impersonal being.'[1] What Baudrillard appeared to be saying is that the departure of the corporeal Artaud has led to a transubstantiated reversal; in the process, Artaud has achieved almost mythological status, a conclusion echoed by others, including those closest to Artaud. In April 2012 Artaud's nephew, Serge Malausséna, his last living relative, alluded in conversation with me to the existence of two Artauds: the one who lived and the one of our ideas. In other words, Artaud has become something of a palimpsest upon which we inscribe what we want to find in him, and maybe even find in ourselves.

In some respects, Artaud facilitated this in a couple of ways. First, his choice of literary expression was compelling, and at the same time it was head-spinningly confusing. Much of what he wrote was in the service of transcending the boundaries of conventional communication: a cocktail of obtuse symbolism, intentional obfuscation, sexual prudery and weird scatological analogies, followed by references to 'curses and spells' as a chaser – and yet, this strange admixture was so well written. Second, in a paper he wrote to accompany an exhibition he organized on the work of the Mexican Surrealist María Izquierdo, Artaud noted that, as they travel, objects exchange their properties and metamorphose.[2] Why would it not be the same for him that his peregrinations, whether within this dimension or – after his death – outside of it, have caused a corresponding alteration of his persona?

It is pretty clear that Baudrillard had no intention of wiping away the occluding mud Artaud seemingly placed intentionally on the window into his thoughts, and I must concur that to study Artaud means respecting the impenetrability of his seemingly Kevlar-shrouded head; but all the same, the more I read, the more I began to find a logic to his thoughts. For purposes of literary clarity, the pre-asylum Artaud is a snap in comparison to the guy who, during nearly a decade of confinement in French insane asylums, had existed alone, in his head. Whether or not he was insane when first institutionalized in 1937, his years in the precariousness of wartime French asylums did no favours to his mental health. The electroconvulsive therapy administered to him in Rodez during the last years of his confinement might have rewired him and prepared his re-entrance into society; but to Artaud this was yet another example of the individual's vulnerability to *envoûtements* (spells). While it is tempting to put these references to spells down to his penchant for spiritualism, given the impact of hegemonic forces on him, how else could Artaud make sense of it all?

From start to finish, there is constancy to Artaud's writings and ideas; they scream (sometimes literally) alienation and rebellion: rebellion against the stultifying bourgeois values of his youth; the privileging of Western cultural norms, including reason and rationality; and rebellion against the authorities; the power of wealth; and the subversion of nature. Stripped of their bizarre, if not inaccessible, symbolism and verbiage, Artaud's ideas are consonant with the ideals of the French revolutionary tradition, challenging domination in general, and bourgeois domination in particular; but whereas nineteenth-century French revolutionaries situated their challenge in the social-political realm, Artaud's revolution was over the cultural space of meanings, understandings, representations and signs.

Though surrounded by friends and admirers, Artaud's journey through life was a lonely one in which comfort was fleeting and usually opiate-based. The exposed emotion in his writings, the brutalized genius within him, the rawness with which he verbally articulated his prose, the torment of his sufferings and the ethereal mien of Artaud struck all those who encountered him; to them,

Artaud at the private nursing home in Ivry-sur-Seine, 1947.

he was the genuine article – performative only when acting on the stage or on screen. Artaud saw his life as a prolonged and confused ontological crisis, a violent contest which he could never win between himself and hegemonic forces – forces filled with a coterie he needed, but who, as products of a manufactured existence, could not be fully trusted. To me, Artaud is both the mythic figure whose often-beautiful prose inspires our imagination while his life story draws our curiosity, and the thoughtful writer penetratingly examining and exposing a world, or theatre, of cruelty.

Antonin Artaud, *c.* 1918.

1
Youth

At the end of 1918, nearly one-third of the generation of French-men born between 1880 and 1900 were casualties of a war of unprecedented carnage and destruction, largely fought on French soil. At the First World War's declaration in 1914, many of that generation welcomed it: some as *revanche* (revenge) for the military debacle of 1870; some out of a Nietzschean, testosterone-fortified association of strength, vitality and youth; some in the belief that the war would restore a decayed society. The war, however, was simply the culmination of a series of technological, political and cultural convulsions that influenced this generation.

Though referring to lost spiritual values when, in 1913, Charles Péguy lamented a world that had changed more over the previous three decades than in the nearly two millennia since Christ, he could equally have been alluding to the immediacy and accelerated pace of life made possible by the telephone, telegraph, cinema, automobile, airplane and electricity.[1] Whatever its benefits, the new technology fostered uncertainty – for some an existential crisis, for others a sense of exhilaration over a future that would be decidedly different from the past or the present. Above all, technological change represented a destabilization of the safety and security that anchored the bourgeois world.

Technology aside, nationalist stirrings in, for example, the Balkans portended a reconfigured, conflict-ridden Europe. Political movements presented the prospects of a tectonic structural shift in Europe. Socialism provided the working class with an alternative identity to nationalism. Feminism awakened women to the inequities of a patriarchal society. In France, a tumultuous century of conflict between republicanism and authoritarianism reached its climax with the Dreyfus Affair. Though rooted in the period's rampant anti-Semitism, the injustice meted out to Captain Alfred Dreyfus was an indictment of the monarchic-militaristic-ecclesiastical tradition of unconditional obedience; but for others, the injustice was less important than the nation sliding into modernism and disorder.

Anarchism – a cultural-apolitical-political movement – challenged the state's very existence, condemning the authority that is its *sine qua non* as an inhibition of, if not outright assault on, fundamental natural rights.[2] Over the course of 1893 and 1894, direct action by anarchists literally exploded onto the Parisian scene as anarchist bombs detonated at the French Chamber of Deputies, La Madeleine, popular restaurants and magistrates' homes.[3]

Political and cultural anarchism crystalized when the Théâtre de l'oeuvre, under the direction of Aurélian-Marie Lugné-Poe, staged Alfred Jarry's *Ubu Roi* on 9–10 December 1896 at the Nouveau-théâtre (now the Théâtre de Paris, rue Blanche). *Ubu Roi*'s main character, Père Ubu, pursues power avariciously, gratuitously, cruelly and rapaciously; his objectives and methods straddle wanton brutality and infantile outlandishness, revealing authority as inherently destructive and tyrannical. *Ubu Roi*'s themes were not the most shocking aspects of the production. Freely casting actors as marionettes and employing slapstick – if not scatological – humour and idiosyncratic staging, Jarry's production disorientated the audience's preconceived ideas about theatre and the audience's response to the phenomena on the stage. Every aspect was designed to shock; even the disruptive behaviour of Jarry's drinking pals in the audience was calculated either to attract attention to the play or, by transferring the theatrical event from the stage to the seats, to subvert the theatre experience.[4]

Ubu Roi was a veritable call to war against 'the langour of bourgeois complacency' and the principles upon which it rested – reason, morality, rationality, reality and materiality; out of the ashes of that war, a new age might arise, phoenix-like, to regenerate a corrupt and decadent society.[5] However, the cultural, social and political renewal anticipated by the generation that went to war did not ensue at the war's conclusion; instead, that generation wandered between two worlds, both built on foundations of illusion and disillusion.

The staging of *Ubu Roi* nearly coincided with Antonin Artaud's listed date of birth, 4 September 1896. While there is no dispute – from either the standpoint of biological processes or legal documents – that this was the date he entered this dimension, less than two years before his death, Artaud wrote:

> The civil status of the man I am, Antonin Artaud, problematically bears 4 September 1896 at eight o'clock in the morning as his date of birth. And, as place of my entry in this life Marseille, Bouches-du-Rhône, France, 4 rue du Jardin des Plantes, on the fourth floor. However, I object to all this, I needed more time, I mean tangible, real, verified, actual, authentic time to become the edgy and irrepressible asshole that I am.[6]

Birth and rebirth were central to Artaud's struggle to locate his identity. Prior to his internment at the asylum in Rodez (1943–6), Artaud wrote little, if anything, about his childhood. However, in Rodez, Artaud's most metaphysical musings on existence germinated out of *a posteriori* conflations of the real and the imaginary. Pregnant with anecdotal reconstructions of his formative years, Artaud's esoteric writings during this period are less revelatory of his childhood experiences and more a window into how he processed what remained embedded in the recesses of his memory; something as seemingly axiomatic as his birth date became yet another self-referential contest over his autonomy, a 'being and nothingness' crisis where the objective was transcendence over facticity.

Incessantly struggling for unmediated control over his entire being, Artaud's emergence from the womb was simply a date affixed by the civil authority, a further extension of the control it exercised in arbitrarily defining him. Artaud devoted endless pages to challenging the determinants of identity, thought and self, and the cultural norms that serve as monolithic points of reference.

The bulk of Artaud's ideas – and their almost seamless vacillation between incoherence and lucidity – developed largely during the second half of his life; but it could be argued that those ideas had been in gestation from his earliest years and experiences. As he bifurcated his corporeal and ethereal selves, Artaud's Rodez writings lack coherence and inform us more on his ideas on the temporality and superficiality of tangible existence.

> A soul is not disposed in a body but the soul must give
> rise to the body just as the body gives rise to the soul after
> having lived within me for awhile, not in the state of life,
> but in my eternal state – neither waking nor sleeping –
> that's to say having had to learn to live in my body.[7]

A letter Artaud wrote just four days after learning that he was to be released from Rodez, as he was entering one of his more lucid stages, extended his penchant for attaching mythic and epic proportions to his origins, claiming

> I don't come from this world, that I am not like the other men
> born of a father and a mother, that I remember the infinite
> sequence of my lives before my so-called birth in Marseille on
> 4 September 1896, at 4 rue du Jardin des Plantes, and that the
> other place from where I come is not the sky, but like the hell of
> the land in perpetuity. Five thousand years ago, I was in China
> with a cane history attributes to Lao-Tseu, but 2,000 years ago,
> I was in Judea . . .[8]

Artaud's family roots left an indelible and lasting imprint on both his identity and ideas. On his father's side Artaud's family hailed from Marseille, the chief French trading port on the Mediterranean, while his maternal roots lay among the Greek population in the cosmopolitan Aegean port of Smyrna (now Izmir, Turkey) in the Ottoman Empire, a trading crossroads and meeting spot for different ethnic groups, primarily Greeks and Turks, with a minority of Jewish, Armenian and Western European communities.

According to a French observer:

> by virtue of its geographic position, by the natural richness of its soil, by its dreamlike climate, by the enchanting perspective of its roads and by the interminable and spacious promenade of its quais – incomparable to the world – Smyrna, port of fertile Asia Minor, brings together all the combined and charming aspects of Marseille and the Côte d'Azur.[9]

As a young boy, Artaud and his sister, Marie-Ange, regularly accompanied their maternal grandmother Mariette (known as Neneka) to her native Smyrna; until 1911 Artaud passed holidays, learned modern Greek and soaked in the city's eclectic mix of Eastern and Western cultures. However, the Smyrna of Artaud's youth barely survived his adulthood. By 1922 Smyrna had been denuded of its Greek population, as first Ottoman and then Republican Turkish authorities directly and tacitly 'ethnically cleansed' the city.

Mariette Nalpas (Neneka), the maternal grandmother of Antonin, shown here with her son John.

Whether or not he directly acknowledged it, the Mediterranean exercised a powerful influence on Artaud. Artaud's pursuit of non-Western cultural references, the impact of Greek theatre on his performance theories and his quest for a mystical spiritual experience bore the indelible prints of his family roots and exposure to the exotic mix of cultures and traditions between Marseille and Smyrna. Artaud's use of language was also marked by these seminal experiences. The Greek he learned as a youth reverberates in the consonant-heavy glossolalia that featured prominently in his writings from Rodez. Furthermore, his ironic or self-deprecating adoption of the moniker 'le Mômo' during the last years of his life is commonly seen as a riff on *momo*, the Marseillaise term for 'idiot' or 'simpleton'. However, Artaud's addition of the circumflex also refers to the Greek *mômos* (ridicule), a derivative of Momus, the god of mockery and witticisms.[10]

The Artaud family tree was a nest of endogamous relations. Though separated before either was ten years old, his paternal and maternal grandmothers were sisters; the maternal grandmother, Mariette, remained with her family in Smyrna, Turkey, while his paternal grandmother, Catherine, accompanied an uncle to Marseille, France. Two of Mariette's children married two of Catherine's children, including Artaud's parents, Euphrasie Nalpas and Antoine-Roi Artaud, thus producing two sets of intermarried first cousins. Whether employing incest as a trope in his adaptation of *Les Cenci*, in his translation of Matthew Gregory Lewis's *Le Moine* (The Monk) or in his writings from Rodez, Artaud's fragile physical and mental states suggest unresolved conflict and irreconcilable thoughts on the relationships in the Nalpas–Artaud clan.

After giving birth to Antonin, Euphrasie carried eight more children to term, but only two – Marie-Ange and Fernand – survived to adulthood, the deaths possibly the result of a congenital condition; if so, this might offer an explanation for Artaud's various ailments.[11] At the age of five, Artaud was diagnosed with meningitis. However, given the frequency of such misdiagnoses, coupled with the absence of a treatment (and consequent near-minimal survival rate) and the symptoms he had, it's unlikely that Artaud actually contracted it. Nevertheless, to cure his son's affliction, and probably

Antonin, aged 2 years, in 1898.

Antonin, aged 5 years, with his sister Marie-Ange.

to assuage Euphrasie's fear of losing another child, Antoine-Roi procured a static electricity-producing machine, a panacea at the time for curing all sorts of ailments.

The death of his seven-month-old sibling Germaine exactly two weeks before his ninth birthday left a lasting impression on Antonin. Germaine had become the focal point for the family, which had already gone through three stillbirths and the death of a newborn. After being violently handled by her nursemaid, Germaine died of internal haemorrhaging. Six years later, Artaud's maternal grandmother, Neneka, died in Smyrna. While Artaud had a very close relationship with Neneka yet barely knew Germaine, both deaths had an impact on his perspective on matters of life and death.

As Artaud recommenced writing in Rodez, Germaine became both a quasi-homonymic symbol for his literary germination and, in her innocence and purity, an apparition for his body's resurrection after more than fifty electroshock treatments.[12] In the preamble to the proposed publication of his collected works, Artaud wrote of a vision he had 'in 1931 where, while seated outside at the Dôme, at Montparnasse, I had the impression that she looked at me from nearby.'[13] In the same passage, Artaud referred to Germaine, his grandmother Neneka and the art critic Yvonne Allendy as having been societally strangled.[14] Although none had, in fact, been strangled, for Artaud strangulation symbolized a means of depriving the soul of its essence and of removing 'all those [society] wanted to get rid of or to protect itself from, because they refused to become accomplices in its great dirty tricks'.[15]

In many respects, Artaud was product and victim of his bourgeois family's norms and values. As the bourgeoisie rose to political, social and economic authority over the nineteenth century, its cultural currency became the measure of its hegemony over society. Order, stability, rationality, consumerism and a commitment to progress – ideals that were incubated in the household and largely enforced and reinforced by the authority of the family patriarch – defined the bourgeoisie. In his relations with his father, the male child, in particular, 'found himself suffocated. Devoid of an identity, he exists only in a virtual state: one day he

From left to right: Antonin, Fernand, Euphrasie, Marie-Ange, *c.* 1918.

will be identical to the paternal figure . . .'.[16] Befitting Antoine-Roi's social and cultural status, his family was a crucible for perpetuating bourgeois values. According to Marie-Ange, Antoine-Roi followed the maritime commerce of his male forebears, 'men of honour, men of serious probity, men of duty . . . who, when the time came to follow in their father's footsteps, knew how to be bosses in every noble sense of the word'.[17]

From an early age, however, Antonin was not destined to follow in the grand maritime tradition of Artaud males. By the time Artaud reached his eleventh birthday, there was not much left of the Artaud–Nalpas enterprise. The principal part of the family business – shipping – had been sold in 1906, leaving Antoine-Roi with only the insurance of it; furthermore, instability in the Ottoman Empire was threatening the Mediterranean shipping industry. All of this must have been distressing to Antoine-Roi as he struggled to fulfil his role as family patriarch: the family's once-secure social standing and ensuring his eldest son's economic future became less and less realistic.[18]

Antoine-Roi's rigid subscription to the model of bourgeois fatherhood mandated a distant and formal relationship with his son in matters outside of schooling and professional development. For Artaud, the dissonance between the bourgeois facade and the absence of any substance epitomized the hypocrisy of his father's world. Described by Marie-Ange as 'cultivated, erudite, open to the arts, [but], consistent with the proper society of his era, a little rigid', Antoine-Roi was likely disappointed by his inability to provide his son with a career and with Antonin's failure to measure up to his expectations. That said, Antoine-Roi's financial support during the early 1920s was crucial for Antonin's commencement of his artistic ventures.[19]

Antonin would later write disparagingly of fathers, in general, and Antoine-Roi, in particular.[20] In a series of lectures on Surrealism he delivered in Mexico City in 1936, Artaud wrote:

> The family is at the foundation of social constraint. The absence of all fraternity between fathers and sons has been the model of all the social relationships based on authority and the contempt of bosses for their fellow men. Father, fatherland, patron, this is the trilogy upon which the old patriarchal society was based, and today, the bitchiness of fascism.[21]

Further on in the same lecture, Artaud wrote specifically of Antoine-Roi:

> I have lived for 27 years with the concealed hatred of fathers, of my father, in particular. Up to the day when I saw him die. Now, the inhumane cruelty, by which I accuse him of oppressing me, has subsided. Another being left his body. And for the first time in my life, this father extended his arms. Self-conscious of my body, I understand that his body vexed him his whole life and that we are born to resist against a deception of the soul.[22]

A distant presence during Antonin's formative years, never cultivating an affectionate parent–child connection, Antoine-Roi loomed as an ominous spectre over his son's identity and future; the world that brought Antoine-Roi success, and the values that defined that success, were antithetical to his son and his son's cohorts. By the time Antonin articulated his thoughts on patriarchy during those lectures in Mexico, Antoine-Roi had been

Antoine-Roi Artaud, the father of Antonin Artaud.

dead for a dozen years, and the society and culture over which he and his ilk presided had been left in tatters by a world war and its consequences. The questions posed and the contradictions exposed during those first two decades of the twentieth century placed Antoine-Roi's world in relief; order, security, stability and Western triumphalism were simply veneers barely hiding the decadence and vacuity lurking beneath the surface.

In contrast to his relationship with Antoine-Roi, Artaud's relationship with his mother was close, almost to the point of obsession. If Antoine-Roi exemplified the *fin-de-siècle* father, Euphrasie conformed to the prevailing model of bourgeois domesticity. Her life rarely extended beyond the household, and much of her time was devoted to Antonin, who mastered the art of maternal manipulation, feigning nervous disorders to instil fear in, and attract attention from, Euphrasie.[23] Marie-Ange recalled that Artaud had for his mother 'an exceptional tenderness as if his

Antonin's mother, Euphrasie Artaud-Nalpas.

subconscious already foresaw what his sorrowful life was going to demand of this admirable woman'.[24] And according to Marie-Ange, upon Antoine-Roi's death in 1924, Artaud wrote countless letters to Euphrasie imploring her to live with him in Paris; until the commencement of Artaud's sustained period of asylum commitments in 1937, mother and son were nearly inseparable.[25]

Owing to Euphrasie's intense mystical Catholicism, Artaud's childhood was largely steeped in religion. Artaud's adolescent education commenced in 1907 at the Collège Sacré-Coeur (a middle school), a choice that reflected both the Artauds' social standing and affirmed their religious convictions: Sacré-Coeur's student body was drawn from the bourgeoisie of Marseille, and to send a child to a parochial school at the *fin de siècle* was a strong statement on a family's piety, if not hostility to the secular values of the French Republic.[26] At Sacré-Coeur, Artaud discovered poetry and collaborated with several classmates on a journal. Artaud's contributions reflected the terrains of his familiarity – Marseille, its culture and maritime environment – and his favourite poets: Edgar Allan Poe, Charles

Baudelaire and Maurice Rollinat, all of whom mined the supernatural, the subconscious and the macabre. Exposure to the works of Arthur Rimbaud and Stéphane Mallarmé heightened Artaud's entry into the interplay between conscious and unconscious states of mind in poetic expression and the limitlessness of expressive possibilities if unhinged from linguistic conventions. It is hardly surprising that Artaud's adolescent discovery of poetry led him to canon-challenging poets. In these formative years, however, marked as they were with a heavy dose of Catholic mysticism, Artaud appeared confused and unable to process the seemingly incompatible forces competing for, and ultimately shaping, his thoughts.

Artaud's early, adolescent poetic forays naturally bear the signs of his literary influences; but with respect to one theme, Artaud appears to have found his own voice. In several of these early poems, Artaud wrote despairingly of the stagnancy of existence and of a world that was seemingly dead. In these works, one can, perhaps, evince a connection between women and death, where the separation that occurs at the moment of birth presages the individual's separation from its essence, a theme Artaud fleshed out more fully in the poems he produced during his first few years in Paris.[27]

During his final year at Sacré-Coeur, in 1914, Artaud's behaviour underwent a perplexing shift; he destroyed most of his writings and divided his book collection among his friends. The final year at school might have signified a turning point for Artaud, a purifying moment lest his intellectual and artistic maturation be encumbered by the appetites of his youth; yet, in a sign of his confusion, Artaud signed a letter he wrote to his parents on 1 January 1914 with both his juvenile pet name 'Nanaqui' and his proper name, 'Antonin Artaud', signifying, perhaps, a hesitancy over transitioning into adulthood.[28] The war that would define and transform Artaud's generation commenced in 1914; even though the cause or trajectory of the war would not have been actualized during the first six months of that year, a broader sense of uncertainty permeated French youth.

If the dispersal of his library and his own artistic output were any indication, Artaud's ever-changing moods provided an almost prescient glimpse into his future. During his adolescence, Artaud

From left to right: Antonin, Fernand and Euphrasie, *c*. 1913–14.

became extremely pious, prayed daily and planned to become a priest, but then abruptly abandoned that plan of action. The adult Artaud's spiritual quest vacillated wildly between bouts of extreme religious devotion, pagan esotericism, non-sectarian spirituality and atheism. This, 1914, was also the first year when Artaud and his family began to notice the first signs of the psychological distress and depression to which his posterior persona would be anchored.

Artaud's condition manifested itself in withdrawal, isolation and anger. His parents consulted a psychiatrist, who, according to Fernand, concluded that Artaud did not like his parents.[29] In response, in 1915, Antoine-Roi and Euphrasie sent Artaud to the Montpellier clinic operated by Dr Joseph Grasset, the first of a series of psychiatrists in Artaud's life to correlate nervous disorders with cultural genius. To Grasset, Artaud must have appeared as living proof of the theory Grasset advanced in his book, *Thérapeutique des maladies du système nerveux* (Therapy for Ailments of the Nervous System, 1907), that nervous disorders often result from consanguineal kinships and through indulgence in religious excesses.[30] Grasset diagnosed Artaud as a neurastheniatic. Characterized by nervous exhaustion, lethargy, fatigue, anxiety and depression, neurasthenia is today rarely treated as a mental disorder, and is often dismissed as a contrivance of the leisure class. Grasset prescribed a bewildering assortment of treatments for Artaud – hydrotherapy, mineral baths and various narcotics and stimulants – and suggested that Artaud spend some time at the sanatorium in La Rouguière, a Marseille suburb, where the course of treatment largely centred around hydrotherapy and isolation from the source of agitation: in Artaud's case, his family.[31] However, La Rouguière was just the start of a five-year sojourn for Artaud as he shuttled between various clinics and sanatoria throughout a wide swathe of the south of France (Provence, the Pyrenees, the Savoie) and Switzerland.

In August 1916 Antonin Artaud was less than a month away from his twentieth birthday, and deep into treatment for neurasthenia, when he was conscripted into the Third Regiment of the Infantry. Despite being treated for a recognized nervous disorder, the French military deemed Artaud suitable for military service – the urgent need for soldiers in the midst of the bloodbath at Verdun and Artaud's possession of a driver's licence were likely the determining factors. Beyond this, doctors correlated nervous disorders in men with the 'female malady' of hysteria, a sign of social degeneration and society's decline through emasculation; the 'war was supposed to be an invigorating male experience that could revitalize, even re-masculinize, French men and help rebuild a failing French society'.[32]

The privations and dangers of war promised to deliver Artaud, and countless others like him, from their slide into effeteness, and in the process restore French society.

Stationed at Digne in southeast France, Artaud had a short and uneventful stint in the military. Within five months of his induction, he was temporarily released from military service for an unspecified health reason, and by the end of 1917 he received a full discharge. Artaud later stated that he had been discharged for sleepwalking, but his mother, when interviewed by psychiatrists during one of Artaud's commitments, claimed it was 'because of his nerves'.[33] Artaud's dismissal from the military was likely the result of his father's influence, as few would have been afforded similar treatment in that pivotal year of 1917, when the French military was desperate to compensate for the tremendous losses of 1916.

The features of the First World War were traumatizing for nearly all its participants. The destruction enabled by technological progress psychologically scarred a generation, who no longer viewed war with a sense of adventure and anticipation. The high number of casualties and the mental terror of the war helped the psychiatric profession to grow. Very few records remain of Artaud's brief appearance during the war; consequently, it's impossible to determine whether or not he contrived or sincerely experienced the mental or physical anguish that led to his discharge. As previously stated, though, by the time of his conscription, Artaud already had an established track record of neurological disorders, beginning with the migraines he suffered at the time of the meningitis diagnosis; his psychological treatments continued nearly uninterrupted until the end of 1919.

Later in life, Artaud wrote of a temporal correspondence between the war and his sexual awakening, and the two 'catastrophes' were inextricably intertwined. Claiming to have experienced puberty in 1914 (though it is unlikely that this would have occurred at the age of seventeen), Artaud was likely conflating his sexual awakening with the physiognomic processes associated with puberty. In a letter to gallery-owner Colette Allendy, Artaud obliquely requested 'blood' in order 'to make up for the flask that someone had stolen from him at Marseille in 1915'.[34] His first sexual encounter – an experience upon which he never really elaborated, though to which he frequently made vague reference – was one source of anguish, and we can only wonder whether the other source was the war, his fragile mental state or a combination of the two.[35] In any event, Artaud's persistent linkage of the loss of his adolescence with the war seems to represent a longing for youth over which he never had control, a formative period prematurely cut short, and a quest for self-definition that never reached fruition.

Although Artaud was not injured during the war – and, for that matter, might not have seen any action – in later writings he seemed to yearn for a vicarious association with injury. During the Second World War, while in Rodez, he wrote of being stabbed, for no apparent reason, in Marseille in 1916:

> Among the blood spilled, mine fills a lot of pints, and I still have two scars in my back from a knife wound which you can't say I dreamt up, and that I hallucinated, although the circumstances where I received them are, were, naturally weird. The first was given to me in Marseille during the other war in July 1916 by a pimp whom I saw for the first time in my life . . . passing by him anonymously, and who saw me, as well, for the first time.[36]

Artaud's belated recollection of the foregoing incident, after he had already been institutionalized for years, might have resulted from a repressed memory. On the other hand, the incident might never have occurred: there is no official record of it. Was it a non-cognitive exaggeration of the past, the result of Artaud's inflated imagination and psychological burden at having avoided a war that produced a staggering casualty rate of 71 per cent of mobilized French soldiers? Had Artaud simply transferred onto himself, and absorbed, the victimization of so many others from his age cohort, placing himself in the galaxy of wartime casualties?

Artaud would later write of his shame, upon his return to Marseille in January 1917, when Dr Grasset informed him that he bore the symptoms of syphilis. In a letter from 1943 to Dr Jacques Latrémolière, who administered the electroshock treatments in Rodez, Artaud wrote:

According to certain pathogenic signs that you have noted on me, you have suspected the existence of a syphilitic malady. THIS CANNOT BE TAKEN FOR GRANTED because I avoid and I despise as disgraceful all human sexual relations, of any kind, and it gravely offended me to believe that my body is capable of giving itself freely at any moment of its life and, as to my case, my hereditary syphilis, doctor, is an old history known by a good number of French doctors, the first of whom was Professor Grasset of Montpellier, who, in 1917, because of my irregular pupils, as you noted, prescribed a long series of biniodide mercury shots.

Artaud cast doubt on the initial diagnosis, disputing that he was a syphilitic, hereditary or otherwise, but instead the victim of 'hundreds of injections . . . that have gravely injured the marrow and the brain'.[37] By the time Artaud wrote this, his views on sexuality were well formulated – and at least tangentially related to this diagnosis. Grasset's initial tests produced positive results; the following year, after receiving the anti-syphilis injection regimen then in vogue – twice-weekly administrations of various pharmaceutical cocktails, mercury injections and cyanide chasers – he tested negative for syphilis. While it's possible that the treatments cured Artaud, it's also possible, as he suspected, that he never had the condition in the first place; at the time, doctors often attributed inexplicable emotional disorders to syphilis.[38] If the syphilis diagnosis hung over Artaud and influenced his antipathy towards, and fears of, sexuality, it is possible that it contributed to his definition of sex as an irretrievable loss of essence.

Towards the end of 1918, Artaud arrived at the relatively new Chanet clinic near Neuchâtel, Switzerland. There, he had his first tastes of morphine and laudanum and decided to pursue literature as a career. In March or April 1920, Artaud was discharged from the Chanet clinic. While his condition had improved, he was not cured; the clinic's director, Dr Maurice Dardel, conceivably concluded that he could offer no more assistance to this patient. In any event, Dardel put him in contact with Dr Édouard Toulouse, the director of the asylum at Villejuif, a suburb south of Paris. The choice of Toulouse was more than simply fortuitous; Dardel recognized Artaud's literary interests and, since 1912, Toulouse had edited a partially literary, partially scientific journal, *Demain*. If Artaud's emotional state had plateaued in the sedentary environs at Neuchâtel, perhaps the more vibrant cultural life in Paris and the guidance of Dr Toulouse would provide the patient with a therapeutic artistic outlet.

While Artaud's move to Paris opened up new vistas for artistic expression, his essence had already been determined. Though Antonin was unable, or perhaps unwilling, to conform to his family's bourgeois mores, paradoxically, he had imbibed them. Resigned to the idea that his thoughts and behaviour were abnormal, Artaud understood the abnormal to be pathological. Implicitly, he endeavoured to absorb and accept the prevailing norms and institutions, but through every effort at conformity, he set himself in conflict with himself. Although Marseille was a trading crossroads, a meeting place of various cultures and seemingly a mecca of freedom, for Artaud it was a space of confinement where his personal liberation was constrained by the reality of what was expected of him and the irreality of reaching what he had come to expect of himself. Coinciding with the resumption of pre-war cultural experimentation, Artaud's emergence in Paris also allowed him to explore and extend the depth of his literary and theatrical ideas and to decentre himself from the normative bourgeois regime's hegemony.

Sketch by Antonin Artaud, 'Malade B', from Dr Dardel's clinic, 1919.

2

Paris

Prior to the First World War, Dr Édouard Toulouse surveyed the sorry state of French psychiatric care. At the *fin de siècle*, psychiatry in France lacked the prestige and urgency of other forms of health care. At best, the French public and government ministers were indifferent and, at worst, insensitive to the plight of the mentally disturbed. However, the unfathomable casualty rate, economic dislocation and shell shock suffered by demobilized soldiers left France with a 'pool of citizens who needed psychiatric care'; the time appeared propitious for the types of change envisaged by Toulouse and other reformers. Most particularly, Toulouse hoped to transform asylums of confinement into hospitals of mental health care. Furthermore, those in need of such care could freely avail themselves of it without having to be judicially committed to an asylum; thus psychiatric care would be available to even the mildly disturbed who lacked the resources to pay for private care.[1] While Toulouse's objective of providing access to outpatient psychiatric treatment to patients of moderate incomes might not have had much impact on the Artaud family, his larger objective – to remove the social stigma attached to a recipient of mental health care – provided them with some relief.

Toulouse was also one of the first psychiatrists to explore the correspondence between artistic production, physiognomical characteristics and psychiatric diagnoses. In his early adulthood, Toulouse was a literature and theatre critic for newspapers in his native Marseille and perceived psychiatry as straddling the line between art and science, the psychiatrist as 'a novelist whose work was based on exact observations'.[2] In 1896 as part of an intended, but uncompleted, series examining the physical and psychological conditions of men of 'superior intellect' entitled *Enquête médico-psychologique sur les rapports de la superiorité intellectuelle avec la néuropathie* (A Psycho-medical Inquiry into the Relationships between Intellectual Superiority and Neuropathy), Toulouse profiled Émile Zola, painstakingly delineating the author's physiognomical and psychological characteristics. Toulouse's objective was to identify and establish that genius, whether literary (Zola, Daudet), musical (Saint-Saëns), visual (Rodin) or mathematical (Henri Poincaré), shares certain explainable characteristics. Among the methods employed by Toulouse was a pre-Rorschach ink-blot test; rather than distinguishing between social normalcy and pathology, however, Toulouse used the test as a gauge of creative impulses. Two years after embarking on this project, Toulouse was appointed head of the modern clinic in the Villejuif.

Accompanied by his father, Artaud arrived in Paris in the first half of April 1920. According to Toulouse's wife, her husband almost immediately glimpsed qualities of creative genius in Artaud, though could offer no more insight than oblique references to Artaud

Artaud photographed in 1920 in the consulting room of Dr Toulouse.

Sketch by Artaud of Dr Toulouse, 1920.

being of the same 'race' as 'Baudelaire, Nerval, or Nietzsche',[3] a 'race' defiant in its embrace of 'unreason' and visionary rejection of rationality's privileged position.[4] Toulouse brought Artaud into his home, a more conducive environment than Villejuif for channelling and encouraging the patient's creativity.

In 1912 Toulouse had launched *Demain*, a fortnightly journal whose objectives were to inspire 'a more complex intellectual life, deeper, clearer, more independent' and to invite the reader to become 'an active agent of propaganda'.[5] Toulouse conceptualized happiness as harmonizing intellectual curiosity, republican morality, and physical and psychological health. Ever the positivist, Toulouse placed the accent on science as the principal agent for ensuring global happiness, a position that was hard to reconcile with his idealization of cultural irrationality. But for Toulouse, the universality of science would liberate humankind from ignorance, bigotry and fear. Consonant with his holistic view of science, *Demain* was thematically diverse: in its first year of publication, *Demain*'s 68 articles covered theatre, literature, political authority, class and gender inequality, juvenile criminality, anarchism, war in the Balkans, eugenics, fashion and the psychology of cinema.[6] A year into *Demain*, Toulouse introduced the term 'biocraty' as a descriptor for his scientific-technocratic society. Biocraty shared many objectives with communism: both were anti-capitalist and anti-bourgeois, and both promoted internationalism as the final stage of historical evolution. However, in Toulouse's estimation, applied communism (through Bolshevism) elevated the uncultured and unrefined to unwarranted positions of authority.

The devastation and irrationality of the First World War provided a sense of urgency to Toulouse's message; from 1919 onwards, he became more steadfast and proactive in his opposition to the bourgeois regime. Though never specifically acknowledged by Artaud, Toulouse's influence over him is palpable. In 1923 Artaud assembled and wrote an introduction to a collection of Toulouse's texts on the destructive nature of prejudice – be it predicated on class, gender or ideology – *Édouard Toulouse, Au fil des préjugés* (Édouard Toulouse, in Pursuit of Prejudices):[7]

> Some things must be destroyed. There are distortions of thought, mental habits, in short, vices that contaminate the judgment of man at its inception. We are born, we live, we die in an environment of lies. Our teachers, who through blood are our kin, were, we must say, not consciously, but unconsciously, by ancestral habit, bad advisors . . . To battle prejudice is an admirable task, but the completion will come from a sweeping redress of social and moral wrongs.[8]

Within months of arriving at Villejuif, Artaud was contributing to *Demain* on topics ranging from a new curriculum for the baccalaureate to art criticism.[9] However, one contribution to *Demain*, above all others, conveys Artaud's dismay over bourgeois style, and unveils the significance of culture in the anti-bourgeois zeitgeist. In 'Le Grand Magasin empoisonneur' (The Poisonous Department

Store), Artaud took exception to 'Le Grand Magasin éducateur' (The Educational Department Store), a piece where Toulouse extolled the aesthetic and hygienic virtues of department stores. In despairing over bourgeois tastelessness, Artaud evinced a growing independence from Toulouse:

> The department store bears an enormous share of the responsibility for the widespread degeneration of taste in France.
>
> With its moderate prices and delivery services, the department store has, so to speak, inflicted on the bourgeois home and the country cottage, alike, the silly buffet, the fake antique brass lamp and all the hideous décor of today's apartment.
>
> It has organized the general intoxication of taste by the elimination of small shops, those isolated foyers of personal style . . .
>
> People are stupid, people are blind. They do not know that one does not furnish simply in order to furnish and that furniture is made to be useful, and that it can deviate from this very strict functionalism only if it is an art object or of an undeniable aesthetic.

Artaud then chastized Aristide Boucicaut, the entrepreneur behind Le Bon Marché, the world's first department store, for vulgarizing, cheapening and homogenizing household aesthetics, solely for the purpose of filling his coffers.[10]

Disdain for the commodification and banality of performative culture also preoccupied Artaud; drawn to theatre, he was attracted both to new currents and by the prospects for even more radical conceptualizations. During the two decades prior to the First World War, French theatre was divided between 'boulevard theatre' – highly commercialized, traditional, alternatively melodramatic and comedic, modestly priced productions – and avant-garde theatre, a creature of nineteenth-century bohemianism, which endeavoured to connect theatre to new currents in art and psychologism.[11] As *fin-de-siècle* France became more politically polarized, the avant-garde became more revolutionary, viewing theatre as the optimal forum for subverting cultural norms and challenging social and political conventions.[12] Artaud's introduction to the avant-garde theatre in Paris piqued his interest in drama, and his more expansive ideas on its significance gestated.

In 1893 Aurélien-Marie Lugné-Poe had launched a veritable assault on French theatre with his subscriber-subsidized Théâtre de l'oeuvre. Introducing French audiences to works by Scandinavian symbolists such as Henrik Ibsen, and staging Alfred Jarry's controversial *Ubu Roi*, Lugné-Poe envisaged melding cultural and political anarchism through nihilistic portrayals of oppressive and corrupt authorities. Lugné-Poe's cultural anarchism emphasized 'action and the gestural dimension over speech', diminishing the prominence of dialogue in favour of the mise en scène.[13] In Ibsen's *An Enemy of the People* and in *Ubu Roi*, Lugné-Poe fetishized and anaesthetized violence; the violent act became a gestural end in itself, devoid of instrumentality, an act of terror at once unsettling and destructive, yet purifying. Anarchists and symbolists both privileged gesture's timelessness and universality over rhetorical contrivances, though dramatists might have stopped short of advocating physical violence.

As a reflexive impulse, gesture restored communication to its primal essence; commensurate with this, by abandoning speech's reflective imperative, gestural communication expressed what was buried in the subconscious. New directions in the arts were merging with new currents in psychiatry, and Toulouse was at the vanguard of this synergy of science and culture, devoting space in *Demain* to both literary and theatrical works.

In 1913 Jacques Copeau took over and gutted a rundown theatre in the 6th arrondissement, purposely maintained it in a tastefully austere condition and named it the Théâtre du Vieux-Colombier. Copeau's dream was to return artistry to theatre; the stripped interior would facilitate a return to 'primal integrity' and regenerate actors and audience alike. Untethered from the artifices and superficialities that have 'mechanized' humankind and rendered theatre a banal imitation of life, the actors would uncover the essence of the human condition; vicariously, for the audience, theatre would be a revelatory experience, raising it from the complacency of commercialized reductionism.[14]

Through Copeau's theatrical sensibility and Lugné-Poe's politicized conception, the course French theatre had been following was re-channelled. Toulouse saw it as a crystallization of his beliefs on 'the salubrious ideas of regeneration which are in the air'.[15] For Artaud, the naturalness with which Copeau's actors adapted to their roles, together with the elegant simplicity and imaginativeness of the sets, foretold a new beginning from which French theatre could advance – even if Copeauean theatre was, perhaps, too driven by text.

A refugee centre during the First World War, the Vieux-Colombier reopened as a theatre in February 1920. In the war's aftermath, Copeau demonstrated an almost absolute indifference to the audience, be it its physical comfort, its judgement, its expectations or the accessibility of the material. The stage became a self-contained setting, bereft of any semblance of decor and alien to the outside world; the text and the acting were all that mattered. Between 1920 and 1923, admittance to the Vieux-Colombier was one of the most sought-after tickets in Paris; in 1924 Copeau, perhaps frustrated that commercial success entailed compromise, ended his association with the Vieux-Colombier Theatre.

Shortly after arriving in Paris, Artaud, after attempting to sneak into a production at the Théâtre de l'oeuvre, had a chance encounter with Lugné-Poe; he made an immediate impression on the director. In no time, Artaud was working gratis at the Théâtre de l'oeuvre, behind the scenes and occasionally as a walk-on actor. In a rare reminiscence about the French theatre of the 1920s, Artaud recalled how, in Lugné-Poe's direction of Fernand Crommelynck's *The Magnificent Cuckold* (one of Artaud's first stage roles), the director emphasized gestural expressiveness in his actors over textual fidelity:

> Lugné-Poe created an unforgettable type of intellectual buffoon, introducing to the French stage a Bruegelian-like composition, with a kind of voice that seems to snarl from a dark place, and a succession of laughs followed by a cascade of expressions that travelled from the head to the feet.[16]

Artaud's tenure at the theatre was not particularly long and in June Lugné-Poe wrote to Toulouse, confirming his interest in

Artaud, enquiring, 'What will become of him?'[17] Though Artaud's feelings towards Lugné-Poe ultimately turned decidedly critical (Artaud chastized the Théâtre de l'oeuvre for 'commodifying the beautiful Nordic tragedies'), two years after Artaud's departure from the Théâtre de l'oeuvre, Lugné-Poe wrote the following:

> He has brilliance, a rare quality among young actors who imagine that their craft is only a profession that will produce rapid and lucrative results. I have signalled to my comrades the fiery poetry of Antonin Artaud, but his laboured diction rendered the first steps clumsy . . . At the time of the *Scrupules de Sganarelle*, Henri de Régnier and I smoked, charmed by the silhouette of this surprising artist, still just a walk-on, playing a bourgeois stimulated by the night. His make-up, his bearing was that of a painter, led astray, amid a group of actors.[18]

In May 1921 Artaud attracted the attention of Firmin Gémier, director of the Théâtre national populaire (TNP). As an actor, Gémier originated the role of Père Ubu in Lugné-Poe's staging of *Ubu Roi* in 1896. Similar to Lugné-Poe, Gémier saw theatre as a vehicle for revolution, for challenging the mediocrity of bourgeois society. A committed socialist, Gémier envisioned theatre as mass spectacle, staged under enormous collapsible playhouses that would move around the country; it would be reminiscent of Jacques-Louis David's orchestrations during the French Revolution, cast and audience unifying in tribal pageantry, their collective participation overwhelming the last gasps of egoistic individualism. Above all, for Gémier, theatre must untether language from its bourgeois moorings, and render it more resonant with the cacophony of the collective. The end of the war created a propitious atmosphere for Gémier's vision; after all, the carnage had seemingly discredited all elements of bourgeois values. In 1920, with state support, Gémier founded the TNP, an enterprise designed to celebrate the nation's collective spirit, a theatre of the proletariat.[19]

After auditioning Artaud in October 1921, Gémier recommended him to Charles Dullin, formerly with the Vieux-Colombier, now director of the Théâtre de l'atelier in Montmartre. While

Artaud distilled his ideas on the relationship of theatre to society from Copeau, Lugné-Poe and Gémier, Dullin provided the most formidable influence on Artaud's understanding of theatre. Artaud first mentioned Dullin in a letter in October 1921 to Yvonne Gilles, a young woman he met during his pre-Paris institutionalizations, waxing enthusiastically about Dullin's novel approach to the theatre: everything the actor does comes from 'the soul'; the aesthetic choice is modelled on the simplicity of Japanese theatre; and the material is not drawn from 'Tolstoy, Ibsen, or Shakespeare, but [E. A.] Hoffmann and Edgar Poe'.[20] Writing in the journal *Action*, Artaud described Dullin's mission as the 'decontamination and regeneration of the morality and the spirit of French theatre'.[21]

In particular, in Dullin's quest for a more authentic, less contrived, less reductionist theatrical experience, his ideas were more focused on the actor and less text-centric. To accomplish this, he established a theatre laboratory, initially relocated away from the pressures of Paris, where his actors would live communally and rehearse together.[22] Two years after Artaud's death, Dullin recalled that, while Artaud shared in the materially austere communal existence of the Théâtre de l'atelier and his clothes were often dishevelled, he maintained the 'aspect of a dandy'. Dullin prescribed a heavy regimen of improvisation for his young actors as a means for getting them to discover their interior selves before exteriorizing what they had discovered through these exercises. If improvisation for Dullin was merely a honing exercise limited to the workshop, Artaud viewed improvisation as a window into the actor's character.[23]

Dullin's emphasis on theatre as metaphysical experience and his employment of the techniques of East Asian theatre (including Japanese masks) piqued Artaud's interest in the mystical and magical. Writing to the poet, painter and avant-garde gadfly Max Jacob, Artaud said, 'One gets the impression, while listening to Dullin teach that he has rediscovered some old secrets and a forgotten mystique from the mise en scène', yet because theatre had strayed so far from these principles, they appear to be innovations.[24] Gratified as he was by Artaud's openness, respectful of his holistic view of theatre (even commissioning Artaud to design the costumes for a production of Lope de Rueda's *Les Olives*) and appreciative

Study for theatre costume, 2 March 1922, by Artaud for *Les Olives*, a production of the Théâtre de l'atelier.

of his gifts on the stage, Dullin was also troubled by his protégé's extremes:

> Even though I was attracted to the Oriental theatre, he [Artaud] went much further in this direction than I, and from a practical point of view, it became dangerous. For example, in Pirandello's

La Volupté de la Honneur, where he played a businessman, he arrived on the stage with a make up inspired by the little masks Chinese actors use as a model – a symbolic make up which was slightly out of place in a modern comedy.[25]

For Artaud, it was not enough that French theatre adopt some of the practices of East Asian theatre; to realize and recapture theatre's ancient secrets and magical and mystical propensities and potentialities, it had to be inspired by and replicate it. Whatever disagreements they might have had, two years after Artaud's death Dullin wrote that he felt privileged to have known the charming, young Artaud, 'at the moment of the blossoming of a genius'.[26]

East Asian culture's influence on Artaud increased significantly in 1922. In mid-July, Dullin's troupe performed in the south of France. Artaud used the journey as an opportunity to make an excursion to Marseille, his hometown and the host of the Colonial Exposition of 1922, a showcase of the reciprocal economic relationship between France and its empire. In addition to the economics of imperialism that had dominated pre-war colonial expositions, the Exhibition of 1922 celebrated the contribution of the colonies to the French war effort and the culture and histories of the colonies; but rather than focusing on Indochina's minor wartime role, the Colonial Exposition highlighted its architecture and artistry.

Dominating the Indochinese section of the Marseille Colonial Exposition (and perhaps the entire Exposition) was a replica of Angkor Wat. While this alone would have been enough to attract throngs to the Exposition, the organizers enhanced the exoticism quotient by arranging performances of Cambodian and Vietnamese dance companies. King Sisowath's Cambodian Royal Ballet garnered the most attention, and 'the charming dancers were the "must see" of the exposition.' For French governmental officials, these performers exemplified the image of the colonies they wanted to project to the public: graceful, talented and exotic, but not primal.[27]

A decade later, Artaud compared watching the dancers to being touched by grace and 'wondered if the final happiness is not comparable to the solution of this particular Nirvana'.[28] However, as profound an impact as the Cambodian dancers had on him at the time, Artaud could not shake a sense of emptiness, a feeling of melancholy and loss so intense that it overwhelmed whatever wonderment he might have felt while watching the dancers. During the spring season, Artaud had fallen for Génica Athanasiou, an actress in the Théâtre de l'atelier. Separated from Athanasiou while the troupe was on hiatus, he could think of little but her. Artaud wrote to Athanasiou that the Colonial Exposition had left him with a 'feeling of hopelessness (or despair), but of calm and clarity as well. Sunny, some bright gowns. I have thought of your dresses.'[29]

Born in Bucharest, Romania, nearly four months to the day after Artaud, Athanasiou immigrated to France in 1919 to pursue an acting career. By most accounts, Athanasiou was the first, and perhaps only, woman with whom Artaud was intimate; their relationship lasted until 1927, when Athanasiou could no longer withstand Artaud's idiosyncratic (to say the least) views on sex and his addiction to opiates. Nonetheless, their letters reveal an intimacy and tenderness that is often lost in the larger Artaud story. Artaud's passion and longing for Athanasiou when the two were separated also expressed the ideas at the core of his being. In July 1922 Artaud wrote to Athanasiou, 'More and more I need you now more than ever. It appears as though I am separated from my body . . . I have become a little child again as when my mother was everything to me and I could not separate myself from her. Now you have become her, so indispensable, and before you, I am yet more innocent than at that time.'[30]

Artaud's separation from Athanasiou, and the barrier he encountered when endeavouring to express his love and anguish in writing, caused him to ruminate (in a depersonalized way) on the superficiality of language. Unable or unwilling to verbalize his internal sentiments externally, Artaud instead pegged the thought processes necessary for verbal expression to an intrinsic corruption of the purity of emotional feeling. In August 1922, while in the Var, Artaud wrote to Athanasiou, 'Therefore, be in peace, be silent if the silence pleases you; our love will be better when we don't write because all the words are a lie. When we speak we betray our soul . . . One feels some things, but the *effort* alone that one extends to express them is already a betrayal.'[31]

More than a geographic gulf separated Artaud from Athanasiou. Artaud's burgeoning relationship with Athanasiou might have been the first casualty of the ubiquitous presence of narcotics throughout his life. Although he first wrote about his substance issues during those initial years at Paris, there is no certainty as to when Artaud first used. On a hospital admittance questionnaire in December 1932, he stated that he had never taken morphine and, after insisting on laudanum, had been prescribed it in 1919.[32] Artaud regularly imbibed opiates during his two years at the Théâtre de l'atelier. It is strictly a matter of conjecture as to whether his usage was purely for medicinal purposes or to enhance his creativity. In 1921 Artaud commenced an article on author Maurice Magre by discussing the 'unreal' and its daily significance in Eastern cultures, critiquing Magre's more recent forays into the 'unreal' and finishing by reflecting on the positive influence of opium on Magre's work: 'And, since he has sung the praises of opium, he has been able to draw, from daily occurrences, an unprecedented reverberation.'[33] Artaud acknowledged the relationship between drugs and alternative forms of consciousness that had stoked the creative output of Magre, Baudelaire, Poe and Lautréamont. However, according to Toulouse's wife, Jeanne, Artaud used opiates simply as 'an analgesic', to relieve the pains in his head. 'He became terribly angry when anyone mentioned drug addiction. He found fault with the laws that regulated the sale of narcotics: "I understand prohibiting the sale to addicts, but not to an unfortunate type like me who needs it so that he no longer suffers."'[34] On the hospital questionnaire of 1932, Artaud wrote, 'Had I not been in this chronic state of depression and of all sorts of moral and spiritual suffering [between 1915 and 1919], I would not have taken opium.'[35]

Suffering from fatigue and headaches during the spring season of the Théâtre de l'atelier, Artaud was prescribed a twice-weekly regimen of arsenic and bromide injections; in between, he self-medicated with laudanum and opium. Attempts at detoxification during his summer stay in Marseille, primarily to appease Athanasiou, who steadfastly believed that his need was psychological, not physiological, were never successful for more than two weeks.[36] If, initially, the principal reason behind Artaud's use of opiates was therapeutic, he nonetheless maintained a lifelong attraction to, and use of, narcotics.

With some misgivings, Artaud returned to Paris in November 1922, when Dullin commenced the new season of the Théâtre de l'atelier. On at least three different fronts – economic, creative and, for lack of a better expression, domestic – Artaud was becoming more distant from Dullin. Before returning to Paris, in *Le Crapouillot*, a Marseillaise theatre publication, Artaud praised Dullin's effort to create 'a total theatre', in the mode of the 'fantastic illumination' of life that Japanese theatre produces.[37] However, in his letters to Athanasiou, Artaud was less charitable towards Dullin, and less optimistic that he could remain with him. Prior to the troupe's departure for the south of France, Artaud, always notoriously short of cash, lived with the Dullins before trying his hosts' patience with 3 am rehearsals and middle-of-the-night discussions with Charles about articles Artaud was writing on Japanese Noh theatre. The breaking point came when Madame Dullin found Artaud, apparently emulating her six apartment-bound dogs, urinating on the rug in the living room.[38]

On 19 December 1922 the Théâtre de l'atelier premiered Jean Cocteau's adaptation of *Antigone*, featuring decorative pieces (including masks) designed by Picasso, costumes by Coco Chanel and music by Arthur Honegger.[39] Artaud appeared as Tiresias, the blind prophet of Thebes. Just before the production opened, Artaud wrote enthusiastically about its novelty, and later recalled (a decade afterwards while in Mexico) Athanasiou's performance in the lead role:

> Moans came from times beyond, as if carried by the froth of a wave on the Mediterranean Sea, on a day drenched by the sun; this is like the music of the flesh extending towards chilly darkness. This was, effectively, the voice of the ancient Greek, when it saw the Minotaur suddenly crystallize at the bottom of Minos' labyrinth in the virginal flesh.[40]

Artaud's enthusiasm for *Antigone* did not alter his increasingly dim view of Dullin; the definitive break occurred during the production of *Huon de Bordeaux*, after *Antigone*'s run had ended. Cast as Charlemagne, Artaud looked forward to playing 'an old visionary king, whining, blustering, hateful and tortured. This is the first time that I have found a role adapted to my skills.'[41] Within a few performances, Dullin replaced Artaud, ensuring Artaud's break with the Théâtre de l'atelier. For Dullin, Artaud constantly pushed performances to extremes; for Artaud, Dullin had compromised the guiding principles of the Théâtre de l'atelier. As Artaud wrote to Madame Toulouse in January 1923, with neither artistic integrity nor the monthly income promised him by Dullin to keep him at the Théâtre de l'atelier, 'I will go soon where one is paid.' Artaud's choices were not singularly determined by mercenary considerations; he also criticized Dullin for following in the grand affective, amateurish tradition of the Vieux-Colombier: 'one does not remake the theatre with apprentices who will never become artists.'[42]

After leaving Dullin's company, Artaud attracted the interest of Georges and Ludmilla Pitoëff, Russian émigrés, and former students of Konstantin Stanislavski, who were now showcasing the works of non-French playwrights at the Comédie des Champs-Elysées. Artaud profiled Georges Pitoëff in *Le Crapouillot*, discussing his accentuation of the actors' expressions through creative lighting: 'to go to the bitter end of nature, this is the heart of Pitoëff's art.'[43] Originally cast as 'the Prompter' in the Pitoëffs' staging of Pirandello's *Six Characters in Search of an Author*, Artaud's disappearance for a few days before the opening performance foreclosed any role beyond a bit part.[44] After bombing at its premiere in Pirandello's native Italy, the play was a huge success in Paris. Though this might have been a missed opportunity for Artaud to distinguish himself on the stage, in other ways his celebrity in Paris was growing.

Just as Artaud's relationship with the Théâtre de l'atelier was winding down, his first book of poetry was published. Daniel-Henry Kahnweiler, an art dealer and director of a small arts publishing house that had produced works by Georges Braque, Juan Gris, Fernand Léger, André Masson and Pablo Picasso, published, in 1923, eight of Artaud's poems under the title *Tric trac du ciel*. Written in slant rhyming verses – very similar to the poems he penned as a teenager – Artaud demanded their exclusion from his *Oeuvres complètes*, claiming they did not represent him 'in any way'. At the time of publication, in a letter to Kahnweiler, Artaud wrote that a poem's value should be conditioned on the expression of its sentiments, rather than the form of the expression:

> What is of personal interest to me (perhaps this is an error) is, above all, to have some thoughts from a durable and real framework, rather than from affectations, being most persuaded that the real (in the sense that I understand it) is, by definition, beautiful.[45]

Artaud was clearly tortured by the writing process, and, as this letter reveals, he was especially fixated on the symbiotic relationship between beauty and truth and how the contrivance of one compromises the integrity of the other. Writing in *La Vie*, reviewer Francis de Miomandre cited Artaud as 'a true poet', calling the work 'strange, diverse, chaotic, as well, and which makes no effort to give us even a little helping hand'.[46] In spite of his stated insecurities, Artaud was not without a measure of hubris. Masson recalled Artaud enquiring of Kahnweiler, 'Do you think that I am a better actor, artist or poet?', to this anecdote Masson added, 'How do you respond to this? Under the circumstances he was not humble, persuaded that he had a great role to play.'[47]

In March 1923 Artaud sent two short poems to Jacques Rivière, the editor of *La Nouvelle Revue française* (NRF). Although Rivière passed on publishing Artaud's poems for reasons not altogether clear (given the relative standing of the two men), Rivière wanted to meet him. During this time, between 1 May 1923 and 8 June 1924, the two engaged in regular correspondence. In a letter to Athanasiou, Artaud wrote that 'perhaps a new door is going to open.'[48] He was correct: prior to his death from typhoid in February 1925, Rivière published the exchange of letters in the NRF.[49] The publication of these epistolary missives catapulted Artaud to literary prominence.

In the letters, Artaud offered a preview of the tormented thoughts that bedevilled him and defined the ideas with which he is inextricably associated. The letters are punctuated with meditations on the inadequacy of language and on his sense of nothingness, of non-existence, of the beauty of pure – though imperfect – expression and of literary nonconformity; they convey the urgency of a young man who foresees that his inability to reconcile his thoughts with their expression will result in a personal holocaust. At the same time, he refuses to compromise the integrity of those thoughts or his personal sensibilities for the sake of comprehensibility. Rivière, however, would prove to be less than sympathetic, telling Artaud that he lacked the requisite discipline over his thoughts that would put better order to his ideas.

Artaud began his correspondence with Rivière by writing of the dissonance, for him, between the 'simple fact of thought' and its 'external materialization in words'. For Artaud, this failure 'results from the profound uncertainty of my thoughts'; he queried with Rivière whether 'one can concede less literary authenticity and value to a poem that is imperfect, but cultivated with great beauty, as opposed to a perfect poem that lacks an internal reverberation?' From there, Artaud wondered whether, despite its 'overall beauty', his poetry's failure to follow certain canons diminishes its literary value. Rivière's response could not have been too comforting. Referring to 'clumsiness and disconcerting weirdness' in Artaud's poems, Rivière doubted that they resulted from Artaud's inability to control his thoughts, but rather from a calculated decision by Artaud, perhaps, to claim an inner demon as compensation for lassitude.[50]

Artaud wrote back, denying that he lacked the intellectual rigour, diligence and will to control his thoughts. He felt hurt, misunderstood and judged: 'I have presented myself to you as a mental case, a veritable psychic anomaly, and you respond to me with a judgment on the literary merit of the poems which I do not esteem, which I could not esteem.' Seeking to clarify, but probably only reiterating, Artaud introduced a concept to which he would return in future: that there is a 'furtive' source 'which snatches the words I have found, which reduces my mental tension, which destroys, simultaneously and proportionately, in its substance the body of my thoughts'. Artaud did not yet delineate what furtive force deprived him of his ability to express himself; however, he wrote, 'though I can judge very well my mind, I can only assess the production of my mind to the extent that it blends with it in a sort of blissful unconsciousness. This will be my criterion.' In a poem that he attached to the letter, 'Cry', Artaud wrote, presumably of himself:

The little lost poet
Abandoned his celestial position
With an other-worldly idea
Pressed to his hairy heart

Two traditions met
But our padlocked thoughts
Do not have the space,
An experience to begin again.[51]

When Rivière finally answered, two months later, and at
Artaud's prompting, he renewed his accusation of artificiality: 'One
thing strikes me: the contrast between the extraordinary precision
of your self-diagnosis, and the vague, or at least the shapelessness
of your efforts.' Ultimately, Rivière acknowledged the sincerity
of Artaud's 'mental erosion', but cautioned him against allowing
his mind too much time to wander, too much autonomy and not
enough structure.[52]

In his penultimate letter to Artaud, Rivière broached the idea
of publishing their correspondence, but doing so under fictitious
names. Responding to Rivière, Artaud affirmed that he, too,
thought the letters publishable, but rejected the idea of using
false names, claiming it would give the reader the impression that
the whole correspondence had been manufactured. Of course, if
published under a pseudonym, Artaud would be deprived of the
distinction of being published by Rivière.

Artaud made reference to the psychological damage suffered
by his generation, but nonetheless viewed his turmoil as unique:
'I can truly say that I am not in this world, and this is not simply
intellectual posturing.'[53] In his last letter to Artaud, Rivière finally
struck empathetic chords, admitting to suffering the pangs of
self-doubt Artaud had continuously expressed, but conceding that
Artaud experienced a more profound torment, the annihilation of
the soul. If it was any consolation, Rivière offered a ray of hope for
Artaud's creative output: 'Who does not know depression, who has
never felt the soul impaired by the body, invaded by its weakness, is
incapable of perceiving any truth of the nature of man.'[54]

Self-portrait, *c.* 1921.

The exchange of letters between the aspiring, though tortured, poet and the doyen of avant-garde Parisian literature provides a remarkable window into Artaud's state of being. It is possible that, for Artaud, Rivière was more than simply a renowned mentor and prospective publisher; instead, he was a surrogate father for Artaud, yet another substitute for the biological one who, his son believed, did not listen to and could not understand him.[55]

During his correspondence with Rivière, Artaud continuously wrote to Athanasiou. The letters are often heartbreaking and tender in their declarations of desire, longing, pain and sorrow, without discussing his correspondence with Rivière or confiding in Athanasiou his difficulties in expressing himself. Throughout much of the period between May 1923 and April 1924, Artaud and Athanasiou were apart – he was in the south of France when she was in Paris, and she was in Romania when he was in Paris. The letters reference Artaud's physical separation from Athanasiou and the accompanying emptiness he felt. However, Artaud also wrote, in July 1923, of being physically out of sorts, of a

> sensation of numbness, of *separation* of myself from each of my limbs, from my organs . . . that when I touch myself I don't have the feeling to touch ME, myself, but to encounter a conscious wall, that gives me the sensation of being a skeleton with neither skin nor flesh, or rather a living void.[56]

In October he wrote of barely being able to function and feeling 'stripped of his being, stripped of his life'.[57] Although Artaud did not directly peg his feelings of disorientation and loss to his absence from Athanasiou, it is nearly impossible to conclude otherwise.

However, Artaud's addiction to opiates casts a ubiquitous shadow over this series of letters. Artaud's responses allow a glimpse into the substance of Athanasiou's letters; to her, their relationship could only endure if Artaud abstained from narcotics. Artaud, however, steadfastly refused, claiming in one letter that he would 'separate himself from the poison when [his] state of health permitted him to do so', imploring her to not abandon him during his 'misfortune'. He concluded this letter, as he would subsequent letters, with a plaintive plea for understanding: 'Help me, instead of adding to my unhappiness, understand in order to conclude that all your reasons cannot have any effect on me because my dreadful destiny has, for a long time, put me *beyond human reason*, outside of life.'[58]

By November 1923 Artaud claimed to be doing better, feeling vindicated that the injections were working as he had expected.[59] This was not the type of message to mollify Athanasiou; she understood that in spite of Artaud's reassurances, as long as he pegged his physical and mental well-being to opiates, he would remain forever a junkie. Artaud's reaction mixed anger, desperation, pleas for understanding, reminders of their past together and threats to break off all communication; but as the letters from Athanasiou assumed a more distant tone, and as their frequency diminished, it became clear that Artaud's expectations of a lifetime with Athanasiou would not materialize. He had poured his soul into his letters, even signing off with the familial diminutives 'Nanaqui' and 'Naky'; however much Athanasiou harboured reciprocal feelings for him, the relief he obtained from the junk flowing through his veins would forever trump anything she could offer him. In August 1924 Athanasiou appeared jealous of a relationship Artaud developed with the pianist Aline Panthès. In two letters, Artaud told Athanasiou that her mistrust of him was hurtful and clarified that he 'did not call [Panthès] his girlfriend (*amie*), I said soul (*âme*)'. Artaud then went on to say, 'But don't harass me with complaints, my life is still too insecure, too unhappy to be so troubled.'[60]

The publication of Artaud's correspondence with Rivière left an impression on André Breton, one of the leading figures of the Dada movement. Breton's first encounter with Artaud occurred at the premiere of *Antigone*; prompted by his long disdain for Cocteau, whom he struggled to keep out of Dada circles, Breton disrupted the performance. However, by 1922 Breton had publicly eschewed his association with Dadaism, sensing that the spirit of the movement was spent and unsalvageable.[61] Breton turned to the creation of a new cultural movement, one that would be uncompromising in the face of the inevitable co-opting forces; Artaud's internal conflicts and his determination to reproduce his ideas, purified of thought and form, appeared to Breton to coincide with the ethos of Surrealism.

3

Beyond

Six months older than Artaud, born in Normandy and raised in the suburbs of Paris, André Breton, like Artaud, chafed under the dictates of his family's bourgeois aspirations. There the similarities ended. Breton was more engaged in pre-First World War France's political currents, particularly anarchism; though he would later refer to this as a 'confused admiration', Breton credited anarchism with being one of the seeds out of which Surrealism sprouted.[1] In contrast, political debates did not appear to have entered Artaud's pre-war universe. During the war, Artaud and Breton were on opposite ends of the psychiatric spectrum; Artaud was institutionalized for his nervous disorders, while Breton was employed as an assistant at the psychiatric centre at Saint-Dizier treating soldiers for shell shock. It was through this experience that Breton's worldview began to crystallize, as he combined his artistic inclinations with an interest in Freudian theories on irrationality.

In February 1916 a group of exiled artists and writers, disillusioned by nationalism and the war it produced, met at Zurich's Cabaret Voltaire. The group, employing literary and visual arts to expose the moral vacuity of Western logic and reason, and the banality of its cultural output, brought Dadaism to life. In 1917 Breton dismissed Dadaism as unoriginal, but shortly after the armistice of 1918 he reconsidered his earlier assessment. Despairing over the opium-overdose death of Jacques Pierre Vaché, his intellectual and cultural mentor, Breton thought he had found a surrogate for Vaché in Dada's guiding force, the Romanian-born poet Tristan Tzara, a kindred spirit determined to subvert the ordered bourgeois world.[2] For Breton, the war had physically and psychically destroyed Europe and laid bare the emptiness of the West and the precepts underpinning its foundation. The question for Breton, however, was whether Dada's emphasis on the absurd was a sufficiently audacious response to the challenges and opportunities of 1919 when the prospects of revolutionary change appeared propitious.[3]

Within months Breton was contributing to Dada's journals and taking an active hand in editorial decisions; however, by late 1921 Breton had grown sceptical that Dada was anything but a theatrical novelty – and a dying one at that – lacking substance, no more than a voice in the cultural wilderness. He had become disenchanted with some of his fellow collaborators and discouraged that Dadaism was stagnating, devoid of a constructive purpose, its challenge never rising above the level of parody. In January 1922 Breton broke with the Dadaists; out of its moribund body he would develop a new movement, replete with the audacity, verve and energy of its progenitor's earliest days.

During the two years after his departure from Dada, Breton sought to train individuals, rather than form a collective, but by 1924 his new philosophical venture – Surrealism – had become a movement. Its defining core was distilled in a manifesto drafted by Breton:

> SURREALISM, *n.* Psychic automatism in its pure state, by which one proposes to express – verbally, by means of the written word, or in any other manner – the actual functioning of thought. Dictation of thought, in the absence of any control exercised by reason, exempt from any aesthetic or moral concern.[4]

For Breton, Surrealism was the product of a ménage à trois between Dada, Freudian dream theory and Breton's literary heroes – Comte de Lautréamont, Arthur Rimbaud, Edgar Allan Poe, Friedrich Nietzsche, Alfred Jarry, Matthew Gregory Lewis and Raymond Roussel. Departing from Freud's employment of dream analysis, Breton envisioned dreams as pods containing the seeds of alternative states of consciousness, a veritable harvest of poetic expression genetically unmodified by reality's adulterating strictures. In contrast to Dadaism's nihilistic focus on society's absurdities, Surrealism assumed a self-consciously revolutionary posture that melded together Breton's political convictions and his definition of poetry. For Breton, poetry was 'a specific solution to the problem of life', a medium 'for acceding to a richer, more fulfilling world . . . and even for creating such a world out of one's own inner resources'.[5] Originating as they do in the unconscious cosmos of irrationality, ideals engendered by poetic thought and expression seamlessly morph into a remonstration against reason and logic; from there, it's but a short step to a revolt against bourgeois cultural, political and social hegemony. The purpose of Surrealism – to challenge and, ultimately, to overthrow the bourgeois cultural regime – necessarily entailed a concomitant revolutionary and regenerative process, though one that remained distrustful of political movements. Fidelity to its anarchist roots, at least initially, required Surrealism to scrupulously avoid party affiliation.

Attracted by the Artaud–Rivière correspondence and the notoriety Artaud garnered from being published in the *NRF*, Breton, on 11 October 1924, invited Artaud to participate in Surrealism. Artaud was indifferent, writing to Madame Toulouse, 'I have met all the Dadaists, who would like to include me in their latest surrealist boat, but nothing doing. I am too much of a surrealist for that. Moreover, I have always been, and I know, what surrealism is. It is the system of the world and of ideas that I have always practiced.'[6] Furthermore, in a letter written to Rivière on 25 May 1924, Artaud distinguishes between the torment from which he suffers and that of the Surrealists:

> The fact remains that they do not suffer and that I do, not only mentally, but physically, in my everyday soul. This lack of connection to an object, a characteristic of all literature, is for me a lack of connection to life. Speaking for myself, I can honestly say that I am not in the world, and this is not merely a state of mind.[7]

Written on the cusp of Artaud's adhesion to Surrealism, this letter underscores Artaud's contention that his condition made him

Artaud with his sister Marie-Ange at her wedding in 1924.

distinct from others of his generation who had suffered from the war and its aftermath. For Artaud, the pain that he endured was both an anguish-causing curse and a creative blessing; it stamped his voice as unique, his expressions of torment shrouded in the language of an artist seemingly plagued by his enigmatic insights and the impenetrability of his thoughts.

By early 1925, however, Artaud was an active member of the collective, having found, at last, a creative space among artists who, like him, were unwilling or unable to conform to society's conventions. Even after his bitter break with the Surrealists, Artaud recalled Surrealism as a deliverance:

> Surrealism came to me at a moment when life had grown absolutely weary, had beaten me down, and where madness or death were the only ways out for me. Surrealism was this virtual hope, intangible, and probably as seductive as any other, but which stimulated you, in spite of yourself, to take one last chance, to grapple with any phantoms if ever they are able to deceive the mind. Surrealism could not restore my lost essence, but it taught me to look no longer for the impossibility of stability in the activity of thought, and to learn to be content with the ghosts that my mind drags behind me. Even more than this, it gave these ghosts a sense, an indisputable and harsh life, and, in point of fact, I have relearned to believe anew in my thoughts.[8]

Artaud had known the artist André Masson since 1922. At the time, Masson, along with Joan Miró, Michel Leiris and other writers and artists, formed a creative collective at 45 rue Blomet. Just as Artaud's paradoxical relationship to writing attracted Breton's attention, so too did Masson's art, in particular his celebration of primalism in *The Four Elements*, which Breton bought in 1924. The inclusion of painters in the Surrealist galaxy was something of a conundrum for the movement. One of Surrealism's guiding practices was automatism – creative production unmediated by thought or consciousness; visual art, by its very practice, is deliberative and evocative of memory. However, to refuse the likes of Masson, Miró, Picasso, Ernst, de Chirico, Dalí, Magritte and Tanguy would have excluded those with the potential and ability to visualize Surrealist imagery and render abstract literary ideas more readily digestible. Previously segregated into cliques of their chosen media of artistic expression, Surrealism offered literary and visual artists the opportunity to coalesce as the vanguard of a transformative movement.

From its headquarters at 15 rue de Grenelle, a few doors down from the headquarters of the NRF, the Bureau of Surrealist Research produced a journal, *La Révolution surréaliste*, to disseminate its work on the unconscious mind, and, above all, to envelop Surrealism in a revolutionary agenda. For Artaud, this was an exciting and fulfilling venture; he was still an outsider to the dominant norms of society and culture, but no longer alone and rejected in a wasteland, no longer confined within the deepest recesses of his troubled mind. Among the Surrealists, his most profound, unexpurgated ideas were true poetry; they assumed an air of purity and honesty, even if – perhaps because – they disregarded form and style. Surrealism for Artaud was, above all, the genesis of a revolution – a 'new declaration of rights of man', as the cover of *La Révolution surréaliste* proclaimed – against artistic contrivances masquerading as objective reality, and, by extension, the calculating, duplicitous, self-interested and smugly over-refined social and political milieu that sustained it. Elevating dreams and automatic writings above contemplation and consideration, Surrealism would uncompromisingly liberate the human spirit from all that stifles its fulfilment.

Breton and the other Surrealists welcomed Artaud's enthusiasm and commitment, but found his personality enigmatic. Shortly after meeting Artaud, Simone Breton described Artaud as 'splendid as a wave, as pleasant as a catastrophe'.[9] According to Breton,

> No one put all his powers – which were great – more sincerely to the service of the Surrealist cause [than Artaud]. Perhaps he was in greater conflict with life than were the rest of us. As handsome as he was then, as he moved about, he seemed to carry around with him a landscape from a black novel, all shot through with light. He was possessed of a sort of rage that did not spare, so to speak, any human institutions, but which could, on occasion, end in a laugh, where the extreme bravado of youth was discernible. Nonetheless, through the astonishing power of contagion, this rage had deeply influenced the Surrealist method.[10]

Sensing Surrealism to be his salvation, and basking in its acceptance of him, Artaud experienced an intense, albeit brief, period of influence over the movement, contributing pieces to various issues of *La Révolution surréaliste* and directing its third issue; Artaud's idiosyncratic vision appeared to have found the family and home that he believed had eluded him to that point. His first contributions to *La Révolution surréaliste* centred on two existential issues of personal significance: narcotics and control over one's existence. In the second issue, Artaud advocated the decriminalization of opium, positing opium's utility as an existentialist dilemma: until 'human despair' is eliminated, opium must be readily available.[11] That same issue also included Artaud's response to an article on suicide that appeared in the journal's first issue. In this piece, Artaud wrote that, as a volitional act, suicide did not interest him; it simply affirmed the reality that torments him. Intending – and likely succeeding – in obscuring the issue, Artaud averred that

> I have been dead for a long time, I am already suicided. In other words, someone has already suicided me. But what would you think of a *previous suicide*, of a suicide that makes us retrace our steps, but from the other side of existence, and not from the side of death. This, alone, will have value for me.[12]

Artaud clarified what he meant in a slightly longer piece for the Belgian monthly literary review *Le Disque vert*. Here the absences in Artaud's life became the subtext of his rejoinder. This discourse introduced themes that became some of Artaud's most profound ideas – reconstitution of the self, a 'body without organs' and the liberation of thought:

> If I kill myself, it will not be to destroy myself, but to reconstitute myself; suicide will be for me only a means of violently reconquering myself, of brutally invading my being, of anticipating God's uncertain advance . . . I would free myself from the conditioned response of my organs, so badly adjusted with my ego, and life for me would no longer be an absurd destiny where I think what I am told to think. I will henceforth choose my thoughts and the direction of my faculties, my inclinations, my reality . . .

Because life itself is not a solution; life is not a chosen, consented, determined existence. It is only a series of desires and opposing forces, petty contradictions that succeed or fail according to the circumstances of an odious fortune.[13]

When writing to Génica Athanasiou, Artaud occasionally alluded to suicide as an escape hatch from his despair over their relationship. However, in this piece, he wrote that in order to consider suicide he would have to be in complete control of his whole being, completely liberated from society's ligatures; otherwise, the act lacks volition. Whereas he once planned to enter the priesthood, Artaud now blamed a malevolent God for having

kept me alive in a void of emptiness, of relentless self-denials; he has extinguished everything in me down to the last surge of my thinking and sentient life. He has reduced me to a walking automaton, but an automaton who feels the rupture from his unconsciousness.[14]

Though carrying 26 names, the Surrealists' 'Declaration of 27 January 1925' was written, at least substantially, by Artaud. The 'Declaration' ratcheted up the Surrealists' commitment to revolution, asserting that they specialized in revolt: 'there is no means of action that we are not capable of employing.' It closed with the following: 'To the Western world we say more particularly: surrealism exists . . . It is a cry of the spirit reinstated to itself and firmly inclined to crush its shackles furiously, if need be with real hammers.'[15] This piece positioned Surrealism in opposition to Western culture and defined Surrealism's objectives as revolutionary; those objectives might have differed from previous French revolutions, but the necessity of violence remained a constant.

Drawn to Artaud's personal investment in Surrealism's revolutionary mission and sharing his weariness of it being led astray by self-indulgence, Breton supported Artaud's appointment as director of the Bureau of Surrealist Research and as editor of the third issue of *La Révolution surréaliste*. But Artaud's embodiment of Surrealism's sense of purpose, and the urgency with which it inhabited his every fibre, was a double-edged sword: tireless in dedicating all his energies towards Surrealism, his low tolerance for deviating views placed unreasonable demands on his comrades and strained the movement's camaraderie. Committed to maturating Surrealism from an idea to a serious challenge to extant orthodoxies, preserving Surrealism's purity and keeping the group cloistered from outside influences, Artaud closed off the Bureau to the public.

The third issue of *La Révolution surréaliste* (15 April 1925) was entitled 'End of the Christian Era'; this issue represented Artaud at the apex of his influence over Surrealism. As was the Surrealist custom, the articles were anonymously penned or collectively signed (based on notes left with Athanasiou, Artaud authored most of the pieces, several treating his growing disenchantment with the West and pursuit of mysticism). Conveying only super-ficial familiarity with Eastern religion, Artaud's 'Address to the Dalai Lama' pleaded for enlightenment 'in a language that our minds, contaminated by Europeans, can understand'.[16] Similarly, in a plea to Buddhists, Artaud extolled what he believed to be Eastern asceticism and rejected Western materialism:

> Our minds suffer from needs other than those inherent to life. We suffer from corruption, from the corruption by Reason.
> European logic ceaselessly crushes the mind between its two extremes; it opens and closes the mind.[17]

In two other pieces addressed to the rectors of European universities and to the Pope, Artaud condemned Western education and Christianity, respectively:

> You know nothing of the Mind, you ignore its most hidden and essential ramifications, those fossil imprints so close to our origins, those traces that we sometimes discover in the most obscure deposits in our minds.
> Your Catholic and Christian God, like all other gods, thought only of evil:

1st You are more than a match for it

2nd We only make shit of your canons, Index, sin, confession, priesthood; we imagine another war, war on you, Pope, dog . . .

From top to bottom what triumphs from your Roman masquerade is the hatred of all immediate truths of the soul, these flames which burn in the same mind. There is no God, Bible or Gospel . . .[18]

These texts convey the Surrealists' abjuration of Western knowledge's theological and pedagogical pillars. In 1924 Breton wrote, 'For my part, I'm pleased that Western civilization is at stake. Today light comes to us from the Orient . . . The *liquidation* of Mediterranean influences is underway and for that I can only rejoice.'[19] Inspired by Abd El-Krim's rebellion, in Morocco's Rif Mountains, against French imperialism, the Surrealists forged an 'imaginary Orient', the East mythologized as a more genuinely spiritual antipode to the decadent West and the antidote to the premium placed by the West on reason and logic. Whether the Surrealists, Artaud included, really understood non-Western cultures is open to conjecture; however, Artaud – more so than Breton, who admitted to being more attracted to the 'image' of Eastern thought – conceptualized an East that responded to his particular needs, and offered a palliative for his torment.

Unlike his fellow Surrealists' flirtation with Orientalism, when Artaud heard Surrealism's abnegation of reason echo Eastern philosophies and religions, the resonance was deeper and more personal.[20] Through his immersion in Surrealism, Artaud experienced an epiphany: until now, he had fretted over his inability to articulate his thoughts according to reason's dictates and solicited advice from Rivière on escaping his torment, but Surrealism had revealed to him that there was nothing inherently superior about logical thought processes. As Artaud expanded his familiarity with Eastern beliefs, he became aware that, like those subjugated by Western colonialism, he was another victim of European intellectual and religious imperiousness. Artaud's inability to locate the words at the core of his being was no longer an impediment, no longer a failure requiring remediation, but evidence of a higher state of consciousness. The sacred books of Hinduism and Buddhism attracted Artaud to the concept of thought and being as separate entities, and that the products of reflexive perception, rather than reflective thought, yield a more elevated understanding of reality:

> You who are not imprisoned in the flesh, and who know at what point in its carnal trajectory, in its senseless comings and goings, the soul finds the perfect way of speaking, the new word, the inner land; you who know how we retreat in our thoughts, and how the mind can save itself from itself; you who are inside yourselves, whose mind is no longer in the flesh; here are hands for which taking is not everything, minds which see beyond a forest of roofs, a blossoming of facades, a nation on wheels, an activity of fire and of marble . . .
>
> Therefore throw into the sea all the whites arriving with their small brains and their behaved minds. These dogs must understand us, that we are no longer speaking of the old human misery. Our minds suffer from needs other than those inherent to life. We suffer from corruption, from the corruption of Reason.
>
> Logical Europe crushes the spirit endlessly between the hammer blows of two extremes, opening and closing the mind. But now the suffocation is at its peak, for too long we have suffered under its yoke. The mind is greater than the mind, life's metamorphoses are numerous. As you, we reject progress: come, tear down our houses.[21]

Mysticism resonated with Artaud as both an alternative to the material world and a means for connecting with an elevated state of reality. It promised him a portal out of the pain and frustration of the material world, a reconciliation of thought with being – a form of transcendence.[22] Mysticism would allow Artaud 'to preserve his being when confronted with the encroaching materiality of outer reality'.[23]

When he entrusted the directorship of the Bureau and the editorship of the third issue of *La Révolution surréaliste* to Artaud, Breton was both discouraged with the direction of the movement and struggling to combat the appearance of micromanaging his cultural progeny. Breton had high aspirations for Surrealism, and he saw these endangered by personal conflicts between members, the complacency of the journal, a lack of commitment and discipline, and the failure of members to internalize Surrealism's core practices, including automatic writing. He feared that Surrealism was replicating the disappointments he experienced with Dadaism, and Artaud shared many of those same frustrations. Therefore Breton turned to Artaud to inject Surrealism with purpose, drive, verve and energy, telling his wife Simone on 22 January 1925, 'He will provide a new basis for the workings of the Central [Bureau], and he seems more resolved than anyone to bring our revolutionary action to the forefront.'[24] Artaud, though, was as apprehensive of his fellow Surrealists as Breton had been. On 14 May he wrote to Athanasiou of

> a crisis of absolute, and otherwise irreparable, disgust that I am going through after a series of ups and downs and disappointments as a result of my dear Surrealists, who, overall, Breton and Aragon excepted, have proven themselves to be the worst bunch of assholes the earth has produced.[25]

However, in spite of the seriousness, if not urgency, with which he approached Surrealism, Artaud's tenure as director of the Bureau would not even last two months. On 20 April 1925 Breton announced that the Bureau would close; a little less than one month later, Breton reopened the Bureau at his home. How and why things went wrong is largely a study in the dichotomous dynamic between Artaud and Breton, a relationship that was at once harmonious and incompatible, and speaks volumes about what each man invested in the Surrealist revolution. Breton objected to the tone of the third issue of *La Révolution surréaliste*, troubled by Artaud's forays into mysticism and his internalized, self-indulgent stance on revolution. Despite Breton's stated aversion to reason and logic, his conceptualization of revolution was a 'revolution of the mind'. Artaud, on the other hand, pursued a cosmos of chaos, a domain of disruption where a knowable reality is persistently inverted into a complex web of abstruse sensations stripped of anything familiar or comforting. Reflecting, years later, on the schism that developed between him and Artaud, Breton stated that Artaud led him to a place that seemed

> abstract, a gallery of ice . . . a place of lacunae and ellipses, where
> personally I could no longer communicate with the innumerable
> things I like – things which, despite everything, keep me on this
> earth. It is too often forgotten that Surrealism loved many things
> and that it angrily condemned whatever was harmful to love.[26]

If Breton is correct, Artaud adhered to Surrealism as a response to his darker impulses. Self-consumed, if not self-indulgent, Artaud could not successfully navigate existence as it is commonly experienced. On one level, for Artaud, these 'lacunae and ellipses' were a more generalized symptom of the human condition, an absence caused by all that interrupts pure thought; Surrealism was its panacea. On another level, though, Artaud identified issues very intimate to him; in personalizing what was at stake, Surrealism was less a panacea, and more a validation of his existence. Less an exit from his own headspace, Surrealism was a vehicle for bringing others into that headspace. Its promise having driven him to dogmatically insist on the actualization of the obtuse ideas he expressed, Artaud would not compromise because his very being could not permit compromise.

Though never entirely in sync with his fellow Surrealists, Artaud's years of association with the movement were formative ones for him. Surrounded by individuals whose ultimate objective was the subversion of their society, Artaud could unleash his thoughts without fear, rejection or judgement. Artaud was simpatico with his fellow Surrealists in believing Surrealism to be a revolutionary, rather than simply a cultural, movement; yet, as conceptualized by Artaud, revolution is not a break between past and present, but, as per its etymological origins, a return to a starting point.[27] Artaud's removal as director of the Bureau was partly due to Breton's desire to reassert control over the movement, but it also signified a more fundamental schism within Surrealism.

Breton's initial eschewal of any political objective to a Surrealist revolution did not last long. Given that, *ab initio*, Surrealism's activities were designed to subvert bourgeois values, it was, at least abstractly, political; but it had not taken an identifiable stance relative to any political issues. That changed, however, in 1924 with Abd El-Krim's rebellion in the Rif Mountains of Morocco against French imperial rule. The French Communist Party (PCF), and the editors of its affiliated journal *Clarté*, actively opposed the war and supported El-Krim's rebellion; but in a nationalistically and patriotically overheated political climate, and bolstered by *la mission civilisatrice*'s (the civilizing mission) undercurrent of imperialist racism, pacifism was largely a voice in the wilderness.

Up to that point, there had been very little, if any, symmetry between Surrealism and communism's ideas of revolution. More inclined towards anarchism and its promotion of pure freedom and exaltation of unconscious thought over reason, the Surrealists saw the Russian Revolution as lacking substance, imagination or inspiration; it was little more than a bureaucratic substitution. Despite this, Surrealism and communism had, at their cores, a mutual disdain for the bourgeoisie and its ideals.

Motivated by opposition to the French government's response to the Rif revolt and sympathetic with the victims of Western imperialist hubris, the Surrealists and the members of *Clarté* joined forces. Breton wrote to Simone: 'After this [the French invasion of Morocco], who can still talk about writing poems and the rest.'[28] Beyond galvanizing the Surrealists in favour of peace, France's military response to the Rif revolt exposed the emptiness of Western cultural superiority, the cornerstone of imperialism. Though this was consonant with Artaud's cultural sensibilities, the increasingly close relationship between the Surrealists and communism, whether with the official PCF or with *Clarté*, was not.

The rising conservative tide in Europe, exemplified by Mussolini's assumption of power in Italy, and the ineffectiveness of France's *Cartel des gauches*, the Radical–Socialist coalition government, equally contributed to the Surrealist–*Clarté* rapprochement. Breton reconsidered his earlier avoidance of ideological issues and comfortably slid into the rigorous dogmatism of *Clarté*. The first fallout from this was a close associate of Artaud, Surrealist playwright and poet Roger Vitrac, who was officially ostracized from

the Surrealists for failing to adhere completely to Surrealism's newly politicized agenda. Even under pressure by Breton to abide by the quarantining of Vitrac, Artaud refused to do so; combined with his removal from the directorship of the Bureau, Artaud was further alienated from the Surrealists.[29]

In 1925 other doors – film and theatre roles – were opening for Artaud. Notably in spring 1925 Gallimard, the most important and influential publishing house for emerging literary voices, published his *L'Ombilic des limbes* (The Umbilicus of Limbo). Although still affiliated with Surrealism, Artaud's level of commitment to it had diminished. It definitively broke in November 1926 after Artaud, along with Vitrac, opened the Théâtre Alfred Jarry, promising a complete psychic transformation of mind, body and senses for its audiences. Two years prior, before schisms within Surrealism surfaced, such aspirations would have fit well with its creed; but as Surrealism became more politicized, increasingly linked to the material concerns of communism, such ethereal – if not spiritually based – ideals had become incompatible with its new direction. Artaud was summoned before a panel of 'judges'. Faced with a variety of accusations, he stated that he had only appeared before the 'tribunal' as an act of courtesy; with that, he resigned, officially ending his more than two-year formal association with Surrealism.

In 1927 Artaud wrote two post-mortems on Surrealism, *À la grande nuit, ou le bluff surréaliste* (In the Dark, or the Surrealist Bluff) and *Point final* (The Final Point). In the introductory portion of *Point final*, he mourned Surrealism's lost potential in very personal terms:

Surrealism came to me at a time when life had perfectly man-
aged to tire me, to discourage me, and when the only solutions
for me were madness or death. Surrealism was this virtual hope,
elusive, and probably also as deceptive as any other, but which
pushed us in spite of ourselves to take one last chance, to hang
any phantoms if ever they are able to slightly frustrate the mind.
Surrealism could not reinstate my lost essence, but it taught me
no longer to search an impossible stability in the workings of the
mind, and to know to be content with the ghosts that my mind
temporizes before me.[30]

Artaud castigated Breton's leadership as absolutist and motiv-
ated by 'personal preoccupations'. Artaud's lament in these two essays was largely focused on revolution and, in particular, how the Surrealists had unwisely strayed from their original conception of revolution:

Wasn't Surrealism, at its origins, a rehabilitation of thought . . .
Yes, the genre of revolution that the Surrealists imagined at the
beginning is impossible in the overall scheme of life. Perceptible

or not, revolution is an affair of the mind, and the practical mind has nothing ever to do therein.[31]

Moreover, Artaud excoriated his fellow Surrealists for their inability or unwillingness to break with materialism, rhetorically querying,

did Surrealism not die on the day when Breton and his adepts believed they had to rally to communism and to search in the domain of facts and of the immediate questions the culmination

Artaud, *c.* 1926–7.

of an action that could normally develop only within the most intimate confines of the mind.[32]

While Artaud appreciated that his idea of revolution was, to say the least, esoteric, he could not support a materially driven revolution:

> They believe themselves free to ridicule me when I speak of a metamorphosis of the inner conditions of the soul, as if I understand the soul to mean the same disgusting thing they understand it to be, and as if, from the point of view of the absolute, there could be the slightest interest to see the world's social structure change or power pass from the hands of the bourgeoisie to the proletariat.[33]

In an extended footnote, Artaud agreed that revolution is a collective enterprise, but 'true Revolution is an individual thing.'[34] Artaud further asked, 'In order to survive, did Surrealism need to embody a material revolt, to assimilate itself with such demands as the eight-hour workday, or the readjustment of wages or the struggle against the high cost of living?' As a Western philosophy, communism was an example of Surrealism's unimaginativeness at commanding a real revolution: 'Marxism is the last rotten fruit of Western mentality. A serious outrage visited on the mind's indiscernibility.'[35]

After his expulsion from the Surrealists, Artaud excoriated his former comrades' lack of spiritual purity, and, by extension, their commitment to the Surrealist revolution, citing that they 'only see love in the coital act'.[36] Beginning with the Surrealist years, and continuing throughout his life, Artaud obsessed over sex. He suffered an almost pathological fear of sex, in general, and of impotence and castration, in particular. In his mind, the two were linked, as sex caused the loss of a vital essence. Over the ensuing decades, he expanded upon and refined his ideas, but during the late 1920s Artaud made persistent references to the fears that would consume him; the spiritual revolution, of which he imagined Surrealism was a harbinger, denied physical and material pleasures, including sexuality.

One of his first published works, *Le Pèse-nerfs* (The Nerve Scale), included a series of three 'letters on the household', directed at, without naming, Athanasiou. Partly motivated by his frustrations with Athanasiou's efforts to stop his drug dalliances, the letters link together romantic liaisons with Artaud's sense of disengagement from his being. Oozing misogyny, Artaud's sexual insecurities bleed through with oblique references to failed or unfulfilling sexual encounters:

> Just like all women, you judge with your clitoris, not with your mind . . . Besides, you have only ever judged me by my external appearance, like all the women, like all the idiots do, while my inner soul is the most damaged, the most ruined.[37]

By his own admission, Artaud was egotistical when he wrote of his 'need of a woman who is exclusively mine and who I can find at my home at any time'. Though he acknowledged that Athanasiou could never satisfy this demand, he confirmed his undying love for her before concluding, 'I only ask to change our relationship, for each of us to make a different life that will not break us apart.'[38] In the third letter of the trilogy Artaud laced into Athanasiou for draining the life out of him with her 'stupid letters, your letters from your clitoris and not from your mind, your letters filled with sexual impulses and not conscious reasoning'.[39] The contradiction between Artaud's previous relentless disparagement of 'conscious reasoning' and his words here is striking. However, in this case, within the taxonomy of things that alienate and corrupt the body (and without really explaining the dichotomy), sex was more deadly than consciousness.

The tragic lives of the Italian Renaissance painter Paolo Uccello and the medieval thinker Peter Abélard also served as a refracting lens into Artaud's struggle between mind and body; sexuality was the subtext. Artaud's interest in Uccello stemmed, in all likelihood, from his familiarity with the fictionalized sketch of the painter in Marcel Schwob's *Vies imaginaires*.[40] Schwob focused on Uccello's confinement in his aesthetic imagination and neglect of life's physical necessities. While Uccello's myopic commitment to his art no doubt attracted Artaud's interest, Artaud embellished it. In the first of his three versions of the story – a prose outline for a play written at the time of his correspondence with Rivière – the conflict revolves around Selvaggia, Uccello's wife, dying of starvation; Uccello, who is either unwilling or unable to feed her; and the Renaissance architect Filippo Brunelleschi, whose lust for Selvaggia would deliver all the sustenance she needs. In contrast to Uccello's ethereality and weakness, Brunelleschi personifies corporeality and strength; Uccello floats in a spiritual domain, while Brunelleschi is grounded in the material. In writing that Uccello cannot feed Selvaggia because 'he has nothing in his robe', Artaud is really alluding to Uccello's inability to satisfy Selvaggia's sexual appetite.[41] Brunelleschi desires Selvaggia both 'terrestrially and sexually. He only thinks of fucking her', while Uccello, though he 'does not ignore sexuality, sees it as glossy and volatile, and cold as ether'. Artaud's prospectus ends as follows: 'All of a sudden Brunelleschi feels his dick expand, becoming enormous. He cannot hold back and he lets fly a big white bird, like sperm, turning and twisting in the air.'[42]

At the beginning of the piece, Artaud indicated that the story is a form of self-representation; he and Uccello are alter egos, just as his later writings on literary or historical figures – whether on Uccello, Abélard, Heliogabalus or Van Gogh, or his adaptations of Matthew Gregory Lewis's *The Monk* and Percy Bysshe Shelley's *The Cenci* – might have been an 'indirect form of autobiography'.[43]

Included in a collection of short stories entitled *L'Art et la mort* (Art and Death) are two that concern the star-crossed romance between Peter Abélard, prolific scholar and theologian, and Héloïse, his talented student. After having impregnated and secretly married Héloïse, Abélard incites the wrath of his love's uncle, who has Abélard castrated. Thereafter separated, Abélard and Héloïse's great love endures, henceforth, as an epistolary romance. Though the stories of Uccello and Abélard could not unfold more differently, Artaud located the common thread between them and himself in corporeal urges: Uccello's abnegation of it, and Abélard's capitulation to it. In Artaud's telling of the story, it is not Héloïse's uncle, but Héloïse, who is responsible for

Abélard's punishment; after having emasculated him, she stands before him, a mocking presence, her beauty, having once attracted Abélard, now turned to ugliness. The final words – 'And here is the wife of Abélard, the eunuch' – are a tragic coda to Abélard's denigration.[44] Abélard's story metaphorically conformed to Artaud's fear of sex; in Abélard's case, it led to the physical loss of his penis, and, in Artaud's, in a metaphysical loss, a spiritual castration, a detachment from his being.

In 1946–7, after nearly a decade of institutionalization and more than fifty electroshock therapy treatments, Artaud extended his quest for 'pure thought' to the construction of 'an immaculate body' (*corps propre*). The body, for Artaud, was an 'unaccomplished work', striving to maintain its limitlessness. When the body is reduced to anatomical functions, sexuality

> inscribes the body in the limited and finite field of psychosocial norms or of the identifying markings of the dominant power . . . this malevolent sexuality is a strategic and rhetorical construction, which wants to mask over, suffocate, and control the body's potentialities.[45]

Artaud's understanding of sex was idiosyncratic to a fault. In 1947 he wrote to Breton that 'the coitus of sexuality, through the erethism of an orgasm, is only to make the body forget that it is a bomb, a torpedo which the atomic bomb of Bikini has no more, and is no more, than the science and the dullness of an old fart let loose.'[46]

In one of the many streams of consciousness he wrote in his notebook less than a year before his death, Artaud asserted

> but <u>shit</u>
>   and damn it
> at any rate i have
> no need to screw
> to please myself
> these are the beings
> who need
>   to screw

but what is within
can also be found in
the nose
in the eyes
       on the forehead
this is also in screwing
that the state described
       as least pure
furthest from
its origin
all that has been
done by beasts[47]

His disappointments with Surrealism's evolution notwithstanding, Artaud remained in contact with several of his Surrealist
comrades, including Breton, throughout his life. Though he
eschewed communism as too material, too Western, Artaud
never wavered in his commitment to the anarchistic ideals that
first motivated Surrealism, never ceasing to consider himself the
one true Surrealist. From his perspective, the individual's psychic
release – what he believed to be the core objective of Surrealism's
revolutionary process – was not compatible with the pursuit of
a collective consensus or the rigid materialism of communism.
Having emerged out of the chaos, confusion and uncertainty
of post-First World War Europe, Surrealism was a product of,
and a reflection on, its times; its revolutionary rhetoric, disdain
for bourgeois conventions and privileging of the unconscious
mind provided Artaud with what he thought would be a space
of validation and inspiration. However, Artaud's investment
in Surrealism – the intensity with which he personalized and
internalized its tenets – rendered his long-term relationship with
it untenable. As inflexible as Breton in his doctrine, Artaud could
not forgive deviations from his cosmos. Amorphous and malleable,
Surrealism created a semblance of symmetry and harmony – albeit
a false one – between Artaud and his fellow Surrealists. Artaud's
vision for Surrealism required a loftiness and ethereality that rose
above quotidian experience and events; but as it had been at its

inception, Surrealism would remain a creature of its time, adapting and responding to the exigencies of its period, in the end returning Artaud to the isolation he inhabited prior to his stint with the Surrealists. 'For me, disregarding all collective enterprises, I plunged uncompromisingly into the search for the magic in a solitude.'[48]

4

Performance

The break with the Surrealists, though inevitable and disappointing, liberated Artaud. The final years of the 1920s witnessed Artaud's validation by the prestigious publishing house Gallimard. Meanwhile, through theatre – a cultural medium particularly scorned by the Surrealists – Artaud strove to realize his artistic vision. Finally, from the middle of the decade onwards, Artaud expanded his cinematic repertoire, acting in more films, writing screenplays and imagining the potential for visualizing and representing alternative forms of consciousness.

After Jacques Rivière's death in 1925, Jean Paulhan, his secretary for the previous five years, became director of Gallimard's *Nouvelle Revue française* (NRF). For authors in France in the 1920s, being published in the NRF 'conferred a form of literary apotheosis'.[1] While Artaud did not actively pursue notoriety within the rarefied world of French letters, he revelled in the attention and his burgeoning reputation. Before personally becoming acquainted, Artaud and Paulhan travelled in concentric cultural circles. During the war, Paulhan was an editor for Édouard Toulouse on *Demain*, and towards the war's end Paulhan corresponded with Breton.[2] Upon assuming the editorship of NRF, Paulhan published two small books by Artaud, *The Umbilicus of Limbo* and *The Nerve Metre*; André Masson illustrated the covers of both works, with a rendering of Artaud gracing the former. Artaud's burgeoning association with the NRF commenced – and perhaps facilitated – his definitive parting with the Surrealists and expanded the scope of his audience. It also lay the foundation for a lifelong collaborative relationship and friendship with Paulhan. Although the two had been in correspondence since

1924, the relationship crystallized during the summer of 1926, when Artaud mediated between Paulhan and Breton over a collaborative venture between the Surrealists and the *NRF*. Negotiations broke down over Paulhan's and Breton's respective assertions of editorial control; Artaud, in an uncharacteristically obsequious response, peppered with apologies for a previous correspondence, reassured Paulhan, 'I am not chained to Breton. I love my independence too much and I am not always in agreement with him.'[3] Paulhan responded that he was willing to disengage his disappointment with Artaud from his respect for his writing.[4]

Surrealism's adoption of a more political posture during the autumn of 1926 frayed Artaud's connection to it; Artaud's interest in theatre snapped the thread. Breton targeted theatre as another bourgeois cultural contrivance and thus anathema to Surrealism's increasingly political objectives. Artaud remained committed to theatre, seeing in theatre's regeneration a vehicle for revolution. Together with another excommunicated Surrealist, Roger Vitrac, and Robert Aron (secretary to Gaston Gallimard), Artaud approached René and Yvonne Allendy in September 1926 about financing a new theatre venture, the Théâtre Alfred Jarry (TAJ).[5] A prospectus for the theatre appeared in the issue of *NRF* of 1 November 1926:

> Theatre is the most impossible thing in the world to save. An art based entirely on a power of illusion that it is incapable of delivering can only disappear.
>
> Words either have or don't have their power of illusion. They have their own individual value. But sets, costumes, gestures and fake cries will never replace the reality we expect. What is urgent is the creation of a reality, the unprecedented eruption of a world. Theatre must give us this ephemeral, but real, world, this world in tangent with reality. Either it will become this world, or theatre will cease to exist.[6]

In Artaud's prospectus, theatre is an interactive experience; the audience is a participant in the production – it is not simply the spectator, not just entertained, but is viscerally and ontologically transformed or destabilized by the experience, leaving the theatre in '*human* anguish'.[7] In contrast to the blueprint for the Theatre of Cruelty that he would develop years later, in 1926 Artaud privileged text over all other matters:

> For this definition that we try to give to the theatre, one thing seems invulnerable to us, one thing appears true: the text. But the text, as a distinct reality, existing by itself, is self-sufficient, not in terms of its spirit – that we do not tend to respect – but simply in terms of the displacement of air created by its enunciation. Enough said.[8]

Artaud's *Manifeste pour un théâtre avorté* (Manifesto for an Aborted Theatre), produced on 13 November 1926, alternatingly aspired to reorient Surrealism back to its original mission (and harmonize it with a regenerated theatre) and expressed frustration over the unlikelihood of his project reaching fruition. Artaud wrote that the TAJ would be neither a business nor a space for staging plays, but would provide a metaphysical experience, physically manifesting 'all that is obscure, hidden, and unrevealed in the mind'.[9] Referring to the Surrealists as 'toilet paper revolutionaries', Artaud explicated the different approaches to revolution between him and his former comrades:

> There are several ways to understand the Revolution, and among these ways, communism, seems to me, the worst, the most reductionist. A revolution of slackers. It makes no difference, I strongly proclaim, if power passes from the hands of the bourgeoisie to those of the proletariat. For me, this is not a Revolution. This is not a simple handing over of power. A Revolution that puts at the top of its concerns the necessities of production and which persists in grounding itself on mechanization as the means of bettering the condition of the workers is, for me, a revolution of eunuchs . . . At all stages of reflection we are driven to despair by mechanization. But the true roots of evil run deeper, and it would be necessary to produce a volume to analyse them. For now, I will limit myself to say that the most

urgently needed Revolution consists of a sort of regression in time. Let us return to the *mentalité* or the simple customs of the Middle Ages, genuinely and by a transformation in our natures, and I will guess that we will have accomplished the only revolution worth mentioning.[10]

When the Manifesto was published – more than two months later in the Marseille-based *Cahiers du Sud* – Artaud's break with the Surrealist movement was complete, though his personal estrangement from his former comrades, including Breton, would be temporary and fluctuating. More importantly – at least in the immediate sense – Yvonne Allendy supplied a 3,000-franc disbursement for the TAJ in March 1927.

In its first production, on 1 and 2 June 1927, the TAJ staged three works, one by each of its founders. Reviews were mixed. Literary critic Benjamin Crémieux, a contributor to *NRF*, disparaged Aron's and Vitrac's pieces as lacking originality but liked Artaud's contribution, calling it 'a brief hallucination without text, or nearly so, in which the author has condensed a synthesis of life and death'.[11] However, after having lost 7,000 francs, the prospect of the TAJ's survival was slim. Artaud, though, remained committed to the larger purpose of the theatre to convey 'a certain spiritual desperation which comes to life only in performance'.[12]

The second TAJ production on 14 January 1928 at the Comédie des Champs-Élysées featured a screening of the Russian film-maker V. I. Pudovkin's adaptation of Maxim Gorky's *La Mère*, a film about the Russian Revolution that had been banned by the French censors, as well as a piece by a playwright whose identity Artaud kept under wraps, not even revealing it to his actors. Intent on disrupting the performance, the Surrealists were disarmed when Breton realized the performance was a parody of Act III of *Partage de midi*, written by Paul Claudel – poet, playwright and, at the time, France's ambassador to the United States. Breton admired Claudel's poetry, but was put off by Claudel's political conservatism and Catholicism; Claudel's recent comparison of Surrealism to pederasty deepened the chasm. Upon the performance's completion, Artaud appeared on stage and identified Claudel, an 'infamous traitor', as the author.

Artaud's remarks provoked a public outcry, but raised the profile of the theatre group and paved the way, in the very short term, for a rapprochement between Artaud and Breton.[13] On the other hand, in addition to the *NRF*'s scathing review of the play, Artaud's characterization of Claudel personally appalled Paulhan:

> So to you it is treasonous to serve France as an ambassador; this is to change oneself. Artaud, isn't this you who has, all of a sudden, abandoned your thoughts to these facilities, to these absences of the soul, to these ruses: anticlericalism, political revolution? I can only say to you how irritated I am.[14]

Artaud provided Paulhan's letter, along with his response to it, to Breton, who published them in *La Révolution surréaliste*.

The second performance at the TAJ actualized theatre's revolutionary and subversive potential and temporarily facilitated Artaud's reconnection with the Surrealists. But even subversive theatre required financing. Conditional upon it staging a work by August Strindberg, the TAJ procured funding from some Swedish expatriate friends of Yvonne Allendy. Combining elements of Eastern mysticism (though from a decidedly Orientalized vantage point), social criticism, the collapsing of time and space, and alternative realities, Strindberg's *A Dream Play* had obvious appeal to Artaud. The set for this production was inspired by, in Crémieux's estimation, the Italian Surrealist Giorgio de Chirico.[15] That aside, barely six months after Artaud's and Breton's reconciliation, the choice of material and source of funding drove another wedge between them. Since it was partly funded by the Swedish consulate, Breton promised that the Surrealists would disrupt performances. At *A Dream Play*'s premiere at the Théâtre de l'Avenue on 2 June 1928, the audience included the Swedish ambassador, Swedish aristocrats, the duchess of La Rochefoucauld, the princess of Polignac, Prince George of Greece, Paul Valéry, André Gide, Abel Gance, François Mauriac and an assortment of other dignitaries, as well as international journalists; a coup for Allendy, the illustrious list of attendees was a burden for Artaud. As the Surrealists took seats in the orchestra reserved for the glitterati and shouted about the production's co-option by Swedish capitalists, Artaud appeared on stage and declared that the piece had been deliberately selected because 'Strindberg was an insurgent, as was Jarry, as was Lautréamont, as is Breton, as am I. We stage this piece in so much as it vomits on its country, on all the countries, on the society!'[16] With these words, the Swedish delegation left the theatre, but afterwards sent a note to Allendy complimenting the production as superior to the one staged by Max Reinhardt in Stockholm! Four days later, Artaud lamented insulting the Swedes, clarifying that while he was in 'revolt against all organized society', he would not have expressed this publicly had it not been for 'the perfidious provocations of the surrealists'. For good measure, Artaud offered to recompense the Swedes for the funds they had expended.[17]

Though Breton and the Surrealists warned Artaud not to stage the second performance of *A Dream Play*, the TAJ went ahead with the show on 9 June, and, much to Breton's consternation, with police protection. The production degenerated into a fight, and five Surrealists were arrested. The entire affair proved to be too much for Robert Aron, who affirmed his support for the TAJ, in principle, and his continued friendship with Artaud, but tendered his resignation to Allendy. For the Surrealists, acrimony towards Artaud ran deeper; days after the second performance of *A Dream Play*, Pierre Unik, a young Surrealist, physically attacked Artaud in the company of Breton, in the stairwell of the hotel where Unik and Artaud lived, while Breton, in the twelfth and final issue of *La Révolution surréaliste*, chastised Artaud as unsuitable for the Surrealist movement.

In late December 1928 Allendy agreed to finance another TAJ production, a play written by Vitrac entitled *Victor ou les enfants pouvoir* (Victor, or Power to the Children). In spite of some theatrics – including, for dramatic effect, the lobbing of stink bombs – there was less press coverage; with that said, reviews were enthusiastic, if not hyperbolic (comparing it to Alfred Jarry's *Ubu Roi*). Such accolades notwithstanding, the TAJ folded after *Victor*'s three-performance run. Though the Count and Countess of Noailles offered to fund the TAJ to the tune of 20,000 francs, Artaud's cultural interests and financial needs had already moved him into the relatively new medium of film.

Artaud's film career began in 1924 when he was cast as 'Monsieur II' in Claude Autant-Lara's short film *Faits-divers*. Autant-Lara had been warned that Artaud was 'a pretty difficult lad'; yet in recounting his first meeting with Artaud, he recalled

> facing a strange person, a bit distant. He had the appearance of floating one or two metres above the ground. He gave the impression of not always listening; in fact, he listened very well. My proposal intrigued him, and he soon accepted to make this film with me.[18]

Two months later – in July 1924 – Artaud was in Bretagne to film Luitz-Morat's pirate epic, *Surcouf, roi des corsairs* (Surcouf, King of the Pirates); filming would last through October and, consistent with the frenetic post-production pace of early cinema, *Surcouf* was released in February 1925. Artaud landed this role through the help of his maternal uncle, Louis Nalpas, artistic director for the Société des cinéromans, a cornerstone of French film during the silent era.[19] In his letters to Génica, Artaud relished the experience of working on *Surcouf* and the strong impression he made on the other actors. The Bretagne sea air was doing wonders for his health, and he even wrote of being tanned. However, to fellow stage actor Armand Salacrou, Artaud complained that Luitz-Morat, as punishment for Nalpas' intervention, exploited Artaud's vertigo by having him do scenes on roofs and towers.[20] All was apparently forgotten by the time of Artaud's next screen role in Luitz-Morat's loose adaptation of Eugène Sue's nineteenth-century novel *Le Juif errant* (The Wandering Jew, 1844).

A powerful and formidable figure in early French cinema, Nalpas is credited with amplifying the role of film producer to the lynchpin of a production. Nalpas' support for a production could be crucial to its materialization, while his confidence in a film-maker could be decisive to a career. In 1915 the 26-year-old Abel Gance, inspired by the pioneering cinematic work of Georges Méliès, conveyed madness in his direction of *La Folie du docteur Tube* (The Insanity of Doctor Tube) through a series of distorted images. Nalpas was 'horrified by its confusing imagery' and did not allow the film's release, but trusted Gance's talents and kept him on at the studio –

though on a tighter leash – issuing the following directive: 'Above all, no more theories or psychology.'[21]

Artaud met Gance through Nalpas in September 1924. By then one of France's most renowned directors, Gance's success allowed him to test the limitations of French film and to broaden the cinematic idiom. Gance's *J'accuse*, an anti-war film released in March 1919 – barely six months after the armistice that ended the war – redefined French cinema; for the director Léon Poirier, through Gance,

> the [film] industry had given birth to a new art form. From this point onwards, one could nuance sentiments, express thoughts, give birth by the silent play of rhythm and light waves of emotion developing in intensity in a veritable human crowd. This was authorized, the public followed, the true revolution was accomplished.[22]

In cinema Artaud found a vehicle for his revolutionary vision. In the issue of *Théâtre et comoedia illustré* from March 1923, the director René Clair asked readers to list their favourite kinds of film and the kinds of film they wanted produced. The journal published the reactions of a variety of cultural icons, including Fernand Léger, Jean Cocteau and Paul Valéry; Artaud's responses were not printed, but they reveal a shift in his focus from theatre to cinema. Affirming that he 'likes *cinema*', Artaud characterized cinema as a

> total reversal of values, a complete disarrangement of optics, perspective and logic. It is more exciting than phosphorus, more captivating than love. Its galvanizing force cannot be indefinitely destroyed by employing subjects that neutralize its impact and that really belong to theatre . . . Cinema is a remarkable stimulant. It acts directly on the grey matter of the mind. When the taste of art is sufficiently blended with the psychic ingredient that it contains, it will surpass theatre, which we will relegate to the attic of our memories . . . Cinema has, above all, the virtue of an inoffensive and direct poison, a subcutaneous injection of morphine.[23]

In the silent era, filmic expression depended on corporeal and facial reactions; although speech could be conveyed by inter-titles, these were few, and the words printed on them rarely, if ever, dominated the physical action. For Artaud, the visual image, unlike theatre and literature, was an antidote to the empire of reasoned, verbal expression; by necessity, if nothing else, silent film allowed the body to give meaning to experience, to probe deeper states of consciousness without the imposition of words or vocalizations.

After procuring a next-to-impossible meeting with Gance, Artaud gushed to Madame Toulouse:

> My visit with Gance has been crowned with success . . . My face is of great interest, he said – so too my *mentalité* – and he finished by promising me a role in one of the six films he is preparing on the life of Napoléon.[24]

In early 1925 Gance selected Artaud for the role of the French revolutionary Jean-Paul Marat – 'the Friend of the People' – forever immortalized in Jacques-Louis David's *La Mort de Marat*. Sometime between January and July, however, Gance decided to switch Artaud to the role of Camille Desmoulins, a far less prominent and less dramatic personage. Artaud wrote to Gance, imploring him to reconsider:

> I see so many moral and material impossibilities to playing this role [Desmoulins], and, on the other hand, it will be so disastrous to abandon a role that is far more ideal, far more characteristic, in brief, far more remarkable, of Marat, that it is absolutely necessary that I have a conversation with you before you make your final decision.[25]

Artaud expressed one of his principal convictions regarding acting: that an actor must embody, not simply portray, a role. Artaud was recast as Marat.

In November 1927 Artaud wrote to Gance requesting his intercession in the casting of Jean Epstein's screen version of Edgar Allan Poe's *The Fall of the House of Usher*. 'I don't have a lot of claims in this world,' Artaud wrote, 'but I claim to understand Edgar Poe and to be a type like Master Usher. If I am not this person in the flesh, nobody is. I am him physically and psychically.' Artaud then went on to say that while the American actor John Barrymore would play Usher 'magically' and 'externally',

> I would incarnate him internally. My life is that of Usher and that of his sinister cottage. I have the plague in the soul of my nerves, and I suffer from it. There is a quality of the nervous sufferance that the greatest actor in the world cannot portray on the screen if he has not experienced it. And I have experienced it. I think like Usher.[26]

As Gance sought funding for his ambitious production, Artaud, in need of money, took the role of Cecco in *Graziella*, a film inspired by a work by the nineteenth-century French Romantic poet Lamartine. The eight-day exterior shoot took place on the island of Procida, off the coast of Italy, in less-than-comfortable conditions:

> You're devoured by fleas in your sleep, you eat in the manner of pigs, fifteen seated around the same table. The houses stink like straw, dust and shit. Barely any water to wash. A bed that is no more than a hammock.[27]

Filming of *Napoléon vu par Abel Gance* began in spring 1925, and two years later the film's premiere at the Théâtre national de l'opéra de Paris took place on 7 April 1927. Over 2,000 spectators attended the premiere, including political and cultural dignitaries, as well as several American film personalities.[28] The years between the start of production and the film's release was, by industry standards, excessive. Although the end product was, on the level of narrative, one of Gance's most conventional works, in every other conceivable way it was a testament to all Gance's expectations for the visual potential of film. In *Napoléon*, the camera became more than simply a recording instrument – for example, to symbolize the instability of the Convention of 1793, Gance attached the camera to a pendulum, allowing it, rather than actors or set pieces, to dictate the mood. However, the most memorable scene occurs at the film's end: Gance created a triptych sequence – tripling the width of the screen – by the simultaneous projection of three reels of film in a horizontal row, culminating in the colourization of each reel in simulation of the French Tricolour. The film was originally meant to cover, in six different segments, the life of Napoléon; Gance envisioned that each segment would exceed the duration of his longest film to date, *La Roue*, which clocked in at a little more than four and a half hours. In the end, only the first segment was completed – a five-and-a-half-hour exposition of Napoleon's life in military school, through the French Revolution and ending with his successful Italian campaign in 1797.

Of his experiences filming *Napoléon*, Artaud said little (other than to complain to Athanasiou that he had not been paid). However, in an interview with *Cinémonde* in August 1929, Artaud reflected upon the personal importance of playing Marat:

> This was the first role in which I had a sense of being myself on the screen, where I had the opportunity to be true to the character, to express the conception that I have of a figure, a person, who appears as an incarnation of a force of nature, and disinterested and indifferent towards all but his deepest passion.[29]

Although Marat did not feature prominently in the film, Gance recreated Marat's bathtub assassination by Charlotte Corday, leaving audiences with a memorable impression of Artaud's performance. Film reviews made brief but favourable mentions of Artaud's performance: 'Marat, this is Artaud, a terrible Marat, implacable.'[30] 'Van Daele, Koubitzky, Antonin Artaud and Philippe Hériat have engraved the etchings of Robespierre, Danton, Marat and Salicetti, personalities so difficult to animate.'[31] In May 1931 Jean Cocteau, writing in *NRF*, remembered Artaud's performance as the work of 'an alchemist. I can still see hanging from the edge of the bathtub this divine figure who combines the strange childlike figure in David's painting with the dormant upright profile of the interpreter.'[32]

Antonin Artaud as Marat in Abel Gance's *Napoléon*.

Two months after the premiere of *Napoléon*, Artaud landed a role in the Danish director Carl Theodor Dreyer's first production in France, *The Passion of Joan of Arc*. The author of the book upon which the film was based, Joseph Delteil, had been a member of the Surrealists; though Delteil's portrayal of Joan was unorthodox, Breton condemned his book as 'a gigantic fuck' and kicked Delteil out of the Surrealists. When Dreyer landed in France in April 1926, he was already well known to French film audiences; his arrival coincided with an announcement that he had been hired by the Société générale des films (the same company that produced *Napoléon*) to direct a new film penned by 'one of [France's] most famous authors'. *The Passion of Joan of Arc* was a visual triumph; its inter-titles were drawn directly from the transcripts of Joan's trial, though words were secondary to the minimalist set design. Above all, Dreyer's use of the close-up humanized his characters and reduced the distance between audience and images on the screen.[33] According to André Bazin, Dreyer's close-ups allowed the actor to truly embody the soul of the character, to transcend the limitations of playing a role.[34] Cast as Massieu, a priest sympathetic to Joan, Artaud's extraordinary facial expressions underscore his character's compassion and emotional torment when faced with Joan's suffering; the publicity posters featured Artaud and the film's star, Maria Falconetti, personifying the film's principal themes: stoicism, iconoclasm and spiritualism.

Artaud's turn as Massieu was a contrast to his previous screen roles, whether as the pirate in *Surcouf* or Marat in *Napoléon*; in an interview from 1929, he characterized Massieu as 'a saint who is no longer in turmoil, full of rage or perpetually uprooted from himself, but, on the contrary, calm'. During the shooting of the film, Artaud wrote to Athanasiou of his irritation with Dreyer (he never elaborated, but years later complained about Dreyer's insistence that the actors shave their heads up to the tonsure).[35] However, in that interview of 1929, Artaud lauded Dreyer's direction as providing him with 'unforgettable memories':

> This time I have dealt with a man who was able to make me believe in the justice, the beauty and the human interest of his conception. And whatever had been my ideas on cinema, poetry, life, for the first time I took stock that it was no longer a matter of aesthetics, bias, but of a work of art, with a man determined to elucidate one of the most anguishing problems that there is: Dreyer was determined to demonstrate Joan as a victim of one of the most abominable distortions that has occurred: the distortion of a divine principle passing into the minds of men, whether called Government or the Church or any other name. ... Dreyer was committed to insinuate the spirit of a scene to the actor and allow him the latitude to realize it, to give him some personal interpretation, provided he remain faithful to the spirit demanded.[36]

With the ensemble cast garnering strong reviews, Artaud's performance was rarely singled out. One of the rare reviews to have noted Artaud called his performance 'memorable, even though he does not try to stand out'.[37] In 1952 Cocteau stated that the performances of Falconetti, Silvain and Artaud still, decades later, amaze and induce tears from audiences while riveting them to their seats.[38] Though Artaud did a masterful job of embodying Massieu's

Artaud as Massieu in *The Passion of Joan of Arc*.

combination of sympathy, faith and sincerity, the most lasting impression is his visage as seen in a still photo. While cleaning her closet in 1934, Anaïs Nin, who had just met Artaud the previous year, found the now-iconic photograph of him as Massieu:

> His cheeks looked hollow, his eyes visionary and fanatical. Antonin Artaud had always refused to give photographs of himself because he feared voodoo curses (*envoûtements*, as he said) and believed that harm could come to him if some demonic person stuck pins into the portrait. And here was the beautiful monk at my mercy. I would not even put a thumbtack through it. I stored it away.[39]

Two more roles rounded out Artaud's film career in the silent era – 'the Intellectual' in Léon Poirier's *Verdun, visions d'histoire* (1928), and a small role in Marcel l'Herbier's contemporary version of Émile Zola's nineteenth-century novel *L'Argent* (1928).

Although l'Herbier lauded Artaud's acting skills ('merely with his presence, his look and the intelligence of his movement, he gave an unforgettable dynamism that was a little unsettling to the role of the secretary'), he was less enamoured with his unreliability in arriving on set.[40]

Artaud's role in *Verdun* was yet another flashpoint for conflict between him and the Surrealists. Although Poirier dedicated his film (which, like *Napoléon*, premiered at the Opéra de Paris) 'To all the martyrs of the most hideous of human passions: war', his film was less an exposition of the First World War's toll on the *poilus* (French soldiers), and more the presentation of a noble war. For having appeared in the film, Artaud came under attack from the Surrealists. Writing to film-maker Roland Tual, Artaud defended the film as 'not a patriotic film made for the exaltation of the most ignoble civic virtues, but a film of the left made to inspire "the horror of war to conscious and organized masses"'.[41]

Mixing footage from the war with dramatic representations shot on location in Verdun, *Verdun* recreated the experience of the war and its impact on a cross-section of society. For Artaud, whose experience in the war was marked by bouts of somnambulism and stays in clinics, the film provided a vicarious, though unreal, connection to the war. 'The intellectual' enthusiastically enlists in the 'righteous war', but dies on the battlefield, prostrate in a Christ-like pose, a martyr for a more transcendent cause. In spite of Poirier's direction that the actors draw from their personal experiences in the war, Artaud appeared to have channelled those of André Masson, who, after being gravely wounded in 1917, lay on the battlefield contemplating the horrors he had encountered and the senselessness of it all.

As Artaud's interest in cinema crystallized during the second half of the 1920s, he wrote two screenplays. The first, *Les dix-huit secondes* (Eighteen Seconds), written between 1925 and 1926, is, in length and format, more of a treatment than a screenplay. The autobiographical undertones could not be more obvious. The story begins with a man, an actor, looking at his watch; when he next looks at the watch, only eighteen seconds have passed, though on screen much will have occurred, all of it inside the actor's head. As

Artaud describes it, the actor is on the precipice of achieving great renown and the love of the woman he has pursued for so long:

> He is struck by a strange malady. He has become incapable of reaching his thoughts; he is completely lucid, but no matter what thought occurs to him, he can no longer give it an external form, that is to say to translate it into appropriate gestures and words. . . . He cannot find the necessary words, they no longer respond to his call; he is reduced to watching a procession of images, a surplus of contradictory images, none with much connection to the other.[42]

Eighteen Seconds is akin to a snapshot of Artaud in the mid-1920s: an actor on the verge of success, tormented by his inability to materialize his thoughts. The actor's romantic life nearly parallels Artaud's relationship with Athanasiou, while references to Kabbalah and the actor's suicide at the end of the eighteen seconds anticipate two of Artaud's later preoccupations. Reliant on imagery and absent speech, the eighteen seconds unfold on the screen in an almost nightmarish, surreal fashion. The actor migrates through a succession of seemingly incongruous circumstances ultimately leading him to the realization that existence is a Faustian bargain with one's mind, the thoughts that go with it the price.

Whereas *Eighteen Seconds* was never committed to celluloid, Artaud's next screenplay – *Le Coquille et le Clergyman* (The Seashell and the Clergyman) – would be the only one of his screenplays to make the transition from page to screen; its release, however, came amid a whirlwind of controversy and chaos, largely generated by Artaud himself. On 16 April 1927 Artaud deposited his screenplay for *The Seashell and the Clergyman* at the Association of Film Authors; three weeks later, *Cinémagazine* announced that Artaud and famed director Germaine Dulac would make 'an original film whose screenplay was inspired by a dream. There will only be one performer: Antonin Artaud.' Two weeks later, *Comoedia* clarified that Artaud and Athanasiou would be the performers.[43] Dulac accused Artaud of having placed these notices in the press; she had no intention of collaborating with him.[44]

Artaud, *c*. 1927–30 (left), and *c*. 1928 (right).

In a letter to Dulac, Artaud denied having anything to do with the notices and protested that he had 'no pretention to collaborate with [Dulac]. This would be a stupid pretention.'[45] He blamed the rumours on 'people who want to harm me, who personally hate me' before closing, 'the film you make will be something absolutely sensational.'[46] Other letters to Dulac reveal something different: that Artaud had definite ideas about the film's direction. In his final letter to Dulac, on 25 September, Artaud objected to her intention to include an explanatory text at the beginning of the film: 'I have never considered this film as the demonstration of any kind of theory. This is a film of pure images. There are no psychoanalytic, metaphysic or humane implications.'[47]

Artaud would have no role in the film, whether behind or in front of the camera. He was given a two-week break from the filming of *The Passion of Joan of Arc* to work with Dulac; whether for artistic differences or personal reasons, the director delayed the production long enough to make it impossible for Artaud to be near the Gaumont Studios during its filming.

Between her visual sensibility and cinematic experience, the choice of Dulac to direct Artaud's screenplay made sense. Though she directed her first film in 1918, Dulac's screen adaptation of André Obey's play *La Souriante madame Beudet* (The Smiling Madame Beudet) in 1923 substantially elevated her profile. Under Dulac's direction, the story took on feminist hues; it was an edgier version of *Madame Bovary*, with Dulac making full use of the visual possibilities offered by cinema to convey the unrealized dreams of a protagonist frustrated by a stifling, provincial bourgeois life.

Expecting a more prominent role in the conceptualization of his screenplay, Artaud did not take his exclusion from the film's production with equanimity or humility. On 25 October 1927, Dulac finally acceded to Artaud's requests to view the film. Predictably, Artaud claimed not to have been at all pleased by the finished product. In particular, Artaud claimed that Dulac turned the film into a prolonged succession of dreamlike sequences, sucking the life out of his screenplay, turning a potentially revolutionary script into another example of cinematic banality (however, the British Board of Film Censors, in banning the film, called it 'so cryptic as to be almost meaningless. If there is a meaning, it is doubtless objectionable.')[48]

Dulac originally planned the premiere for 23 November 1927 at the Salon d'automne at the Grand Palais but delayed the premiere until 9 February 1928 at the Studio des Ursulines, a theatre that first opened in 1925 expressly to screen avant-garde films. Several Surrealists, including Breton, Robert Desnos and Louis Aragon, showed up to support Artaud (this was just weeks after the TAJ's production of Claudel's play and the Artaud–Surrealist reconciliation). Accounts of what followed vary, but the most oft-repeated story relates that, as the film was projected, Breton, seeking to underscore Artaud's vision and Dulac's debasement of it, read aloud a copy of Artaud's script.[49] When some audience members tried to quiet Breton, another Surrealist – possibly Desnos – shouted, 'Who made this film?' After a third Surrealist identified Dulac as the film-maker, Desnos asked, 'And who is Madame Germaine Dulac?', to which Breton replied, 'Madame Germaine Dulac is a cunt.' At that, the Surrealists either left of their own accord or were booted out of the theatre, while scuffles broke out, mirrors were smashed and the police were summoned. While Artaud was present at the screening, it is unclear whether, as some accounts hold, he ran wildly amid the chaos of the theatre, screaming about Dulac, or, as others claim, he sat quietly in the back with his mother.[50]

In the aftermath of the affair at the Studio des Ursulines, Yvonne Allendy, with the probable collusion of Artaud, accused Dulac of having 'violated the spirit of the script and to have distorted, by her pig-headedness, poetic images whose meaning she does not understand and for the execution of which she refused all suggestion' leading to 'the violent reaction by poets desiring to disconnect Artaud' from Dulac's erroneous film.[51] Whereas Artaud might, too, have distinguished his vision for his script from the one produced by Dulac, he fully basked in the notices *The Seashell* was generating. Allendy's leaflet contained reviews from eighteen publications (including one each from Belgium and Austria), excerpted to highlight Artaud's role in the production and to minimize Dulac's contribution to only five mentions.[52]

The old adage that there is no such thing as bad publicity did not apply to *The Seashell*; the film did not benefit from all the histrionics surrounding its release, and within sixteen months it was eclipsed in importance by Luis Buñuel's *Un Chien andalou*, whose first screening also occurred at the Studio des Ursulines, but in far less tumultuous conditions. Artaud, of course, continued to defend the originality of the film he wrote, contending that, while all avant-garde films are *The Seashell*'s progeny, they 'are without the spirit of *The Shell*, which they all failed to recapture'.[53]

In several texts in which he alternated between specific and oblique references to *The Seashell* (but never mentioning Dulac), Artaud clarified his intention in writing the screenplay, contrasting his idea with the film that was produced. In an introduction entitled 'Cinema and Reality' that accompanied the screenplay's publication in *NRF*, Artaud argued against the tendency of film-makers to conceive of alternative states of reality only in dreamlike sequences; by contrast, Artaud stated that it was his intention to unleash cinema's visual flexibility, to enable it to convey more primal forms of expression and communication and to disengage it from text, whether conveyed by the movie's narrative or its subtitles:

even in films without subtitles, emotion is verbal and calls for the clarification or support of words, because the situations, the images, the action turns completely on a clear meaning . . . It is not necessary to find in visual language an equivalency to written language, of which the visual language would be a poor translation, but to reveal the strict essence of language and to move the action to a level where all translation would be unnecessary and where action would work nearly intuitively on the mind.

After denying that his screenplay was meant to recreate a dream, Artaud stated that cinema 'does not detach itself from life, but rediscovers the original ordering of things', citing as examples of this the early films of Buster Keaton and Charlie Chaplin.[54]

Artaud's apparent rejection by Dulac was compounded by more oscillations in his relationship with Athanasiou. He had strongly recommended Athanasiou for the female role in *The Seashell*, but his exile from the production accentuated his romantic insecurity; in his mind, he had become alienated both from his creative work and from the woman in his life. Whether Artaud really loved Athanasiou – and was willing, or able, to make the sacrifices she asked of him – is questionable; at a minimum, his drug addiction was an insurmountable obstacle. With that said, Athanasiou might have represented the one source of stability in his otherwise frenetic existence. In a letter from September 1927, Artaud wrote of a book – possibly Nathaniel Hawthorne's *The Scarlet Letter* – in which 'one lives, one dies, one is restored to life in reading it'. He then proceeded to denude his heart of every emotional fibre to Athanasiou ('The proof of our cohabitation, of our impulses towards each other, of our conflicts, as well, is a perfect representation of love as I imagine it'), before alternating between hopeful ('But I appreciate that you already became, in some way, as alone as me, and I ALONE can fill this solitude, as you, alone, can fill mine') and disconsolate, if not melodramatic:

I assure you that since our break-up, I often think of Death, or Life (it's the same thing), and this thought, that in the infinite, in the absolute, I will be alone, without you who was my soul, without the counterbalance and the compensation of your presence, this thought was, for me, perfectly heartbreaking. What do you want me to be in the face and the service of Death?[55]

This letter was one of Artaud's last *cris de coeur* to Athanasiou; by April 1928 Artaud had all but given up on anything but a working relationship with her:

I cannot prevent myself from thinking that you live an *abominable* life, and I can only say that you cannot be my lover . . . Anyone who has been my lover and who lives and sleeps with another man who is unworthy of her can no longer exist in my life . . . You have never been MY woman at any moment before the spirit or in the eyes of God, as I had believed, because if you were this woman, you would never have left me or you would have returned to me. To me, my solitude is without a name, without limits, and it increases twofold the horror to think that I have always in *reality* been alone and that, for five years, someone made for me and who has known me intimately did not perfect my life . . . You have allowed me to realize the illusion that I lived in your spirit. Woman is an inferior being who has botched her destiny since the first days of the world.

Curiously, Artaud closed the letter, 'I kiss you in spite of all and FROM MY HEART.'[56] Though he claimed to be in despair over his relationship with Athanasiou, during the second half of the 1920s Artaud appears to have had at least two other romantic dalliances. In 1926 he pursued, unsuccessfully, a relationship with Janine Kahn, the younger sister of Breton's first wife, Simone. Born into a prosperous Alsatian Jewish family, Kahn, through her sister, travelled in Surrealist circles. Beginning in late July 1926 and until 1 January 1927, she received around twenty letters from Artaud. Ostensibly writing to Kahn about the revelations of Madame Angelina Sacco – the clairvoyant to several Surrealists (including Breton), and the first of a number of psychics he consulted – Artaud's letters soon became romantic, expressing his desire for

Kahn and claiming that Madame Sacco insinuated they were not destined to marry because 'you find me mysterious, and, above all, you would like to know my soul'.[57] At times, Artaud's letters to Kahn boil over with violent passion, and he claimed he wanted to verify the 'science' to Madame Sacco's clairvoyance:

> Some of my dreams appear to me too bitter, too *remarkable* (opium aside) in order not to contain some powerful affirm-ations. Imagine that I have seen in a dream . . . you on my bed covered in red in the process of consummating a terrifying union. That was the substance of my dream, just as in the mass of my soul. But physically, objectively, I am still only able to squeeze you in my arms with fierce passion.[58]

In addition to expressing unrequited desire, Artaud's letters to Kahn are filled with excuses for missed meetings, pleas for her to write to him (or to forgive him) and requests that she procure laudanum for him from a doctor friend (after first telling her that he dreamt of her as a wild queen!).[59] Less than two years after this string of correspondence stopped, Kahn married the novelist and poet Raymond Queneau.

Also in 1926 Artaud made the acquaintance of Alexandra Pecker. Daughter of Russian émigrés, former law student, beauty queen and Folies-Bergère performer, Pecker had a small role in *Le Juif errant* as a romantic interest of Artaud's character.[60] The following year, during the filming of *The Passion of Joan of Arc*, Artaud and Pecker exchanged letters and met frequently (often at Le Select, 99 boulevard du Montparnasse). Pecker recalled Artaud having been carefree and mischievous, but capable of brief, directed outbursts. Their relationship was also professional, as Pecker played two roles in TAJ's production of *A Dream Play*. According to Pecker, Artaud was 'courteous towards his actors' and 'demanding, yet convincing, capable of making actors more talented than they were. His touch was inspiring.'[61] Pecker may have expected more permanence and commitment from the relationship than Artaud was prepared – or able (given his busy schedule at the time) – to give.[62] Much to her apparent chagrin, no romantic relationship developed between them; however, she remained in his constellation of friends until the end of his life.

Scandals over the TAJ and *The Seashell* elevated Artaud's significance, but at the same time labelled him erratic and unpredictable. His acting career included important roles in two of France's greatest contributions to silent cinema, but Artaud never really considered screen acting as anything beyond a means for generating an income. It is doubtful that Artaud was trying to cultivate an image, much less to contrive his 'brand'; instead, he was largely caught up in the contentious atmosphere of cultural politics and the politics of culture. In cinema and its ability to express matters non-verbally, Artaud saw the potential for returning to a more primal and pure form of communication; but as the 1930s approached, he revisited theatre as the locus for revolutionary change.

5

Cruelty

By the end of the 1920s, financial difficulties were putting a
crimp in the realization of Artaud's grander schemes, while his
reliance on opiates – particularly laudanum – was becoming more
pronounced. In spite of the interest of some well-heeled backers,
Artaud lost interest in the Théâtre Alfred Jarry (TAJ) and was
devoting more of his energies to writing film scripts. He remained
confident in cinema's culturally redemptive potential but had
become increasingly pessimistic about the future of film, realizing
that, as with most other cultural forms, it had become a creature
of its own popular success: productions getting more expensive,
projects feeling the weight of bottom-line thinking and the artistic
nature of film yielding to its commodification. The introduction
of sound to film further threatened to compromise its expressive
distinctiveness; the visual medium succumbed to the text. With that
said, Artaud continued to act in films, if only as a means of financial
support. However, it was after encountering a Balinese theatre
group at the Colonial Exposition of 1931 that Artaud was again
inspired to produce a series of essays that re-conceptualized theatre
as a conduit for revolution.

    While in Nice from February to late April 1929 for the filming of
Raymond Bernard's *Tarakanova*, Artaud wrote a series of letters to the
Allendys on cinema. In March 1929 Artaud wrote to Yvonne Allendy
that the creative value of an actor, a director or a script had become
no more than a commodity to be sold and that, in spite of the 'quality'
of his own work, he had to endure humiliations 'because I am not a
movie star and commercially one cannot count on my name TO SELL
a film'.[1] A little more than four months later, in an interview with

Cinémonde, Artaud complained, 'Film is a wretched business' with 'too many financial contingencies' hindering creative expression. He, however, would not compromise his ideals: 'This is why cinema is a business I will certainly give up if I find a role restraining, weakening, cutting me off, from what I think, from what I feel.'[2]

Almost from its onset, film had commercial appeal, and movies were produced that catered to public demand. For Artaud, commercialization sacrificed film's artistic integrity, higher concepts and emotive mission; he was careful, though, to distinguish between purely commercial films that 'diminish and devalue' the artist by forcing him to go 'against his nature, and by consequence against the purpose of his spirit', and films whose success was not a function of commercial calculations at their inception.[3]

Artaud broached the idea of forging a production company with the Allendys, insisting that it had to remain true to artistic integrity. Encouraged by the Allendys, Artaud wrote screenplays, some in the advertising genre (for Peugeot motorcycles and air travel),[4] others – such as his adaptations of Robert Louis Stevenson's novel *The Master of Ballantrae* and Shalom Ansky's play *The Dybbuk* – intended for theatrical production. It made little difference to Artaud if his vision was designed to promote consumption or to tell a story; what mattered was that the cinematic medium – through editing and image manipulation – be employed to its fullest visual potential. Consequently, even though advertising promoted consumption, the prospect of representing the unconscious (even if it is material desire) was the ultimate objective.[5]

Though Artaud was, at best, hesitant about the introduction of sound in film, his treatments of *Ballantrae* and *Dybbuk* did incorporate elements of sound:

I have decided to introduce some sound effects in all my screenplays, and even some dialogue, because there is a movement towards talking pictures and within one or two years, no one will want to see silent films. This is distressing, but it is what it is, and one must be able to live and not be swallowed up in the meantime. But people like us, who have preserved the pure and sincere sense of cinema, need to show the absurdity and uselessness of the non-silent cinema while nourishing the beasts with words, and maintain the *identity* of the other cinema of which they will be perhaps the sole trustees . . . *Everyone* is turning to the talking pictures. It is necessary to follow the crowd so as to direct it.[6]

Speaking at the Studio 28 movie theatre in Montmartre about 'talkies', Artaud either found something redeeming in sound or reconciled himself to its inevitability. He referred to the image as 'a translation, a transposition of reality', whereas sound reverberates with 'a lot more intensity than the image that becomes only a type of illusion of sound'.[7] In margin notes to *Ballantrae*, Artaud allowed for the sound of waves, the silence of the desert and the wind, and also for the soundtracking of emotional outbursts; in those situations, the oration mattered less than the acoustical intonations accompanying the words. For *The Dybbuk*, a Yiddish play about demonic possession within a Russian Hassidic community, the roles of those possessed by the dybbuk and the conspiring spirits could speak 'with cries and appropriate voices'. He further asserted that this film 'would be to the glory of the Jewish people'.[8]

As strong as his desire was to reveal his creative vision in these works, Artaud was also in desperate need of money. Writing to Yvonne Allendy in late July 1929, Artaud referred to meetings she had with film-makers regarding his script for *Ballantrae*, exhorting her, 'don't forget that this is above all *a business* for us and that I have a MONSTROUS need for money at this moment'.[9] Though the Allendys promoted Artaud's work – even entrusting one of the short scripts, *Thirty-two* (a vampire tale set against the backdrop of the war), to an American friend in the hope of getting backing across the Atlantic – nothing came to pass. Besides their interest in producing dreamlike films, the Allendys were also concerned over Artaud's financial state (which was always on the wrong side of precarious); his income was derived exclusively from the paltry earnings of his film and theatre roles.

Artaud's dependency on opiates was also increasing. In a wrenching letter to René Allendy, written on 30 November 1927, Artaud wrote that, notwithstanding the appearance of being in a resplendent phase of my existence . . . there is in my psychism a sort of fundamental vice that prevents me from enjoying what destiny offers me. It is a fact that I am no longer myself, that my true ego sleeps . . . These images given value by truth, no longer have value; they are only effigies, reflections of former thoughts pondered, or pondered by others, not currently personal THOUGHTS. Understand me. This is not an issue of the quality of the images, of the quantity of thoughts. This is a question of the electrifying vivacity of truth, of reality . . . I sense that my soul is dead. And I suffer at each of my mental exhalations, I suffer from their absence, from the faculties in which my thoughts inevitably pass, in which MY THOUGHT is buried and led astray.

He closed by telling Allendy that a three-week stay in Cannes – possibly at a spa – will do him good because as 'you imagine I have relapsed hard back into laud'.[10] There is no evidence that he made it to a detox clinic.

Writing from Nice on 24 February 1929, Artaud complained of terrible physical ailments and a life in torment and anguish. A month later he wrote again, mentioning 'violent gnawings that shift about from one minute to the next from the arms to the legs. The spinal column full of cracklings, painful at the top.' The problem – withdrawal – was clear to Artaud. 'And it has been some weeks since I have stopped using any drug. What a waste of time.'[11] Less than two weeks later, however, in a postscript to Madame Allendy, he wrote of feeling considerably better: 'Very tangible improvement achieved following some injections. In the space of 24 hours the worst of my sufferings have yielded and life has become more tolerable.'[12]

Once the filming of *Tarakanova* had wrapped up, and he was back in Paris – still in pain – Artaud made another attempt at drying out, but at the end of August he complained to René Allendy of 'a pressure in his head, a tightening of all the nerves so painful that I have lost all sensibility'. His closing statement that he planned to enter a detox clinic was, in all likelihood, due to the inaccessibility of drugs. René Allendy typically bought drugs himself and personally gave them to Artaud; however,

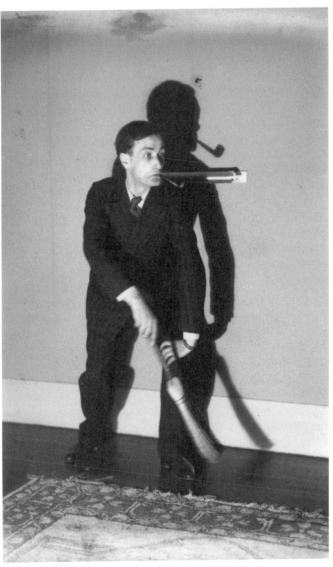

Image from the prospectus brochure produced by Artaud and Roger Vitrac for the Théâtre Alfred Jarry, 1929–30.

desperate to get laudanum at a local pharmacy, Artaud demanded a prescription. 'If this worries you, send me to the devil.'[13]

Artaud also wrote paeans to the consciousness-raising properties of opiates. While still part of the Surrealists, he wrote eight prose poems, which, in 1929, were published by Éditions Denoël et Steele under the title *L'Art et la mort*.[14] In the first of the poems, Artaud described childhood experiences that belong 'to a wholly psychic reality'; as 'the world of appearances advances and overflows into the indiscernible, into the unknown', they recede from the conscience, only recurring 'through the grace of an absolutely abnormal lucidity brought on by narcotics', 'liberating, heightening the mind'.[15]

In November 1929 Artaud wrote to Jean Paulhan, seeking a reconciliation after the deterioration of their relationship in January 1928. Artaud stated that, had he written earlier, his contrition would not have appeared sincere; in spite of the fame he had achieved over the previous two years, and the following he had attracted, Artaud had never been so 'depressed and helpless. You cannot imagine the depths to which I've sunk and I think it's about time I leave from this mediocre romanticism.'[16] To assuage Paulhan's suspicions that he had ulterior motives (such as getting published again in *NRF*), Artaud assured Paulhan, 'This is neither to the writer, nor to the editor-in-chief of an important review that I speak, but to an old friend; this is to a man.'[17] The reconciliation was complete; though Artaud protested that he had no other desire than friendship, Paulhan and the *NRF* would very soon be publishing his works again.

Artistically, though, matters were not breaking as Artaud might have hoped, or expected. He remained, at least ostensibly, committed to the TAJ; together with Roger Vitrac, he planned for another season in 1929 and announced the staging of two works for the coming season – *Ubu Roi* and Vitrac's newest work. The resulting brochure covered Artaud's reimagining of theatre in light of his discouragement from film:

We want to break with theatre as a distinct genre, and bring to light this old idea, never realized in substance, of a *complete show*. Absent that, of course, and theatre becomes confused with music, pantomime or dance, especially with literature.

When under the pretenses of talkies, the displacement of images by words in an art that has become hybridized divides the elite from the public; only this formula of a *full show* can boost interest.[18]

Differences soon developed between Artaud and Vitrac over a range of issues: respective responsibilities, artistic differences and Vitrac's inability to conclude his play, *Le Coup de Trafalgar*. Above all, perhaps, Artaud sensed that Vitrac still subscribed to the Surrealist notion that theatre should be ideologically driven:

> I will not follow if you want to make a theatre in order to defend certain ideas, political or other. As regards theatre, I am only interested in what is essentially theatrical; to use theatre to launch whatever revolutionary idea (except in the domain of the mind) appears to me the lowest and most repugnant form of opportunism.[19]

Still interested in staging Vitrac's play, Artaud wrote, a little further on, that it was possible to conciliate their opposing points of view. Another brochure – for the 1930 season – was produced, but its tone was decidedly more desperate, listing all the obstacles it had confronted since its inception (lack of capital, unavailability of actors, censorship, the police, 'systematic sabotage' by *agents provocateurs* and fellow avant-gardists, critics) before addressing its objectives (artistic liberty, exposing the 'present condition of the French') and ending with an appeal to the public.[20] There would be neither a season in 1929 nor in 1930 for the TAJ.

After Yvonne Allendy suggested staging a play at the Théâtre de Belleville (on the border of the 11th and 20th arrondissements), Artaud envisioned this theatre – in a *quartier populaire* (working-class area) – offering both popular melodramas accessible to popular tastes, and artistic spectacles, as he described in the brochure; the result, Artaud expected, would be the mixing of social classes at the theatre, producing 'a jolt of unprecedented

Artaud as Tzigane, 'the Bohemian', in Raymond Bernard's *Tarakanova* (1930).

snobbery' in the 'socialites' and confirming 'that the people and the non-intellectual are human'.[21] That, however, also did not materialize. During the second of two stays in Berlin in October and November 1930, Artaud approached the famed German director Max Reinhardt about staging and directing *Le Coup de Trafalgar*; he even tried to interest René Allendy in financing it, even though, as Artaud complained to Vitrac, 'I don't understand anything in your play; what's more, I no longer recognize it.'[22] The entire experience of the TAJ had been draining, and, as Artaud wrote to Paulhan, 'The Théâtre Alfred Jarry has been ill-fated, and I don't want it to push away my last remaining friends.'[23] Pecker noted that 'without a doubt, the friend that [Artaud] liked the most was Roger Vitrac';[24] when *Le Coup de Trafalgar* was staged in Paris in 1934, Artaud savaged its execution, but lauded Vitrac's work as a departure from the 'banalities and the trifles' of typical avant-garde theatre.[25]

Although disillusioned by the evolution of cinema, Artaud continued to act in films. After playing a bohemian in *Tarakanova*, he had minor roles in two films shot in Berlin in 1930. Arriving in Berlin on 4 July, Artaud appeared in another Marcel l'Herbier-directed film, the German version of *La Femme d'une nuit* (The Woman of One Night). Years later, l'Herbier reflected on why Artaud never had anything more than small supporting roles in films: 'he had a continual tendency to bring out the double that he felt at his core . . . it is necessary that the actor offer to the public a unified interpretation of a role, and Artaud had still not found the means to knit together the two personae that he fundamentally was.'[26] While Artaud was in Berlin, Allendy put him in contact with the German psychoanalyst Hans Sachs, a colleague of Freud, who in turn introduced Artaud to the German director G. W. Pabst.[27] After a brief return to Paris, Artaud was back in Berlin in October for the next two months, acting in Pabst's French version of *The Threepenny Opera*. Shortly after viewing, and criticizing, *The Threepenny Opera*, Artaud wrote to Paulhan trying to convince him to start a critical film journal under the NRF banner, predicting it could be 'commercially advantageous' and saying that his experience gave him insight:

> For a long time, mainly for food, I gave up acting in a profession that is rotten to the core. And it will be good and refreshing for me and for everyone, to say that the world of cinema is more putrid than anything imaginable.[28]

Artaud's return to Paris from Berlin in November 1930 simply magnified his difficulties. Given how little he was earning, film acting was both financially insufficient and artistically draining. Various other collective cultural endeavours had ended in failure and broken friendships, while his relationship with Athanasiou had collapsed amid a barrage of letters, alternatingly conciliatory and accusatory.

In between his trips to Berlin, Artaud (who was trying to find a way to make money, get his own accommodation and move off Robert Denoël's sofa) heeded Denoël's suggestion and began an adaptation of Matthew Gregory Lewis's late eighteenth-century Gothic tale *The Monk*.[29] Replete with depictions of sadism, explicit sex, sorcery, Satanism and phantasmagoric occurrences, Lewis's work, branded immoral for years after its publication in 1796, resonated with Artaud.

In the forward to the book, Artaud wrote of how the story responded to his mystical sensibility:

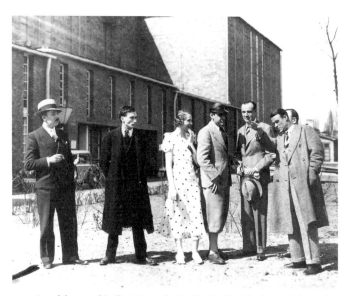

Antonin and the cast of the film *Coup de feu à l'aube* (Gunfire at Daybreak) in front of the UFA film studios, Berlin, 1932.

I don't know if the state of mind that I evoke is intellectualist, spiritualist or mystical or whatever you want. I know that I believe in ETERNAL LIFE, and that I believe here *in its entire meaning*. I regret to live in a world where witches and wizards hide, and moreover, where there are so few true wizards. A book like *The Monk* (novel) gives me a lot more of a sensation of the depth of life than all the psychological, philosophical (or psychoanalytical) surveys of the unconscious . . .[30]

Artaud tried, unsuccessfully, to interest Paulhan in publishing at least some of the chapters; after its publication by Denoël et Steele, Artaud wrote to Paulhan, defending *The Monk* against its critics and praising it as 'hallucinatory and authentic poetry from the upper reaches, from deep invisible circles'.[31] Supernatural and mystical, *The Monk* was, to Artaud, a rejection of Western logic and rationality.

In 1931 at the Bois de Vincennes on Paris's eastern edge, a space 6 kilometres (3.75 miles) long and 3 kilometres (2 miles) wide, was reserved for visitors to experience *Le tour du monde en un jour* (A World Tour in One Day). The Colonial Exposition, an Orientalized showcase of imperialism, provided attendees with a global experience beyond those regions under French hegemony; indeed, the Exposition was an homage to Western imperialism writ large with all European imperial powers (except Great Britain, sensitive to Gandhi's civil disobedience campaign) represented, along with the United States and Denmark (showcasing, respectively, igloos and Greenlander Inuits). Above all, unlike previous colonial expositions (including the two hosted by Marseille in 1906 and 1922), this one neither consciously contrasted colonizer and colonized nor promoted the assimilation of the non-Western world to Western culture, but emphasized French imperialism's new ideal of 'association', the preservation of indigenous cultures within a French imperial context. The Exposition still celebrated the West's authority to appropriate the 'other', and to exoticize the culture of the colonized and the concomitant adaptability of the colonized to evolve from primitive to civilized under the aegis of Western authority.[32]

The Colonial Exposition attracted close to eight million visitors, with many paying multiple visits.[33] The Surrealists urged a boycott of it, condemning it as a celebration of imperialistic exploitation; their own alternative anti-Colonial Exposition – *La Verité sur les colonies* – accented colonialism's brutality and zeroed in on the 'chauvinistic and commercial values' that the Exposition promoted.[34]

Economic benefits derived from imperialism was certainly an element of the Exposition, but another raison d'être for it was to captivate attendees with architecture, art and cultural presentations, vicariously transporting visitors to distant lands they would probably never experience. No pavilion or exhibition space attracted more attention than the Dutch East Indian Pavilion. In addition to being one of the most exquisite structures (as befitting the third-biggest colonial power behind Great Britain and France), it drew headlines it might sooner have avoided: less than one month after the official opening of the Exposition, the pavilion burned to the ground. Quickly reconstructed, though on a slightly smaller scale than the original, the notoriety caused by the fire contributed to it becoming, arguably, the most popular pavilion at the Exposition. Then again, the Dutch East Indian Pavilion's popularity cannot be pinned simply to misfortune: it also featured one of the Exposition's most intriguing performances – a Balinese dance troupe performing a mélange of Balinese dance theatre, including both traditional seventeenth-century dance and contemporary dances choreographed in the 1920s.[35] Reviews of the performance proliferated, gushing over with exuberance after the fire; newspaper reviews, 'no matter how spiced with journalistic fervour, clearly show that this exhibition event was not a case of mere exoticism'.[36]

On 1 August Artaud attended a performance of the Balinese dance troupe. The following day Artaud wrote to Louis Jouvet (administrator and director at the Comédie des Champs-Élysées and, formerly, of Copeau's Vieux-Colombier):

> for theatre to try to represent some of the strange aspects of the unconscious, both in depth and in perspective, on the stage, in gestural hieroglyphics that are unbiased and absolutely new constructions of the mind, all this is fulfilled, satisfied, represented and beyond by the remarkable stagings of the Balinese Theatre . . .[37]

Though Jouvet's more traditional, conservatory-based approach to theatre did not jibe with Artaud's revolutionary vision, beginning in April 1931 Jouvet tentatively and temporarily took on Artaud as an assistant. Although it provided Artaud with an income and connections, it also accentuated his despair of French culture and his inability to influence it. However, having witnessed the Balinese theatre, Artaud realized that his vision for theatre's future already existed and an appeal to Jouvet, an influential director, might reorient French theatre. Three days after writing to Jouvet, Artaud started a letter to Paulhan, stressing the Balinese theatre's revelation of a 'kind of authentic theatrical language of such power that it appears to eliminate the very mental gestures that seem to have given birth to it, that it renders all translation into words impossible and useless'. Marvelling at the physicality of the performers, Artaud referred to 'the nobility and total audacity of their intentions' as separating Balinese from European conceptions of theatre.[38] Exactly two months after he observed the Balinese performers, NRF published Artaud's essay, *Le Théâtre Balinais à l'exposition coloniale* (The Balinese Theatre at the Colonial Exposition).

The tone for Artaud's essay was set by its opening words:

> The spectacle of the Balinese theatre, drawing from dance, song, pantomime – and very little from theatre as we understand it here – restores, following the processes of a proven and ancient efficacy, theatre to its original purpose, presenting theatre as a combination of all elements founded together under the aspect of hallucination and fear.[39]

Throughout the essay, Artaud identified elements of the Balinese production he found invigorating, refreshing and spellbinding – its physical, nonverbal language; its use of intellectual, as opposed to sensual, signifiers; and its real, as opposed to artificial, purpose. Above all, Balinese theatre was a spiritual, consciousness-raising experience in the infinite, whereas Western theatre was simply puerile entertainment of no enduring consequence. More precisely, Artaud marvelled at the actors who 'through their labyrinth of gestures, attitudes and sudden cries, through gyrations and turns that leave no portion of the stage space unutilized, liberate a new physical language no longer based on words, but on signs'.[40] To understand the performance,

> a new language seems to have been invented: the actors with their costumes constitute veritable living and moving hieroglyphics. And these three-dimensional hieroglyphics are, in their way, embellished by a certain number of gestures, of mysterious signs that correspond to some unknown, imaginary and obscure reality that we, in the West, have completely repressed.[41]

Above all, to Artaud, 'in the Balinese theatre, one senses a state prior to language and which can choose its own language: music, gestures, movements, words.'[42] Unlike the text-driven Western theatre, this was primordial, a return to the past before thought was restricted by words, when thoughts and ideas were symbolically expressed through hieroglyphics, when the 'maze of the unconscious' guided thought and signified pure intellect, rather than sentiment.[43]

Did Artaud correctly surmise the meaning and significance of the Balinese theatre, or had he gone into that Dutch East Indies pavilion predisposed to find a challenge to Western theatrical practice? Susan Sontag questioned whether it made any difference if Artaud saw a Balinese dance troupe, a tribal dance from Dahomey or a shamanistic ritual from Patagonia; all that mattered is that what he saw had to be both 'non-Western and non-contemporary'.[44] In fact, the dance that most profoundly impacted Artaud – and that he waxed lyrical about – was the *janger*, a kind of dance and spoken drama devised by a group of Balinese dancers in the early 1920s, and lacking 'the most sacred and mysterious rituals'.[45] Though tightly directed and choreographed, the *janger* did not lack intensity and revealed, to Artaud, 'the idea of pure theatre, where both conception and achievement have value, have life, only through the degree of their materialization on stage'.[46]

Artaud was not alone in his enthusiasm for non-Western culture, nor were his writings on Balinese theatre his first challenges to Western hegemony. Surrealism was rife with Orientalist motifs and influences; in 1924 Breton summoned the Orient as a muse: 'Orient, victorious Orient, you who have only symbolic value, do with me as you please. Orient of anger and pearls! Orient, lovely bird of prey and innocence, I implore you from the depths of the kingdom and shadows! Inspire me!'[47] And Artaud, while part of the Surrealist group, in both his 'Address to the Dalai-Lama' and 'Letter to the Schools of the Buddha', pleaded for Eastern enlightenment to liberate the West from its confinement in the present.[48]

The experience with the Balinese dance theatre might have been a turning point for Artaud; it's hard to say if it was completely responsible for the burst of creative energy that would follow, but if it had not acted therapeutically on Artaud (after all, he had not given up opiates), it inspired and invigorated him. Through René Allendy, he met George Soulié de Morant, former diplomat in China, Sinologue and promoter of acupuncture. Artaud undertook a series of acupuncture treatments that, while apparently improving his physical condition, did not have any impact on his fragile mental and emotional states. In a series of very long letters to Soulié de Morant, Artaud reprised many of his old themes – despair over his inability to form coherent thoughts and the dissonance between his internal consciousness and its external expression.[49] However, having personalized his condition for so long, he now began universalizing his torment, attributing it to the ills of Western culture.[50]

While Artaud continued to act in films, he believed that the medium had run its course, writing to Jouvet that 'cinema is and will remain an art of the past. No one can work in it without shame.'[51] Having abandoned cinema as the tool for redeeming Western culture, Artaud, still euphoric over the Balinese performance, turned again to theatre. Beginning in 1932, he drew upon a variety of phenomena that had influenced him, experienced a rush of creative energy and produced some of the most notable and memorable works of his career. Finding the necessary financing for his projects, though, still proved elusive; for Artaud, this confirmed the relationship between Western culture's vacuity, the bourgeois régime and capitalism. After his previous collaboration with Jouvet fizzled, Artaud tried a different argument:

> You think that the capitalist and bourgeois order in which we live can still hold up and withstand events. Me, I think it is ready to crack; and, indeed, events, alone, will settle it between us . . .
> 1st because it is no longer able to deal with the present catastrophes,
> 2nd because it is *immoral*, being built exclusively on profit and money.[52]

Given Jouvet's dependency on bourgeois patronage, this was equally bound to go nowhere; there is no indication that Jouvet responded to Artaud's argument.

As much as anything, Balinese dance theatre had exposed European theatre's complacency and confinement in conventional storylines driven by language and wedded to the text. Artaud saw theatre and film as destabilizing forces, shattering an audience's perspective and decentring its worldview; they needed to be shocking, mysterious, frightening or magical experiences. It is not as though examples of this did not exist in Western culture. In the issue of NRF of January 1932, Artaud wrote of the Marx Brothers' films *Animal Crackers* and *Monkey Business*, marvelling at 'the liberation by means of the screen of a special magic that the customary relationships between words and images do not usually reveal', likening the films to 'certain successful Surrealist poems, if any such existed'. Behind the humour and zaniness of the Marx Brothers, Artaud discerned something elegiac: 'the notion of something disturbing and tragic, a fatality (neither fortunate nor unfortunate, but difficult to express) that slips behind it, like the revelation of a dreadful illness on a profile of absolute beauty'. He saw also a hymn to anarchy and total rebellion – 'a kind of intellectual freedom is exercised in which the unconscious of each character, repressed by customs and conventions, avenges itself and our unconscious at the same time'.[53] Artaud might have been channelling the Marx Brothers when he suggested a completely incongruous staging idea to Jouvet for his direction of Alfred Savoir's *La Pâtissière du village* (The Village Pastry Chef):

What do you say that, for the dream at the end, using around twenty mannequins of 5 m [16 ft] in height, six of whom will portray the most distinctive roles of the play with their most unforgettable features, all suddenly appearing, swaying solemnly to the rhythm of a humorously selected military march, packed with Oriental sounds, between bursts of flares and rockets. Each of these personages could have a symbol, and one of them would carry, for example, the Arc de Triomphe on her shoulder.[54]

By 1932 Artaud was ready to move beyond the experimental stage of the TAJ and to challenge current theatrical praxis through a series of manifestos, revolutionary writings that, like the progenitor of all modern manifestos – Marx and Engels's *Communist Manifesto* – posed an alternative to existing society. Given the imperatives expressed in Artaud's manifestos – his denigration of the text, for example – it is indeed ironic that he chose the manifesto, a literary means of communication, as his broadside against theatre. With limited resources, Artaud could not open his own theatre to put his ideas into practice; therefore, he was stuck with manifestos. On the other hand, he might have been tacitly acknowledging both the authority of the manifesto to influence potential supporters and the impossibility of realizing the objectives of his manifesto.[55]

While not a manifesto in the strictest sense of the word (but the springboard for one), 'The Mise en Scène and Metaphysics' evolved out of a lecture Artaud delivered at the Sorbonne on 10 December 1931. This lecture – and later the written text – germinated out of a visit by Artaud to the Louvre, where, after viewing Lucas van Leyden's *Lot and His Daughters*, he ruminated on the elements the work shared with Balinese dance theatre. If the Van Leyden piece 'moved the ear as much as it does the eye', Balinese dance theatre, with its comprehensive assault on the senses, appeared, to Artaud, to be the theatrical twin of the painting.[56] From there, he considered theatre's future:

> I affirm that the stage is a physical and concrete space that must be filled, and be given its own concrete language to speak.
>
> I affirm that this concrete language, destined for the senses and independent of speech, must satisfy, above all, the senses, that there is a poetry of the senses as there is a poetry of language, and that this and the concrete physical language to which I allude are truly theatrical only insofar as the thoughts they express elude spoken language.[57]

Undergirding this piece was the contrast Artaud developed between the psychological theatre of the West and the metaphysical theatre of the East that extends the language of the stage beyond speech 'to gestures, signs, postures and sonorities', to a primarily sensorial language.[58]

After the publication of 'The Mise en Scène and Metaphysics' by NRF in February 1932, Artaud sketched out a manifesto, 'Theatre of Cruelty'.[59] In two manifestos and a series of letters, mostly to Paulhan, Artaud defined his understanding of 'cruelty', contextualized it and explained why it is essential to the theatre:

This Cruelty is concerned with neither sadism nor blood, at least not in an exclusive way.

I do not systematically cultivate horror. This word, cruelty, must be taken in a large sense, and not in the concrete and rapacious way customarily given to it.

Theoretically, cruelty signifies strictness, diligence, implacable decision, a determination that is irreversible and absolute. . . . Cruelty is not, essentially, synonymous with bloodshed, martyred flesh, a crucified enemy . . . Above all, cruelty is lucid, a kind of rigid direction, submission to necessity. There's no cruelty without consciousness, without some kind of applied consciousness. This is the consciousness that gives to the exercise of all life's acts its colour of blood, its cruel nuance, since it is understood that life is always someone's death.[60]

For Artaud, if theatre is to convey a deeper ontological meaning, rather than to wallow in, or to try to bestow unwarranted significance to quotidian trivialities, it must convey the gnostic idea that all creation derives from cruelty. Essentially, to embrace cruelty – or the experience of it – is to return to origins, shedding, along the way, the affectations and artificialities of a corrupted culture. Cruelty, in this context, unsettles and disturbs an audience's expectations and prior knowledge. 'It is fair to say that theatre remains the most efficacious and active passageway for these immense analogical disturbances that stop ideas in flight at some point of their transmutation into the abstract.'[61]

Artaud's 'First Manifesto' on the theatre of cruelty raises the subject of 'cruelty' only once; itemizing the various elements of his ideal theatre, Artaud wrote: 'Without an element of cruelty at the root of all spectacle, theatre is not possible. In our present state of degeneration, it is through the skin that the metaphysical will re-enter the minds.'[62] The 'First Manifesto' concerned itself, in large measure, with a re-conceptualization of theatre into a holistic mass of words, sounds, lights, gestures, music and costumes organized into 'veritable hieroglyphics', where no one element is privileged over another; each is indispensable to the creation of 'a metaphysics of speech, gesture, expression, in order to wrest it from its psychological and mortal paralysis'.[63] As far as the 'language of the stage' is concerned, Artaud noted: 'There is no need to suppress spoken language, but to give words nearly the same importance as they have in dreams.' Thus words would be tonal in the Artaudian theatre, of no greater consequence than any other sound, the playwright's words no more than 'a point of departure for all theatrical creation'. Real authority would rest with the 'unique Creator', a hybridized writer–director, entrusted with full responsibility for the mise en scène, ensuring not that the play would be acted, but rather that the spectacle would be performed. Finally, Artaud would blur the physical space between stage and audience by situating the latter in the middle of the action, ensuring 'direct communication be re-established between spectator and spectacle, between actor and spectator'.[64] There is an obvious paradox between Artaud's combination of a theatre space and a metaphysical theatre; after all, a metaphysical theatre implies a theatre beyond the physical.[65] Though he aimed to produce a metaphysical experience for his audience, transporting it beyond its own corporeality and into the realm of its collective subconscious, Artaud never completely reconciled his pursuit of the metaphysical in a decidedly physical space and genre.

At the end of the 'First Manifesto', Artaud discussed nine productions that would be staged à la Theatre of Cruelty, with no regard for the text. The first would be a Shakespearean play, possibly *Arden of Faversham*.[66] Other works he listed included 'The story of Bluebeard reconstructed according to the archives, and with a new idea on eroticism and cruelty'; a work by the Marquis de Sade in which eroticism would be allegorically presented; and an extract from the Zohar, the most important text of the Kabbalah, the Jewish school of mystical thought.[67]

When diarist Anaïs Nin first met Artaud in March 1933, she observed him as a 'lean, ghostly figure who haunts the cafés but who is never seen at the counter, drinking or sitting among people, laughing . . . His eyes are blue with languor, black with pain . . . Deep-set, shadowy, mysterious'. Introduced to Artaud by the Allendys, Nin noted the consistency between his internal torment and his aspirations for theatre:

The theatre, for him, is a place to shout pain, anger, hatred, to enact the violence in us. The most violent life can burst from terror and death.

He talked about the ancient rituals of blood. The power of contagion. How we have lost the magic of contagion. Ancient religion knew how to enact rituals which made faith and ecstasy contagious. The power of ritual was gone. He wanted to give this to the theatre. Today nobody could share a feeling with anybody else. And Antonin Artaud wanted the theatre to accomplish this, to be at the center a ritual which would awaken us all. He wanted to shout so people would be roused to fervor again, to ecstasy. No talking. No analysis. Contagion by acting ecstatic states. No objective stage, but a ritual in the center of the audience.

Transfixed by Artaud, Nin wondered whether he got it right or whether humanity had become so desensitized that no ritual could be restorative.[68] One month later, on 6 April, Nin attended a lecture on 'The Theatre and the Plague' delivered by Artaud at the Sorbonne (Amphithéâtre Michelet). Artaud's premise was that sublime works of art produced during the plague resulted from humankind's pursuit of immortality as it feared the approach of death. No sooner had Artaud's ideas connected with his audience than he

> began to act out dying by plague . . . He forgot about his conference, the theatre, his ideas . . . He was in agony. He was screaming. He was delirious. He was enacting his own death, his own crucifixion.

Puzzled at first by his performance, the crowd began to laugh; and then hiss; and then leave, slamming the door to punctuate their disapproval. In the end, 'only a small group of friends' remained. Artaud walked up to Nin, kissed her hand and escorted her to La Coupole. There he told her that he wanted to awaken the audience from its lassitude, but that 'They do not realize *they are dead*.'[69] Notwithstanding this, Artaud recognized that, in spite of the profound and critical ideas he was expressing, his performance 'oscillated perpetually between failure and the most total buffoonery'.[70] Describing it to Paulhan, he was a little more understated: 'This conference was not a unanimous success . . . The general impression had been indignation by a certain part, unease and anxiety for the majority, and, I believe, a lasting impression.'[71]

Nin surmised that Artaud was becoming romantically attracted to her, but she was not interested in a physical relationship with him. The day after a nocturnal visit by Artaud left Nin puzzled over the direction of their relationship, they met at La Coupole; they kissed, but as Nin felt his hand on her arm, she 'saw a momentary joy on his face, and [I] felt a terrible pity for the sick, tormented madman, morbid, hypersensitive'. Nin's rejection line – that she was a divided being incapable of loving both humanly and imaginatively – was clearly designed to resonate with Artaud's sensibility; and it worked. As Nin wrote,

> I knew at the moment, by his eyes, that he was, and that I loved his madness. I looked at his mouth, with the edges darkened by laudanum, a mouth I did not want to kiss. To be kissed by Artaud was to be drawn towards death, towards insanity; and I knew he wanted to be returned to life by the love of a woman, reincarnated, reborn, warmed, but that the unreality of his life would make a human love impossible.[72]

At the time, Artaud was writing the story of the Roman emperor Heliogabalus. Originally from Syria, emperor at age fourteen, assassinated after four years of anarchy and misrule, Heliogabalus' rediscovery during the last twenty years of the nineteenth century by the artistic and literary movement known as Decadence elevated him to anti-hero. According to Nin, Artaud saw himself as Heliogabalus's spiritual double, declaring

> 'I am Heliogabalus, the mad Roman emperor', because he becomes everything he writes about . . . 'The revolution will come soon. The world must be destroyed. It is corrupt and full of ugliness. It is full of mummies, I tell you. Roman decadence. Death. I wanted a theatre that would be like a shock treatment, galvanize, shock people into feeling.'[73]

Like Heliogabalus, Artaud aspired 'to lead the world into a chaos and nothingness that corresponds with its reintegration into the unity of the cosmos'; like Heliogabalus, Artaud, with his familial roots in Smyrna, would penetrate into the Western consciousness the unitary mysticism of the East.[74]

Artaud's inspiration for writing the story of Heliogabalus was, in large measure, Artaud's burgeoning fixation on the relationship between theatre and the plague. Two months after that memorable performance at the Sorbonne, Artaud composed another manifesto – 'The Theatre and the Plague'. Published on 1 October 1934 in *NRF*, 'The Theatre and the Plague' did what the Sorbonne lecture did not: calibrate Artaud's theory on the purpose of theatre to the impact of an epidemic on a population. After discussing at length the historical occurrences of the plague, its symptomology and general pathology, Artaud stated:

> The plague takes dormant images, a latent disorder, and suddenly pushes them up to the most extreme gestures; and theatre also takes the gestures and pushes them to their limits: just like the plague, it remakes the chain between what is and what is not, between the virtuality of possible and what exists in materialized nature.[75]

In Artaud's conception, the plague is a harbinger of redemption, but a redemption cast in a mould of pain and despair; it unleashes dark forces in its survivors, who navigate through life in a manner that, under ordinary circumstances, they would not undertake; had it not been for the plague, the thoughts they entertain would not have entered their conscience:

> If the essential theatre is like the plague, this is not because it is contagious, but because it is, just as the plague, a revelation, a promotion, the exteriorization of the depth of latent cruelty through which all the perverse possibilities of the mind are localized on an individual or a people.[76]

Unlike at the Sorbonne, when he connected the plague to moments of great creative impulse, in this text, the plague is a period of intense darkness characterized by conflict, chaos, sexual freedom and a return to origins. If the plague is designed, in Artaud's analogy, to 'drain society's social and moral abscesses', so too has theatre been devised for this purpose. Consequently, to fulfil its function, theatre must be dark 'like all the great Myths . . . which cannot be imagined in an atmosphere outside of carnage, torture, spilt blood and all the magnificent Fables that recount to crowds the first sexual sharing and the first carnage of essences that appeared in creation'.[77] For Artaud, the story of Heliogabalus was fraught with themes of irrationality, cruelty and anarchy, and also matters of apparent urgency, such as castration (a theme Artaud earlier covered in his retelling of Héloïse and Abelard), incest and sexual licentiousness.[78]

Artaud's first foray in putting these ideas into practice was *Les Cenci*, his adaptation of both Shelley's play and Stendhal's novel; in a letter to Jouvet, however, Artaud insisted that his was not an adaptation, but an original piece.[79] Due to its portrayals of incest, parricide and irreverence, Shelley's play did not see the light of day on the London stage until 1922 (as should be obvious, the disturbing themes are what drew Artaud to the work). Interviewed by *Comoedia* on 6 May 1935, Artaud asserted:

> My heroes are situated in the domain of cruelty and must be judged outside of good and evil. They are incestuous, adulterers, rebels, insurgents, sacrilegious, blasphemers. And this cruelty that washes over the entire work, not only results out of the bloody story of the Cenci family. This is a moral cruelty, not purely corporeal, going all the way to the actor's instinct and strength to plunge into the roots of his being so thoroughly that he exits the scene exhausted. Cruelty that also affects the spectator and must not allow him to leave the theatre unaltered, but, exhausted, engaged, transformed perhaps![80]

In assembling his 'team' for *Les Cenci*, Artaud was partly constrained by the expectations of his financial backers, Denoël and Iya Abdy, a stunning and statuesque divorcée and daughter of Russian émigrés who fled to Finland during the Russian Revolution before ending up in Paris in the 1920s. A portrait of Abdy by Balthus

Artaud (left foreground) on stage at Théâtre des Folies-Wagram in the production of *Les Cenci*.

(who designed sets and costumes for *Les Cenci*) attracted Artaud's attention: 'Balthus painted Iya Abdy as a primitive would have painted an angel.'[81] Both Denoël and Abdy had precise casting ideas for the lead: Denoël, his wife; Abdy, herself. Denoël might later have regretted this, as he suspected Artaud of having an affair with his wife.[82] There would also be more professional and accomplished actors involved in the production – at least initially – including Roger Blin (with whom Artaud had been acquainted since 1928) and Jean-Louis Barrault, both of whom remained close with Artaud and would go on to illustrious careers on the French stage and screen.

The rehearsals were fraught with conflict. Barrault's involvement with *Les Cenci* was abbreviated both by a commitment to Charles Dullin's Théâtre de l'atelier and conflict with Artaud over his casting of Abdy as the female lead. Years later, Barrault cited his frustration with Abdy's haughtiness, the authority her investment afforded her over the production and, perhaps worst of all, the distraction of a media frenzy over a well-known socialite starring in an avant-garde production; to Barrault, the production 'fell into high society amateurism, and I could not bear this'.[83] Artaud, on the other hand, found Abdy's stage inexperience well suited for the role she would play – Beatrice, the ill-fated daughter of the patriarch, Francesco Cenci (portrayed by Artaud). Barrault's exit from the

Artaud, *c.* 1930.

production (though he continued to assist Artaud at the rehearsals) was compounded by the slim budget (for example, actors and crew were sporadically paid) and Artaud's erratic direction – alternating between despair and jubilation, providing incomprehensible and insensible instructions, and generally confusing the other actors.[84]

The end product received poor reviews. Opening on 6 May 1935, *Les Cenci* closed after seventeen performances. Whereas the reviews were mixed on the opening night, subsequent reviews panned it. The music, acting and pacing were all excoriated; only Balthus' set and costumes were universally praised. In some measure, the criticisms were beyond Artaud's control: the acoustics of the Théâtre de Folies-Wagram, a music hall, were not conducive to theatrical voices and many of the actors, including Artaud, were barely audible. On the other hand, the publication of some of Artaud's manifestos prior to the opening, while raising the interest of critics, also set him up for expectations that he could not have met; either he was less the innovator suggested by his manifestos, or if he was such an innovator, his audience would not have been prepared for his work. Pierre Audiat in *Paris-soir* referred to Artaud as an 'appalling actor', but then went on to say: 'And yet, with his absurd violence, his disoriented eyes and his fake anguished rage, he brings us with him from beyond good and evil to a desert where the thirst for blood burns us.'[85] Artaud's performance also evoked confused responses from, among others, the novelist Colette and the theatre director Lugné-Poe, both of whom found his acting exaggerated but at the same time strangely compelling.[86] Based on audience reactions and critics' reviews, *Les Cenci* was a bad production, but to measure Artaud by the dissonance between his theoretical statements and his finished product is to place unreasonable demands on his power to transform consciousness without alienating potential audiences, and to do so on a very limited budget. The excited and large crowds that filled the first few performances soon melted away. On 15 May Artaud wrote to Paulhan that he had blown through all his royalties and, if he did not get more financing soon, *Les Cenci* would have to close. Moreover, Artaud felt 'betrayed' by the production.[87]

The paradoxes of Artaud's life and work were encapsulated in the experience of the manifestos and the staging of *Les Cenci*: rather than creating a new theatrical dynamic with originally written works representing his theatrical paradigm, Artaud merely adapted a nineteenth-century play; instead of 'realizing his vision of a new theatre in something akin to Wagner's Bayreuth, Artaud had to content himself with publishing manifestos'.[88] However, it can equally be argued that Artaud's adaptation of *Les Cenci* was an attempt, albeit an ill-conceived one, at employing a century-old drama to break down and then regenerate an audience. Above all, the experience of *Les Cenci* put circumstances into relief: Artaud's exposure to Balinese theatre had been refracted through the lens of the Colonial Exposition; the theatrical practice to which he aspired would, by necessity, be built upon a foundation of Western cultural norms; and the revolutionary regenerative ideals to which he subscribed were alien to Western frames of reference. In the aftermath of *Les Cenci*, Artaud rapidly realized he would have to undertake and undergo a culturally transformative experience, physically separating himself from familiar cultural referents. Only then could he revolutionize society.

6

Voyage

The experience of *Les Cenci* put Artaud at a crossroads. Whether or not he produced an important piece for the French theatre, the public was not ready for something so unconventional; plus, financial backing was proving to be tough to find. Yet through *Les Cenci* Artaud connected with Jean-Louis Barrault, then an up-and-coming stage actor. Like Artaud, Barrault was a student of Charles Dullin and had worked with Jacques Copeau, but Barrault consistently acknowledged Artaud as having helped him hone his craft. Frustrated with the French stage after *Les Cenci*, Artaud became more proactive in his quest for an authentic non-Western cultural experience, travelling to Mexico for a sojourn that was at once spiritual and political.

Barrault first encountered Artaud on the fringes of Surrealist circles at Les Deux Magots or Brasserie Lipp, and he was initially intimidated by Artaud, whom he observed 'from a distance'.[1] Barrault and Artaud formed a symbiotic working relationship – Barrault expanding his theatrical horizons beyond the physical skills gleaned from Dullin, Artaud finding an actor and director who could realize his vision and create performances resonant with the public – and the younger actor mastered the skills of physical theatricality while, at the same time, fully absorbing the 'Oriental wisdom . . . [that] the irradiation of our fleshly being carries much farther than the contours of our skin'.[2] Artaud broadened Barrault's art, exposing him to Eastern and ancient teachings, including 'Tantrist Yoga, Hatha Yoga, the Tibetan *Book of the Dead*, the works of Fabre d'Olivet, the Upanishads, the *Bhagavad-Gita*, *Milarepa* and Pythagoras' *Golden Verses*'.[3]

After Barrault's departure from the cast of *Les Cenci*, Artaud rebuffed his suggestion of a future collaboration, but clarified that, after the experiences of Surrealism and *Les Cenci*, he could not work collaboratively with anyone: 'I DO NOT WANT to trumpet a spectacle staged by myself if there is even a wink of an eye that does not belong to me . . . I no longer believe in the purity of men. And however highly that I esteem you, I do not believe you to be infallible and I do not want to expose myself again to the slightest chance of a risk from that.' With that, Artaud encouraged Barrault to 'direct his own work, with [his] own personal way of understanding certain ideas'.[4]

Interestingly, more than a week prior to writing that letter, Artaud saw *Autour d'une mère*, Barrault's adaptation of William Faulkner's *As I Lay Dying*, a production heavy on corporeal expression, gestural purity and moments of silence at the expense of the text.[5] According to Barrault, Artaud was in 'a state of exhilaration . . . His fever was in accord with my own which had not yet abated, and we paced the Boulevard Clichy as if possessed.'[6] In the issue of NRF from July 1935, Artaud praised Barrault's production, calling it an 'event': 'It is necessary to recognize as an event such a transformation of atmosphere that an irritated audience is suddenly and blindly submerged and utterly disarmed.' Perhaps the biggest compliment was Artaud's comparison of Barrault's piece to the timeless spirit of the Balinese theatre in creating a theatrical space that lives 'magically in and of itself, that an aviary of sound is released from it, that new relationships between sound, gesture and the human voice are found there'. In short, for Artaud, Barrault had succeeded (where *Les Cenci* had failed) in bringing to life – in a way that moved the audience (though not necessarily the critics) – the ideas expressed in Artaud's manifestos.[7]

Barrault's portrait of Artaud, drawn from daily meetings, is at once playful and dark, tinged by his antipathy towards the social elite. For example, Barrault related the story of a dinner at which he and Artaud were guests. The bourgeoise hostess was the mother of a young and attractive actress with whom Artaud and Barrault were acquainted, and the mother was anxious 'to display an enlightened attitude towards our theatrical community'. According to Barrault,

Artaud took her good intentions literally, as no one else could have done. In the middle of the meal, he stripped to the waist, invited me to follow his example and gave a demonstration of Yoga exercises, after which he remained half-naked in front of the elegant hostess, who could think of no better homage to this 'delicious performance' than to wonder, out loud, how it was that the Comédie Française had not yet discovered him. Thereupon Artaud banged the lady's head several times lightly with his dessert spoon and shouted in her ear, in his strange metallic voice: 'Madame, you get on my nerves!'

At a dinner party organized for potential backers of his script titled *The Conquest of Mexico*, Artaud, perhaps recognizing that the well-heeled guests were only there out of curiosity to see him close up, demanded silence and exploded: 'My only reason for letting the lot of you make me feel sick is to give you the chance of returning to the theatre and to humanity a little of the money you extort from the poor.'[8] Artaud did not receive the funding.

Barrault also witnessed Artaud's personal torment, in particular his conflicted relationship with drugs, which for Artaud were indispensable, yet also abhorrent. He noted that Artaud did not take drugs as a portal into the subconscious or to uncover his genius; his drug usage, his 'disease', resulted, like that of many artists Barrault knew, from despair – 'because the fear of living is strangling them, because they want to suppress themselves: an extreme unction'. And yet 'under the influence of drugs, he lost his vitality'. Barrault recalled Artaud telling him something 'overwhelming' about his relationship with drugs: 'To cure me of the judgment of Others, I have this: the whole distance that separates me from myself.' As Barrault saw it, drugs were a conduit for Artaud's goal of internalizing theatre's pathos: 'Tragedy on the stage is not enough for me; I'm going to bring it into my life.'[9]

In 1935 Artaud made another attempt to wean himself off opiates through démorphène therapy. An emulsion of castor oil, olive oil, camphor and vitamins championed by Dr Roger Dupouy at Paris's Henri-Rousselle Hospital, démorphène was administered in a series of painful injections. As a cure for opiate addiction, it was useless; years after receiving démorphène, patients suffered impairment of their vision, diction and sleep. On 17 July Artaud wrote to Dupouy requesting admittance for a full series of démorphène injections, pleading that 'for the past several years, my life has been nothing more than a long, failed detoxification'. At the time, Artaud claimed to be using 40 grams (1.5 oz) once every three days.[10] This was Artaud's second attempt at detoxification at the Henri-Rousselle Hospital. His first try – in December 1932 – ended in failure when he refused to accept treatment. Though Artaud admitted on the clinic questionnaire to dosing approximately every sixty hours, he seemed confused as to why he needed opiates. On the one hand, laudanum prevented him from working, rendered ideas less interesting and nihilistic, made him frigid and indifferent to sex, and induced nightmares featuring strange creatures morphing into human forms before slowly killing him. On the other hand, opiates 'dissolve pain as water dissolves sugar'; while Artaud admitted laudanum's sensation was artificial, he believed this preferable to 'a certain nothingness of the mind'.[11]

In 1935 Artaud's desire to dry out was motivated in large measure by his role in two films to be shot in September and October, Maurice Tourneur's *Koenigsmark* and *Lucrèce Borgia*, the latter one of Abel Gance's more forgettable movies. He was also driven by a series of lectures on Mexican civilization, which he was planning to deliver on 24 August, and by Yvonne Allendy's death. By his own admission, since 1919 he had not gone fifteen days without opiates; yet on 11 September 1935, only five days after entering the hospital, Artaud discharged himself, disingenuously claiming he 'was less obsessed with the idea of drugs. I no longer believe that they are indispensable to my being.'[12]

Artaud seemed to have a tacit understanding that his life was spinning more out of control – no closer either to transforming Western culture or withdrawing definitively from the narcotics that had become both indispensable and debilitating. At the same time as he was seeking admittance to the Henri-Rousselle Hospital, Artaud wrote to Jean Paulhan about a plan to voyage abroad:

For a long time I have heard of a sort of movement at the base of Mexico in favour of a return to the pre-Cortez civilization . . . I might be mistaken, but the pre-Cortez civilization is at its root Metaphysical . . . I don't think that this pre-Cortez movement is aware of the magic it seeks, but when I exposed my project and my ideas to Robert Ricard, a student of Professor Rivet, he said to me, 'In reality, these people don't know what they are looking for. You can help correct their ideas.'

In this lengthy letter, Artaud promoted the idea of searching in Mexico for a '"magic naturalism" found in the statuary of its temples, their forms, their hieroglyphics'. Artaud saw himself as sufficiently motivated and knowledgeable, but because France was still reeling from the Great Depression, there was little public money available. According to Artaud, the newspaper *Paris-soir* was willing to provide him with an advance, provided he receive a *titre de mission* (diplomatic mission) from the French government, something Paulhan could assist him in procuring through a friend at the Ministry of Foreign Affairs.[13]

Artaud's interest in Mexico dated back to his childhood, when he was introduced to the exoticism of pre-Columbian Latin America in the *Journal des voyages et des aventures de terre et de mer*;[14] according to his sister, Marie-Ange, he was particularly obsessed by the book's macabre stories.[15] In his 'Second Manifesto on the Theatre of Cruelty', Artaud included a script, 'The Conquest of Mexico', a four-act didactic treatment on the Cortez–Moctezuma encounter and the damage visited upon the Aztec culture by European colonizers; this was intended to be the first production of the Theatre of Cruelty. In Artaud's recreation, Mesoamerica was a bastion of 'moral harmony' led by an 'organic hierarchy of the Aztec monarchy established on indisputable spiritual principles' predicated on astrology. 'From the perspective of social issues, it demonstrates the harmony in a society that knew how to feed everyone and where the Revolution has been accomplished for a long time.' In contrast to the idyllic pre-Columbian Mexican civilization, Artaud's play would 'revive in a brutal, implacable, bloody way the perennial conceit of Europe' while 'broaching the current question of colonization and the right of one continent to enslave another'.[16]

When his pursuit of a *titre de mission* encountered obstacles, Artaud believed it had to do with suspicions that he was a revolutionary.[17] Sometime in August 1935, he wrote to Pierre Laval, then the Minister of Foreign Affairs (later head of the Vichy government), and asserted that his voyage to Mexico was for anthropological purposes: to understand the secrets of ancient Mexican civilization, its rituals and its magic.[18]

The following month, while still undergoing detoxification, Artaud received his *titre de mission*; the Mexican Legation in Paris commissioned Artaud to present a series of lectures and arranged for his accommodation. The voyage – for which Artaud received a 50 per cent discount – was paid for either by Barrault or by a collection of his friends. On 6 January 1936, four days before his ship was due to leave Antwerp, Artaud wrote to Paulhan: 'Nevertheless, I left with just enough money for my Voyage, decided to risk it all in order to change my life.'[19] Artaud also expressed urgency that Paulhan should publish, without delay, the series of articles and manifestos Artaud had been writing on theatre, lest imitators steal his ideas; he also asked Paulhan to send any monetary advances to him in Mexico. While still at sea, on 25 January Artaud sent Paulhan a title for the book: *Le Théâtre et son double* (The Theatre and its Double).

> Because if theatre duplicates for life, life duplicates for real theatre, and this has nothing to do with Oscar Wilde's ideas on art. This title will respond to all the doubles of theatre that I believe to have found over so many years: metaphysics, the plague, cruelty, the reservoir of energies that constitute Myths, which men no longer embody, theatre incarnates. And by this double, I hear the great magical agent, of which theatre by its forms is only the figuration, expecting it to become the transfiguration.[20]

On 30 January 1936, twenty days after leaving Antwerp, Artaud's ship docked in Havana, Cuba. Almost immediately, Artaud dashed off letters to Balthus, Barrault and Paulhan, requesting money and waxing lyrical over 'feeling himself in the flow of what I'm looking for', 'this adventure having a miraculous character'.[21] He also wrote to Marie Dubuc, a clairvoyant in whom Artaud placed a good deal of trust, informing her that 'I have taken advantage of the twenty days on the boat in order to throw away the poisons, the doses you predicted I would dissociate from in order to work and rediscover myself.'[22] However, as would become apparent, Artaud's optimism at being weaned off opiates was unrealistic.

Once in Veracruz, Mexico, on 7 February Artaud wrote to René Allendy of 'a country of black African rituals' and of a man who told Artaud to 'listen in life, so that the world of images in me plays out in some way . . . I don't have the right to speak, but know that henceforth, in effect, things will play out after some torments without name.'[23] This was possibly the same man who gave Artaud a 12-centimetre (4.75-in.) decorated sword, which Artaud interpreted as a talisman and from which he was inseparable throughout his Mexican journey and beyond.

Owing largely to his *titre de mission*, Artaud received an official welcome from the French community in Mexico, including the French ambassador. The intellectual and artistic circles in which Artaud mingled had limited interest in primal, indigenous cultures; Mexico was still in the throes of political, social and cultural ferment following nearly two decades of revolution and counter-revolution. While many artists aimed to integrate indigenous art into *mexicanidad* (Mexican collective identity), they were largely conflicted by concerns that too much indigenous culture might project an image of backwardness. One of Artaud's principal contacts in Mexico was the Guatemalan-born, French-educated poet and essayist Luis Cardoza y Aragón, for whom 'authentic Mexicanity is a pointless metaphysical and provincial concept'.[24] Yet it was precisely this 'authentic' or indigenous Mexican experience that Artaud hoped to uncover. Mexico City was full of disappointments for Artaud. The influence of modernist European artistic movements in Mexico City was, in his estimation, symbolic of Mexico's degeneration:

If the revolution of 1910 has a meaning, this is not only because it has liberated the oppressed classes from the hold of capitalism

– which, by the way, still exists – this is because it has given rise to the forgotten unconsciousness of race, but how many modern Mexicans understand the need to liberate their unconscious?[25]

The Mexican artists and intellectuals he encountered were fixated on French Surrealism. Largely because of his one-time affiliation with Surrealism, but also through acquaintances of Robert Desnos, Artaud travelled in important cultural circles in Mexico City; in addition to Cardoza y Aragón, this included artists with international reputations, such as Diego Rivera, María Izquierdo and Federico Cantú Garza. Artaud was unimpressed by Rivera's art, finding it 'far from the powerful solar lightning of the original Mexican art'.[26] Izquierdo, who had only been a working artist for four years, was a different story. Izquierdo 'gives evidence of a truly Indian inspiration. That is to say, among the hybridized expressions of current Mexican painting, the honest, spontaneous, primitive, troubling paintings of María Izquierdo have been, for me, a sort of revelation.' Even if Izquierdo's work still bore the marks of European technique and 'the mechanistic European civilization', she 'is in communication with the true forces of the Indian soul'.[27] Izquierdo's art had always been tinged with the metaphysical; the considerable time she spent with Artaud inspired her to incorporate indigenous elements into her paintings, which 'began to express an increased violence and imagery of mysterious astrological and solar rituals', while addressing post-revolutionary proto-feminist themes.[28] Artaud brought around thirty of Izquierdo's watercolours to Paris for an exhibition in Montparnasse in early 1937; Izquierdo hoped to use the exhibition to raise both her profile in Europe and money to send Artaud to a drug rehabilitation facility.[29]

According to Cardoza y Aragón, Artaud's stay in Mexico City was miserable:

He journeyed to Mexico to reassemble the puzzle pieces of his life, without success. What he searched for, he was not going to discover in any reality. No way. What he looked for did not exist. It could only exist in his imagination.[30]

Materially, his life was miserable as well. Cardoza y Aragón recalled that 'he captivated with his dignity, his brilliance', however, 'he was badly nourished. His clothes were in a pitiful condition. I have memories of a thin man, aged terribly, severely worn by his forty years of life. He changed domiciles several times. He rented rooms. He spent his days writing at a café.'[31] For a time, he lived in a brothel, his private space invaded by drunk, naked and raucous customers.

The dissonance between what Artaud expected and what he encountered in Mexico City, together with his loneliness, his alienation and the absence of a familiar support network, returned him to old habits. Soon after arriving, Artaud scoured the city and mined his sources – including Cardoza y Aragón and his circle – for laudanum. Artaud's peregrinations took him to the seedier quarters of the city; on at least one occasion, he ended up in a 'squalid opium den' among overdosed junkies; on another, he exchanged his grandfather's watch for what turned out to be baking soda. With regard to the latter incident, Artaud confided to Cardoza y Aragón, 'Everywhere, the underworld and the drug addicts have an ethic. Things like this only happen in Mexico.'[32] His erratic behaviour – sudden disappearances in pursuit of opiates, outbursts in restaurants – troubled the artists with whom he had become acquainted; Artaud's ability to communicate in Spanish was largely limited to long, theatrical monologues. Cantú recalled one of Artaud's nocturnal visits to Chapultepec Park, when the police stopped him and found heroin. He was allowed to leave only after Cantú informed the police that Artaud was a writer whose byline had appeared in the government newspaper *El Nacional*.[33]

At the end of February, Artaud delivered what amounted to a trilogy of lectures at the National University of Mexico City, each one endeavouring to build on themes broached by its predecessor. On 26 February Artaud's lecture, entitled 'Surrealism and Revolution', lauded the early days of Surrealism, before contrasting the Surrealists' Marxist-inspired conception of revolution with his anti-materialist take on revolution.[34] Artaud continued this theme in his second lecture, 'Man against Destiny' (27 February), calling 'historical and dialectical materialism . . . an invention of the European conscience. Between history's true movement and Marxism, there is a type of human dialectic that is not in accordance with the facts.' Yet Artaud did not entirely blame Marx, claiming that what is commonly called Marxism 'is a false ideology that caricatures Marx's thoughts'. He then launched into an often confusing, at times contradictory jumble of ideas that amounted to an attack on science and reason, closing with a call he hoped would resonate with his audience: 'I would like someone to deliver the occult magic from a land that does not resemble the egotistical world that persists in treading on it, and does not see the shadow that falls from it.' Artaud commenced the third lecture, 'Theatre and the Gods' (29 February), with a pointed message to Mexican adherents to Surrealism, who, no doubt, hoped to see a genuine French Surrealist:

> I have not come here carrying a Surrealist message; I have come to say that Surrealism is out of style in France, and a lot of things that are out of style in France continue to be imitated outside of France as if they represent the current of this country.
>
> The Surrealist attitude was a negative attitude . . .

According to Artaud, it was 'very worrisome' that Europe was in a 'state of advanced civilization': 'the spirit of the French youth is reacting against this state of advanced civilization.' Echoing, in part, sentiments expressed by Rousseau nearly two centuries before, Artaud chastised Western scientific thought and the empiricist tradition as leading society to a disastrous outcome; he indicted written text for 'fix[ing] the spirit and crystalliz[ing] it in a form borne of idol worship'. Contending that life is contingent on metaphysical knowledge or magic, rather than written text, Artaud spoke of the mystical qualities of 'true theatre', a space unconstrained by text, where gesture, movement and noise allowed theatre to liberate life.[35]

Published in *El Nacional*, Artaud's quixotic stance on revolution, rejection of Surrealism and privileging of theatre could hardly have been well received by the artists in Mexico whose revolutionary references were Marxist, as opposed to pre-Columbian; who idolized French Surrealism and thought Artaud might embody it; and whose cultural focus was centred on the plastic arts, rather than theatre and literature. Around a month later, speaking before the Liga de Escritores y Artistas Revolucionarios (League of Revolutionary Writers and Artists, LEAR), Artaud critiqued the Mexican Revolution as aimless and lacking a cohesive message: 'The youth are all in agreement that the life of Mexico must be socialist, but opinions diverge as to the means to reach this Mexican socialism fully and quickly.' Artaud spoke of Europe's optimism for the Mexican Revolution as:

> a revolution of the indigenous soul, a revolution to reconquer *the indigenous soul* that existed before Cortez . . . But it does not seem to me that the Mexican revolutionary youth is very concerned about the indigenous soul. And here is where the tragedy emerges.

For Artaud, the levelling of material conditions promoted by Marxism required a corresponding shared consciousness, an escape from 'this frightening . . . capitalism of the conscience, since the soul is the property of all'.[36]

While Mexican artists and writers, such as Rivera, incorporated indigenous themes in their works, few envisioned Mexico, at this pivotal point in its history, returning to its primitive, uncivilized, simple pre-Columbian past. They aspired to revolutionize the op-pressed indigenous population by improving its material conditions, not glorifying its pre-European culture. By contrast, Artaud hoped to eliminate European references – whether Christian or Marxist – from Mexican culture, and though he might not have said it directly, he did not believe that a revolution predicated on a return to indigenous culture was a regression. As a return to a point of origin, Artaud's vision of revolution implied a revolutionized Mexico rediscovering its indigenous culture. The LEAR, on the other hand, conceived of revolution as a break, a separation of past from future, in which indigenous culture had no role to play, other than as an element in the nation's historical evolution.

Artaud's perception of the indigenous Mexicans as a historically exploited people was detailed in a letter to Paulhan:

There are some School Masters, those that are called here The Rurals, who preach the Gospel of Karl Marx before the Indian masses.

But faced with the Gospel of Karl Marx, the supposedly uncultured Indian masses maintain the mindset of Montezuma confronted by the simplistic preachers of Cortez. Through four centuries, the same eternal White error has not ceased to perpetuate itself.

The Government offers land to the Indians, but it offers them, at the same time, electoral urns, and the Indians protest that they want neither urns nor lands, but simply Freedom . . . Christian fanaticism is the reason the Indians, who are all peasants, refuse the urns and lands and revolt against the envoys of the Government when pushed by Priests. But also because of Pagan fanaticism, they take to their guns to defend their Jiculi (God of Peyote), their Raïenaï (the Sun), their Mecha (the Moon).[37]

Discouraged by the revolutionary vision of Mexico City's artistic community and its reaction to his ideas, Artaud made plans to discover the 'primitive' spirit of Mexico. Uninterested in visiting archaeo-touristic sites, such as Teotihuacan, Artaud wanted an experience with 'living culture'.[38] On 2 April he wrote to René Thomas that he would soon be travelling to the interior of Mexico, as part of a government-sponsored agitprop programme for children in the various parts of the country. In a letter to Barrault, three months later, Artaud wrote of a petition signed by leading Mexican intellectuals to the president of Mexico to provide 'the means to execute a Mission near the ancient race of Indians. It is necessary to rediscover and resuscitate the vestiges of the ancient Solar culture.'[39] As usual, Artaud requested that Barrault help him find some means of financial support.

A subsidy from the Mexican government, possibly arranged by artists and writers in Mexico, enabled Artaud to journey to the Sierra Tarahumara in the northern state of Chihuahua. After a 1,250-kilo-metre (777-mile) rail journey from Mexico City to Ciudad Chihuahua, and then another rail trip to Creel, Artaud had to go by horseback deeper into the Copper Canyon, to the land of the Tarahumara.

Occupying a vast space in what became the state of Chihuahua, the Tarahumara people were chased by Cortez and the Spanish conquistadors from a large portion of northern Mexico to the steepest region of the southwest Mexico chain of the Sierra Madre mountains, spending most of the year in high ground but descending into the canyons during the winter months. The unforgiving land inhabited by the Tarahumara necessitated a negotiation between metaphysical beliefs and a materialist communitarian mode de vie. Voluntarily isolated within the inhospitable geological features of the Sierra Tarahumara, the Tarahumara remained largely unblemished by four centuries of contact with Europeans; try as it might, the Catholic Church never had much success with the Tarahumara, who accepted Christianity only when it could be accommodated within their own system of beliefs and symbols. At the end of the nineteenth century, a Jesuit disdainfully observed the Tarahumara 'entertaining themselves by caricaturing the Eucharist, dividing among the congregation a yellow hallucinogenic mushroom in place of the host, intoxicating pulp in place of wine'.[40] The Tarahumara's separation from outside interference facilitated their preservation of the rituals and beliefs of their ancient civilization, albeit laced with the Catholicism that had been imposed on it; among their indigenous practices was the ritualistic use of hallucinogenic peyote buttons. While the peyote ritual might have induced Artaud to seek out the Tarahumara, his choice was more likely dictated by his understanding that they were less contaminated by European influences than, for example, the neighbouring Huichol tribe, who are credited with having transmitted the peyote ritual to the Tarahumara.[41]

There is no accurate record of Artaud's departure for Chihuahua, but he probably left Mexico City sometime at the end of August. By 7 October he returned to Chihuahua, inquiring of Paulhan whether *The Theatre and its Double* had been published. In between, there is no account of Artaud's activities outside of his own writings, some produced within a year or two of his visit, but most written nearly a decade later while he was institutionalized and receiving electroshock therapy. In fact, there is no tangible evidence that he actually arrived among the Tarahumara; the combination of the region's geographic inaccessibility, Artaud's own physical and linguistic limitations and the Tarahumara's semi-insurrection against the revolutionary government's secular integrationist policies has fuelled scepticism in some quarters as to whether Artaud's account was in fact concocted out of readings, wish-fulfilment and his fertile imagination:

> Strange thing: one finds no trace of this mission in the archives, and the director of the Beaux-Arts, likewise, does not seem to remember the name Artaud. If Antonin Artaud had actually gone to the Tarahumara, he would have had to go alone, or more precisely, without official assistance. This is not impossible, but in any event, difficult. At this time, the Chihuahua–Creel train worked well of course, but to arrive at Norogachi, at the bottom of the canyons, there would have been obstacles. Artaud was ill, weakened by drugs; besides, he spoke neither Spanish nor *a fortiori*, Tarahumara. Norogachi was, at the time, like the majority of Tarahumara villages, under the protection of the Jesuit mission, and it is hard to see how Artaud, apostle of paganism, would have been able to communicate with the Indians or, at least, to assist in the peyote ceremonies.[42]

A couple of witnesses, however, have described the presence of a Frenchman at Noragachi in 1936. Sent to the north of Mexico, near the Tarahumara, by the government in 1936 as part of its literacy campaign, the schoolteacher Felipe Armendariz recalled

> A French poet who lived with them . . . a thin man, with a strange expression, very fixed. The Indians had a great veneration for him and led him through the mountain in a sedan chair. I occasionally assisted at the all-night vigils during which he recited poems in French. They did not understand anything, but listened, spellbound, because his gifts as an actor, his facial expressions, were extraordinary. One could say that he cried the texts, that he meowed them as well.[43]

Lack of direct evidence notwithstanding, there is circumstantial evidence that Artaud stayed at least a month with the Tarahumara.

Beginning with 'The Mountain of Signs', written shortly after his return to Mexico City in early October 1936, Artaud composed around ten essays on his journey to, and his experiences among, the Tarahumara; most of his writings focused on the peyote ritual. Lacking access to heroin and anticipating a completely new consciousness-raising experience with peyote, Artaud discarded his last dose of heroin in a stream.[44] However, withdrawal – his first in eighteen years – was too difficult for his body; he variously described it as '28 days of this unbearable captivity, of this pile of badly assembled organs that I am . . . like an immense ice-scape at the point of its disintegration' and as 'a body wrested from itself . . . deprived henceforth of its essential reflexes'.[45]

According to Artaud's accounts – and, again, many of these were written a dozen years after the events described – it took him six days to descend from Chihuahua to the land of the Tarahumara. Artaud commented on the almost seamless blending and placement of geological and anthropological features:

> To be sure, there are places on earth where Nature, moved by a sort of clever caprice, has sculpted human forms. But here the case is different: because it is along the whole *geographic expanse of a race* that Nature has *wanted to speak* . . . When Nature, by a strange caprice, suddenly shows the body of a man being tortured on a rock, one can think, for starters, this is nothing more than a caprice signifying nothing. But when, during the days and days on horseback, the same perspicacious enchantment repeats itself, Nature *obstinately manifests the same notion* . . . knowing that the first men utilized a language of signs, and rediscovering splendidly enlarged this language of signs on the rocks, admittedly, it is no longer possible to think this is a caprice, and that this caprice signifies nothing.[46]

Whether these observations were a self-fulfilling prophecy or a surprising discovery, Artaud's entry into the land of the Tarahumara was enveloped in the expectation of a mystical experience. And the Tarahumara would not disappoint.

Mysticism aside, Artaud portrayed the Tarahumara as practitioners of pure, unapologetic egalitarianism:

> Communism exists among them in a sentiment of spontaneous solidarity.
>
> As incredible as this seems, the Tarahumara Indians live as if they were already dead . . . They don't see what is tangible and draw their contempt for civilization from magical forces.

Artaud went on to describe how, when the Tarahumara go to the city to beg, they feel no compulsion to thank the giver:

> Because to give to someone who has nothing does not seem to be an obligation to them, but a law of physical reciprocity that the White World has betrayed. Their attitude seems to say: 'In obeying the law, you have done good to yourself; I therefore don't have to thank you.'[47]

Upon the recommendation of the Mexican government, Artaud was permitted to lodge at the local Indian school. Tarahumara resistance to outsiders limited Artaud's contact, initially, to the school director (who was also responsible for order in the Tarahumara community); not until at least a few weeks into his stay would Artaud enter into contact with the Tarahumara. His intervention is credited with leading Mexican authorities to reverse a ban on the peyote ritual it had previously imposed. Eleven years later, Artaud claimed to have urged the director of the school to allow the ceremony or risk a revolt, assuring him that the objective of the ritual is not intoxication, but the realization of *ciguri*, a Tarahumaran concept referring both to peyote and to the god that one experiences after consuming the drink made from peyote. To experience *ciguri*, the Tarahumara limit, rather than abuse, their intake of the dose required by the ritual. Convinced of Artaud's representation and reluctant to spill Tarahumara blood, the director relented, and the ceremony took place the following day.[48] According to Artaud's account, his intercession caused his stock with the Tarahumara to spike.

Discrepancies between Artaud's writings composed nearly contemporaneously with the events described and those written during his confinement in Rodez during the Second World War cast some aspersions over his recitation of the *ciguri* incident. In an article published in *El Nacional*, Artaud wrote that the Tarahumara 'do not believe in God, and the word God does not exist in their language'; instead, they chose Nature as their cult.[49] However, in 1945 during his institutionalization in Rodez – his period of zealous, if not quirky, Catholicism – Artaud claimed a Tarahumara shaman told him that *ciguri* was synonymous with Christ:

> At the heart of Ciguri, and in this Burning Heart a figure, where I could not recognize JESUS CHRIST.
>   With JESUS CHRIST – PEYOTE, I have heard the human body, Spleen, Liver, Lungs, Heart thunder to the four corners of the Divine Infinity.[50]

In a postscript composed in 1947, Artaud wrote that his Rodez compositions 'were written in the foolish mental state of a *convert* taken advantage of by the spells of the priests while his momentary weakness was held in a state of servitude'.[51]

The Tarahumara were very reticent about letting a white man participate in the peyote ritual:

> Peyote, as I knew it, was not made for Whites. It was necessary at whatever cost to prevent me from obtaining a cure by this rite that was instituted to act on the very nature of the spirits. And to these Red men, a White is one who has been abandoned by the spirits. If I profited from this rite, this was that much lost for them.[52]

Having convinced a Tarahumaran priest that his greatest desire was to 'to move closer to the Truth' and that he did not believe this possible without *ciguri*, Artaud was invited to participate in the ritual. Unlike opiates, which Artaud largely took to drive away pain, and unlike the Catholic rituals of his youth, 'peyote returns the self to its origins', providing Artaud with unprecedented clarity, obliterating reality's tastelessness and opening a window into existence transcendent of the material world:

> And the entire series of lustful fantasies projected by the unconscious no longer torments the true spirit of MAN, for the good reason that Peyote is MAN, not born, but INNATE, and that with it, the entire atavistic and personal conscience is alerted and supported.[53]

In revealing infinite knowledge previously inaccessible to him, peyote fuelled Artaud's convictions on another issue that had bedevilled him: gender. 'The root of peyote is hermaphrodite. It carries, as we know it, the shape of both the male and the female gender together.'[54] The shape of the peyote cactus was not merely happenstance; nature, as practised by the Tarahumara, is a mixture of the male and female – dualistic forces, to be sure – but working symbiotically and beneficially with nature's order. This masculine–feminine union is largely within the spiritual realm; civilization, to the Tarahumara, is not limited to 'pure physical comforts, to material commodities'.[55] And, Artaud despaired, in the materialistic West the images he witnessed would have value only as inspiration for advertising posters and fashion models.[56]

In 'The Mountain of Signs', Artaud wrote of an epiphany he had while travelling from Chihuahua to the Copper Canyon. Drawing on Kabbalah's reduction of all phenomena to a mystical numerology, he marvelled at the correspondence of numerical patterns he discerned between the natural features in northern Mexico and the dances and practices of the Tarahumara. Writing to Paulhan after his return to Paris, Artaud described the mathematical symmetry between a sign that appeared in Plato's *Critias* and what he observed in the mountains of the Copper Canyon, as well as the parallel between the Jewish Star of David and a Tarahumaran symbol.[57] If nothing else, this indicated a unity of humankind spanning time, based on mystical rather than cognitive knowledge and the spiritual interconnectedness of geographically disparate peoples. Was Artaud, perhaps, looking for a transcendent idea, one that bridged the divisions of class, nation, race or ethnicity that were responsible for so much conflict and oppression, that were so removed from humankind's origins? Connectedness predicated on ancient knowledge also connected corporeality with consciousness. In 1943, during his institutionalization in Rodez, Artaud wrote that peyote gave him the understanding that 'the liver seems to be the organic filter of *the Unconscious*', a belief shared by the ancient Chinese; but for the liver to act properly, it needs to be nourished. Perpetually hungry, the electroshocks slowly killing him, Artaud recalled a part of his life when he was more psychically balanced:

> We are a long way from Peyote's healing powers. From what I have seen, peyote *stabilizes* the conscience and prevents it from straying, from freeing itself to false impressions. The Mexican Priests have shown me, on the liver, the exact point where *Ciguri*, or Peyote, produces this synthetic concretion that durably maintains sentiments and the desire for truth in the conscience and gives it strength to free itself in automatically rejecting the rest.[58]

Notwithstanding his achievement of psychic equilibrium in the land of the Tarahumara, Artaud's mental state upon his return to Mexico City in early October worried his Mexican friends and personnel at the French Embassy. On 24 October the French ambassador to Mexico asked the Mexican Minister of the Interior if, to facilitate Artaud's repatriation, the twenty-peso exit fee could be waived. On 31 October Artaud embarked on a six-week voyage to France, arriving on 14 November and heading 'suitcase in hand, directly to the Dôme in Montparnasse'.[59]

7

262 602

There can be little doubt that Artaud's experience in Mexico had both confirmed his expectations and transformed him; that his return would be accompanied by an acceleration of his frustration and alienation was not so predictable. Even less easy to determine, though, is the source of that alienation. Artaud's stay in France would last less than a year; armed with the sword he received in Havana (what he believed to be a talisman), he journeyed to Ireland expecting to be welcomed as the bearer of magical and mystical tidings. Instead, his life unravelled at an even more dizzying pace, his alienation morphing into delirium. Deported back to France, Artaud commenced more than eight years of institutionalization in five different asylums.

In October 1935 Artaud made his first reference to Cécile Schramme, a Belgian who had left her bourgeois Brussels family (her father was director of the Brussels tram system). In a short, posthumously published memoir attributed to Schramme, she characterized their relationship as affectionate and playful, Artaud endearingly portrayed as alternatively dandyish (though often penniless) and childish.[1] He was a creature of habit, dining twice a day at Le Dôme or, occasionally, at the Viking-themed tavern, Viking, on rue Vavin (where Henry Miller and Anaïs Nin met), scarfing down his food, spilling some of it on his clothes and indulging his penchant for desserts. He was also appreciative of the speed by which taxis reduce Paris's vastness, equating it, perhaps, to his own frenetic pace.

In Schramme's idyllic, innocent recollections, Artaud comes across as appreciative of the company of pretty women and concerned about their material well-being; yet in his own words, he was disdainful of women. Reminiscent of his letters to Génica Athanasiou, Artaud's letters to Schramme combine his fear of sexuality and unreasonable expectations with his history of tormented relationships with women. Even at their most tender, these letters were sometimes, but not always, laced with doses of contempt. In January 1937 he wrote, 'my love is stronger than my irritation – and this love is not blind, but based, above all, on a very strong feeling about the person you are, and is stronger than all the criticisms that can be said of you.'[2] However, on 3 February, while Schramme was visiting her family, Artaud wrote to her, referring to her as 'this angel who, like all angels, has figured me out, but doesn't know the sound of my voice', and pleading with her to make a hasty return to Paris so that he could see her before attempting another detoxification.[3] On 19 February he wrote her a brief note: 'I love you because you have revealed human happiness to me'; then, six days later, he wrote of a dream in which they were dining at Le Dôme with their child.[4] After Artaud's unsuccessful detoxification attempt at the French Centre for Medicine and Surgery, he checked himself into a clinic at Sceaux. Physically drained and enduring the agony of withdrawal, Artaud wrote to Schramme complimenting her lucidity and intelligence, but accusing her of an 'animal instinct common to a very large number of women [which] is no worse than in other women, *but [which] is more concealed.*' Chastizing Schramme in very general terms, Artaud accused her of dissimulation, deception and betrayal of his trust; a couple of sentences, however, reveal Artaud's unremitting fear of sex as the subtext for his verbal assault:

> And I cannot help you unless you always tell the truth. And unless you don't try to conceal the evil sides of your nature, the sexual and erotic, but also moods and feelings . . . I have confidence in your idea of absolute love, and in your desire to reach it, not in your comportment *which is weak and abandoned to wild beasts*.[5]

It is not hard to discern why Artaud failed at forging lasting romantic relationships. His letters to both Athanasiou and

Schramme were a conflicting mélange of severity and contrition, confusing as they seamlessly went from disparaging reprimands to expressions of deep longing. Artaud's handsome features, esoteric ideas and abandonment of social conventions might have drawn women to him; however, they were offset by his dependence on opiates, idiosyncratic attitude towards sex, demanding and controlling behaviour and jealousy. Tragically, Schramme, who had insisted that he enter a rehabilitation centre, became an opium addict during Artaud's stay in Sceaux; she passed away at age 39 in 1950, two years after Artaud, physically ravaged and destroyed by her years of addiction.[6]

Artaud emerged from the clinic in Sceaux in 1937 cured of his addiction; two years later, at the Ville-Évrard asylum, he surmised that the state of clarity induced by his abstinence from opiates had actually rendered him nearly insane.[7] Incredibly, he planned to marry Schramme. Sometime in May he arrived in Brussels to meet his prospective in-laws and to deliver a lecture at the Maison d'art, entitled *Sur la décomposition de Paris* (On the Decomposition of Paris). Witnesses' accounts of the lecture vary. The Belgian Surrealist poet Marcel Lecomte recalled Artaud announcing at the outset that he was changing topics and, true to his word, straying into a discourse on the Tarahumara. At one point, Artaud, eyes closed, face convulsing, screamed, 'And in revealing this to you, I have perhaps killed myself.' According to Artaud's version, he announced, 'As I have lost my notes, I am going to speak about the effects of masturbation on the Jesuit priests.'[8]

In changing the topic to autoeroticism, Artaud intended to amuse himself and to scandalize the bourgeois Schramme family; he succeeded gloriously. Even before his lecture at the Maison d'art (and either version would have offended the Schrammes), his comportment and statements caused Mr Schramme to enquire of Cécile, 'Are you sure that everything is quite right with this young man?' Mr Schramme's consternation increased when, after taking his prospective son-in-law on a tour of the Brussels tram depot, Artaud asked, 'But do you ever lose these cars in the desert?'

Artaud left Brussels shortly after his lecture and, upon his return to Paris, stayed at Schramme's apartment. Even after all that had transpired in Brussels, Artaud still believed marriage was a possibility, requesting that Paulhan serve as a witness to his impending nuptials.[9] Four days later, on 25 May, Artaud wrote to his clairvoyant friend, Marie Dubuc, about his 33rd day of drug abstinence, his fear of 'a mysterious and terrible being emerging from me', and 'an evening where [Schramme's] monstrous beastliness had made my heart heave once and for all. Beastliness beneath a ruthless and obstinate dissimulation.' Yet, informed by an astrology reading that Schramme loved him, Artaud was willing to leave aside their incompatibility.[10] A few days later, he wrote to Paulhan: 'All these marriage projects are in the water. And rightfully so!'[11]

Under the tutelage of a Cuban specialist in tarot cards, Manuel Cano de Castro, Artaud dabbled in astrology. His enthusiasm for psychic divination – whether tarot, numerology or astrology – and his interpretative skills impressed Castro; however, another current propelled Artaud deeper and deeper into a chaotic vortex that he imagined to be revelatory.

Inspired by his psychic visions, in June Artaud produced a pamphlet, *Les Nouvelles révélations de l'être* (The New Revelations of Being), an apocalyptic and misogynistic snapshot of Artaud as his life rapidly spiralled out of control. The fears at the core of his being became the foundation for his philosophy, his idealistic, though quixotic, ideas morphing into a jumbled mess. Ostensibly inspired by his interpretations of the Tarahumara, the tract reads, dichotomously, like an odd cocktail of Nostradamus and Nietzsche. Employing numerology and relying on his reading of astrological indicators, Artaud predicted an 'infernal destruction' by fire to which humankind must yield to preserve reality at the expense of representations of reality. 'This is to say that burning is a magical act and that it is necessary to consent to burn, to burn in advance and immediately, not a thing, but things, in order not to put ourselves at risk of fully burning.' Artaud anticipated a 'revolution' led 'BY A MADMAN WHO IS ALSO A WISE MAN AND WHO SEES HIMSELF AS BOTH WISE AND MAD', a man whose idea of justice was 'INFERNAL JUSTICE' and 'NO LONGER A QUESTION OF RENDERING IT BUT OF TAKING IT AWAY'. Channelling Nietzsche's misogyny, Artaud predicted, and seemingly relished, authoritarianism:

146

The Right will level the world. And the Left is going to fall again under the Supremacy of the Right. Not *here*, or *elsewhere*, but EVERYWHERE. Because a Cycle of the World under the supremacy of Woman is finished: the Left, the Republic and Democracy.

Echoing Nietzsche's disparagement of women as weak and incapable of higher thoughts, *The New Revelations of Being* is consumed by Artaud's obsession with man's mutilation by carnality and enslavement to lustful impulses; conception, heretofore, would have to be immaculate. The tarots revealed that 'THE ABSOLUTE MALE OF NATURE HAS BEGUN TO MOVE IN THE HEAVENS. HE IS REVIVED FOR THE JUSTICE OF THE MALE.' This 'revolt of nature' would free itself from its alteration by woman: 'This is to say that sexuality is going to be put back in its place. In the place it should never have left. That the sexes will be for some time separated. That human love will be rendered impossible.'[12]

A recent study situates Artaud's screeds against rationality, signed 'Le Révélé' (the Revealed), within fascism, concluding that conventional portrayals of Artaud as an avant-garde radical are ahistorical.[13] At the time that Artaud wrote the pamphlet, according to Roger Blin, he could be a 'monarchist at a given moment', extolling the prospects of General Maxime Weygand (of the ultranationalist, proto-fascist *Action Française*) of imposing 'royal communism on the model of the Incas'. Beyond that, he was hanging out at shady bars in Montmartre and Montparnasse, where, to procure drugs, he kept questionable company with goons and fascists.[14] In December 1943 he dedicated a copy of *The New Revelations of Being* to Adolf Hitler, conjuring up a meeting they purportedly had at the Romanisches Café in Berlin in May 1932, 'because I pray God give you the grace to remember all the wonders by which HE has, this very day, GRATIFIED (RESUSCITATED) YOUR HEART.'[15] Yet on 30 July 1937, two days after the publication of *The New Revelations of Being*, Artaud wrote to André Breton in characteristically obtuse terms:

If I said in the brochure that the leftists are politically doomed, this is not to say that the Right is going to prevail, because the

Right I have in mind is the Right of Man and not the stupid Reaction. *After* having swept out the left for the Natural Right, it is necessary for the Right to be swept out *with* the left because in Nature it is the Right Hand that commands the left generally to reign.[16]

The New Revelations of Being and the letter reveal Artaud's muddled thinking after his return from Mexico; his immersion in mysticism and psychic arts fuelled his detachment from reality, even while permitting him the occasional flash of lucidity.

On 14 August Artaud arrived by ship in Cobh, Ireland; his decision to go to Ireland was an extension of his mission to Mexico: to locate a lost, magically based culture. Both voyages involved objects to which Artaud made reference as talismans in *The New Revelations of Being*: a small sword given to him by a Cuban sorcerer and, after his return to France, a cane he took from the painter René Thomas (originally purchased by the Belgian Surrealist painter Kristians Tonny at a flea market). Artaud believed the cane came from 'the daughter of a Savoyard sorcerer referred to in the prophesy of Saint Patrick . . . This cane has 200 million fibres, and it is encrusted with magical signs'; Artaud took custody of it to return it to the Irish. In Artaud's numerology-dominated cosmology, the thirteen knots on the cane took on special significance, particularly the ninth one, since that was associated with lightning and thus the cataclysmic fire Artaud predicted. Accompanied by his tarot-reading friend Castro, Artaud took the cane to a blacksmith to have an iron tip attached to its bottom – the better to work its magical powers (by emitting sparks whenever Artaud struck it on the pavement); Artaud insisted on doing the work himself, uttering incantations as Castro hammered the iron tip. He refused to allow anyone to touch his cane, viewing it as a surrogate to his penis: 'It is as if you touch my genitals . . . as though a woman makes love with me without my consent.'[17]

Unlike the fair amount of preparation he made before his journey to Mexico, Artaud's Irish voyage was a combination of speculative knowledge and his familiarity with John Millington Synge's Aran Islands-based, anthropologically tinged, poetical, theatrical and literary works. Whereas the artistic community in Mexico City welcomed him, Artaud either lacked contacts in Ireland, or did not follow up with the scholars of Gaelic culture provided him by the Irish diplomatic legation.[18] Artaud wrote extensively during his months in Mexico, but what transpired during his six-week stay in Ireland can barely be discerned from letters he sent to friends; his journeys (to Cobh, to Galway, to Inishmore in the Aran Islands, back to Galway and to Dublin) can be pieced together through unpaid bills and unsuccessful requests for loans from the French Embassy, but his letters are bereft of experiential material. While researching his unpublished doctoral thesis, Robert Maguire, in the mid-1950s, retraced Artaud's steps in Ireland and met some of those with whom Artaud had contact; though memories are often unreliable and fade over time, these are the only sources that shed light, however hazy, on Artaud's quotidian existence in Ireland. Writing to his family from Kilronan, Artaud stated that he came to Ireland to find 'the last authentic descendants of the Druids, those who possess the secrets of the Druidic philosophy and know that man descends from the god of death "Dis Pater" [a Celtic variation of the god of the underworld] and that humanity must disappear by water and fire'.[19] Three weeks later, he wrote to Anie Besnard and René Thomas:

> the cane I possess is the very same one of Jesus Christ and, know-ing I am not crazy, you will believe me when I tell you that Jesus Christ speaks to me every day, reveals all that is going to happen and arranges for me to do what I am going to do. Therefore, I came to Ireland to obey the exact orders of God, the Son, incarnated in Jesus Christ.[20]

While Artaud went to Ireland seeking the pagan history of Ireland – a Western-cultural version of what he was determined to find in Mexico – it is possible that the abundance of Celtic crosses on the Aran Islands inspired him, instead, to restore to Ireland the popular roots of Christianity; armed with 'Saint Patrick's cane', he tramped through the island, a god (or a king) on a mission.[21]

Artaud's letters, for the most part, are a bizarre admixture of spiritual prophecies and political rantings. With the exception of two letters to Paulhan, in which Artaud requested money, his letters to Breton (and Breton's daughter, Jacqueline), Anne Manson and Anie Besnard rail against those who live for the material world (singling out, in particular, Jewish bankers and Spanish anarchists in separate letters), but, towards the end of his stay, his boundless venom bordered on the pathological. On 15–16 September he wrote to Anne Manson, urging her 'to betray him' to their friends at Les Deux Magots:

> They need to know that I will not return alone, but with an army. If they believe me to be crazy, a megalomaniac or a maniac, so much the worse for them. And if they believe that I am boasting, they are imbeciles.
>
> Tell them that for years I have hated them and their political, social, moral, amoral and immoral ideas. Tell them that I take them for lowlifes and jerks.
>
> Tell them that I shit on the republic, democracy, socialism, communism, Marxism, idealism, materialism, dialectic or not, because I also shit on the dialectic, and I am going to prove it further on.
>
> I shit on the Popular Front and on the Government of the Popular Assembly, I shit on the International, 1st, 2nd, and 3rd, but I also shit on the idea of Fatherland, I shit on France and on the French, except those that I have personally informed and with whom I am in correspondence.
>
> The French, whether identifying with the Right or the Left, are all idiots and capitalists, and in that stinking café where I send you, where they have all exhausted and exasperated me with their quarrels and their interests, I have seen only capitalists, *well-off* blinded by extravagance and who left behind the darkness of Existence.[22]

Earlier in September, Artaud alerted Breton of the coming of 'serious occurrences', in which Breton would 'play an active role'; his attention riveted onto Lise Deharme, muse to the Surrealists and unrequited romantic interest of Breton. In 1934 Artaud wrote to Paulhan that Deharme had promised him money for the Theatre of Cruelty but delivered 'no more than a pathetic amount'.[23] Artaud warned Breton of a

> woman [identified as 'L. D.'] you know who is part of current High capitalism and who is going to present herself as the Théroigne de Méricourt of the next upheavals. She will foment a horrible Riot, coalesced with all the forces of the left, and bizarrely allied with High Jewish, and *perhaps Catholic* capitalism, *as well*.

He predicted she would either flee or be 'PUBLICLY MASSACRED'.[24] In another letter to Breton, Artaud included 'a curse' (the first of many *envoûtements*) intended for Deharme, which combined anti-Semitism, extreme sexual violence and his newly discovered messianism. Topped by a numerological diagram, the text read 'I will drive a cross of iron / reddened by fire in your / dirty Jewish pussy / and will then *ham it up* / on your corpse to / prove to you that there are / STILL GODS!'[25]

Lacking money and unable to communicate in English, Artaud's final two weeks in Dublin were difficult; his extreme religiosity was nourished by his delirium and stays in monasteries. By the final week of September, Artaud stopped communicating with friends and family. In November Paulhan wrote to the French consulate in Dublin, expressing alarm that Artaud was both without resources and, based on the last letters received (in September), was 'overly excited'. On 20 November the consul wrote back to Paulhan, stating that in September the Irish police wanted to deport Artaud back to France; he had boarded the American liner *Washington* on 20 September at Cobh.[26]

Though the consul got the date of Artaud's departure wrong by nine days, he was correct that Artaud had been deported and had arrived the following day at Le Havre. Versions abound as to the circumstances behind Artaud's deportation: some monks might have caught him in the act of removing St Patrick's headstone (to retrieve a document); or he might have got into a street fight after the disappearance of the cane; or, in Artaud's account of 1945, the Irish government, on orders from the Intelligence Services, might have requested his deportation because he was 'too revolutionary'.[27] According to the official account of the Irish police, on 20 September Artaud caused a commotion at a Jesuit college and the police were summoned. The following day, while meeting with a French consulate representative, Artaud was hostile and uncooperative and denied being French (he claimed he was Greek and that his passport had been substituted). Upon being informed of this, the Irish Department of Justice recommended his expulsion. Interned at Dublin's Mountjoy Prison, Artaud, again, met with the French ambassador's representative; this time he constructed a more elaborate alternative identity, claiming to be 'Antonéo Arlaud Arlanapulos, born in Smyrna on 29 September 1904', who arrived in Ireland on a self-made boat. On 29 September, escorted by two policemen, Artaud boarded the *Washington* for Le Havre. According to the ship's detective, Artaud was delusional, claiming to be 'a member of the French Royalist party, and feared being guillotined if returned to France'; Artaud's sister, Marie-Ange, claimed that he preferred throwing himself overboard to returning to France.[28]

Though hallucinatory while awaiting his repatriation, Artaud's life spun more rapidly out of control on the short ship journey. Artaud re-entered French soil in a straightjacket; he was remanded to the police as insane and taken to the psychiatric wing of Le Havre's general hospital. In a letter to Arthur Adamov in 1945, Artaud claimed that his detention resulted after he fought with two mechanics who entered his cabin – ostensibly to make repairs – but, in reality, 'to make him disappear'.[29]

The 'Law of 30 June 1838' provided for an individual's involuntary confinement at a mental health facility when requested by either his family or the police.[30] On 14 October an official medical certificate stated that Artaud was suffering from hallucinations and a persecution complex: 'Dangerous to himself and to others, and [I] attest that it is urgent to admit immediately the above-named to the departmental Asylum for madmen.' Consequently, on 16 October Artaud was transferred to Quatre-Mares, the psychiatric hospital in Sotteville-lès-Rouen, and assigned the case number 262 602, a designation that followed him along his peregrinations through the French mental health system. The first doctor to examine him in Sotteville-lès-Rouen wrote of Artaud's 'psychotic state' and paranoiac condition towards 'people hostile to his Orthodox Christian religious convictions'.[31]

The consequences of Artaud's short stay in Ireland echoed throughout the remainder of his life, nurturing his delirium and fantasies.[32] Once the process of his institutionalization commenced, his condition worsened; that neither friends nor family received notice of his return to France until sometime in December likely deprived him of support that might have prevented his involuntary confinement in the almost primordial conditions of the French psychiatric asylums.

As spaces of confinement and examination, rather than remediation and restoration, psychiatric asylums in France subjected internees to a strict regimen designed to reinforce their transition from civil to institutionalized status; their lives were a steady diet of surveillance and monotony and, as Artaud remembered years later, interrupted sleep 'in the midst of [inmates'] farts, burps, snores and night dreams, every night'.[33] With respect to the specific treatments Artaud received at Quatre-Mares, there is a lacuna in the record: a major part of the asylum was destroyed during the Second World War, leaving only his admittance record and speculation as to the whereabouts of his medical dossier and its contents.

Unaware of her son's internment, Artaud's mother, Euphrasie, began a concerted effort to locate him. Through a combination of enquiries and intuition, she arrived at Quatre-Mares, only to find her son unable to recognize her; determined to bring him closer to Paris, Euphrasie arranged for Artaud's transference on 1 April to the Henri-Rousselle Hospital at the Sainte-Anne Psychiatric Centre in Paris's 14th arrondissement.

Artaud's donning of his new persona accelerated at Quatre-Mares. Writing to the Irish Plenipotentiary Minister in Paris, Artaud stuck to his Greek alter ego, Arland Antonéo (Arlanapulos), whose papers were altered by the French police. This new identity coincided with his return to Christianity (albeit an idiosyncratic form of it), an abandonment of his rejection of the Catholicism of his youth and, by extension, a rebirth that required a new persona (at least in his estimation).

Sainte-Anne was a teaching hospital, a diagnostic centre for patients destined for a more prolonged commitment in an asylum, and a pioneering facility in treating diagnosed schizophrenics with a newly devised method for inducing seizures: convulsive therapy. Convulsive therapy entailed the injection of a near-toxic dose of either Cardiazol (Metrazol method) or insulin (Sakel method) – both were used at Sainte-Anne – enough to render the recipient into a comatose state; afterwards, the patient received sugar to bring him out of the coma. During the coma, patients sweated, shook spasmodically, slobbered white foam and contorted violently. The experience was so traumatic that patients sometimes concealed sugar under their beds, discreetly taking it just prior to receiving the insulin.[34] Dr Gaston Ferdière was a resident intern at Sainte-Anne in 1937 and described the Metrazol procedure: 'Cardiazol appears to spread throughout the body, then to explode in the brain. This is horrendous to watch, and we feared that accidents would happen. None did.'[35] In an effort to avoid the physical anguish suffered by recipients of either method, a new procedure – electroconvulsive therapy (that is, electroshock treatment) – was introduced during the early 1940s. Dr Ferdière, then the chief of psychiatric services at the asylum in Rodez, spearheaded its employment; Artaud would be his most notable patient.

As with his stay at Quatre-Mares, only fragmentary information exists on Artaud's experiences and treatments during his eleven months at Sainte-Anne; most of what we know comes from letters he wrote several years later, just after his deinstitutionalization. Artaud wrote of beatings at Sainte-Anne and various attempts at poisoning him through the administration of prussic acid as an antidiarrhoeal; the consequences, according to Artaud, were lapses into month-long comas, lung and heart asphyxiation and bloody dysentery, as well as dental neuralgia, dental cavities that caused him to lose his remaining teeth, sinusitis, asthma, rheumatism and a stiff neck. The better cure, he wrote to his sister Marie-Ange, would have been high doses of heroin, which, 'when it is of good quality, does not bring about drug addiction'.[36] In spite of efforts by family members and friends to see him, Artaud refused all visitors. Blin observed Artaud in the courtyard at Sainte-Anne, 'with a beard, even though he was always impeccably shaved, leaning against a tree. Around him, others were playing football.'[37]

One of the other young psychiatrists with whom Artaud crossed paths was Jacques Lacan, whose revolutionary psychoanalytic theories on the relationship between the unconscious, subjectivity and semantics positioned psychiatry within post-structuralism. According to Blin, Lacan confided in him 'that the excellent physical health of Artaud will permit him to live into his '80s, but his hopeless mental state will no doubt prohibit him from any creation'.[38] Years later, Artaud wrote of Lacan, 'You ordain a conscience that works as a delirium, but at the same time, you strangle it with your disgusting sexuality.'[39]

In 1943 Artaud was moved from Sainte-Anne to the asylum in Ville-Évrard. A few months after being moved from Sainte-Anne to the asylum in Ville-Évrard, Artaud wrote of protesting against his transference and, for his troubles, of being immobilized by three guards who kicked and choked him (while the warden allegedly ordered the guards to 'strangle him'): 'If I did not die of suffocation, it is because of some unconscious contraction of the muscles of my throat.'[40]

For nearly four years – from 27 February 1939 to 10 February 1943 – Artaud was confined at the psychiatric hospital in Ville-Évrard. Built in 1868 and located around 10 kilometres (6 miles) from Paris, Ville-Évrard was bifurcated between a private *maison de santé* (nursing home) and a public asylum. Prior residents of the former included sculptress Camille Claudel, consigned there by her mother (who would never visit her) after her father (who had protected her for years) passed away.[41] Lacking the resources for the *maison de santé*, Artaud ended up in the asylum. His life would be orchestrated by the monotonous rhythms of the clock at Ville-Évrard, which foretold awakenings, meal times and bedtimes, in between hours of aimless walks in the courtyard during which internees' inner torments macerated and metastasized into self-fulfilling truths.

Whether regularizing the internee's day or instituting a regimen of constant surveillance, Ville-Évrard was all about control. From the moment the inmate arrived, he was stripped of his individuality. After he was undressed, showered and

Postcard of Ville-Évrard grounds.

issued regulation attire (shirt, jacket, trousers, shoes, socks and a handkerchief), his personal effects were deposited on a wooden bench, confiscated and inventoried, ultimately being reduced to a numbered packet. Flanked by guards on either side, the new inmate walked through an outdoor courtyard into the interior spaces and on to the dormitory. En route, he experienced a complete sensorial assault; his olfactory senses were 'struck by an indefinable odour of mustiness, of urine, of ether, of disinfectant, of violence that breeds the violence and the repression', while the monologues, screams and cries of asylum veterans provided the accompanying soundtrack.

Whether addressed by guards and nurses by his last name or by the familiar *tutoiement* (use of informal pronoun), or, more humiliatingly, forced to undress and shower in full view, Ville-Évrard stripped Artaud of his remaining dignity and privacy; and yet there is no indication that he was anything but indifferent, if not numb, to his new existence, as his past lost meaning or melded into his growing delirium. When one of the nurses expressed surprise at seeing Artaud in one of the monthly films screened for internees, Artaud, who did not attend the screening, replied, 'That is ancient history.'[42]

With that said, Artaud's fertile imagination and, possibly, his pre-institutionalized renown set him apart from most of the other internees and attracted the attention of the Ville-Évrard staff. From appearances, Dr Léon Fouks, an internist at Ville-Évrard, established a warm personal relationship with Artaud; however, in letters to Fouks, Artaud was scathing, a reflection of either his instability or perhaps his unconcealed feelings towards Fouks. (For example, he accused Fouks of conspiring with other doctors to kill him, and he wrote in one letter, 'Fouks fucked. You are only shit. The shit of a little dog: little Fouks dogs.')[43] Through Fouks's encouragement, Artaud constructed an 'autobiography'. Continuing the practice of referring to himself as 'Antonéo Arlaud, or Arlanapulos in Greek, born at Smyrna', Artaud's elaborate biography combined elements of his Greek heritage, his own past and a large dose of fiction (such as a bachelor's degree in Persian, Egyptian and Semitic civilizations, and a marriage to a Turkish woman that ended with her death two or three years later).

Artaud's construction of alternative identities was a mélange of fact and fiction, perhaps a prima facie manifestation of his detachment from reality. However, it is also entirely possible that this was a deliberate obfuscation on his part, a calculation to maintain a modicum of control while he wended his way through a mental health system designed to predetermine his insanity.[44] On the other hand, Artaud's persecution complex was very real; he imagined his victimization since his return from Mexico by the fabricated machinations of a nefarious group, the Initiates (*Les Initiés*), a shadowy group casting spells on him through the agency of their doubles, or 'straw men'. Sometimes the doubles exercised direct influence over the affairs of Artaud in particular (for example, among those he named were André and Jacqueline Breton, Paulhan, Salvador Dalí, Schramme, Balthus and Lacan); in other cases, they exercised control over global events (Hitler, Anthony Eden, Joseph Stalin). As their weapon of choice, the Initiates engaged in sex at precisely identified locations such as the intersection of Boulevard Raspail and Boulevard du Montparnasse, rue Mazarine, Saint-Germain-des-Prés, the Jardin des Plantes and the esplanade of the Invalides. Artaud alone had the wherewithal to counter the Initiates, but in order to find St Patrick's cane and beat the Initiates with it, he needed a special form of heroin, 'heroin B', to 'rediscover the world's unity' from the consciousness-destroying doubles – 'HEROIN OR A REVOLVER'.[45] Delusions old and new merged in Artaud's warnings of the Initiates; if sex was the tool of the latter, Artaud would counter it with heroin. After not having written to Génica Athanasiou since 1934, Artaud composed a series of letters to her in 1940, requesting heroin and imploring her 'to remain completely pure and chaste and forever'. Only Anne Manson attempted to deliver heroin to Artaud at Ville-Évrard; apparently unaware of the reason for the visit, Artaud refused to see her.[46]

After the German invasion of Poland in September 1939, Artaud, witnessing the mobilization of most of the staff, including Fouks, could not help but sense the dramatic changes that were to come, telling a nurse, 'For me, this is not the war, this is the Apocalypse.' In June 1940 the internees at Ville-Évrard could see Neuilly-sur-Marne's residents, and then French soldiers, fleeing the area, followed rapidly by the advancing German army. A state of panic set in among the internees; many were aware that the Nazis had massacred mental patients in Poland. On 1 July 1939, Artaud wrote to Dr Barrat, an internist at Ville-Évrard: 'You have never been anything more to me than a bag of shit in the sinister shadow of this woman.'[47] However, a little more than eleven months later, when the Nazis rolled into France, and as Ville-Évrard appeared more isolated, more deserted, more abandoned than ever, Artaud fearfully asked Barrat, 'Are we going to be killed?' For Artaud, as for many of the patients at Ville-Évrard, reality had trumped delirium, and anxiety gave birth to reason.[48]

Though the Nazis made only a cursory search of Ville-Évrard and did not murder any of its patients, Nazi policy towards the mentally ill clearly made life at an asylum in the occupied zone of France (including Neuilly-sur-Marne) much more precarious. In the French zone controlled by the Vichy government (not including Ville-Évrard and asylums in the Nazi-occupied zone), starvation diets and general lack of care caused an estimated 40,000 deaths in asylums.[49] Hunger was a persistent scourge, reducing internees to eating grass or animal feed; malnutrition rendered them vulnerable to diseases ranging from dysentery to tuberculosis to beriberi. When Paul Sabourin became director of Ville-Évrard in 1943 (not long after Artaud's departure), he found conditions there akin to those described by his sister at Ravensbrück concentration camp, from where she had returned in 'a total physiological distress':[50]

> At Ville-Évrard our eyes were opened to the pathology abundantly spoken of when the survivors of the deportation returned after the liberation of the Nazi concentration camps. Tremendous loss of weight, whether or not latent tuberculosis has been reactivated, or contaminations triggered by crippling advancement of galloping consumption on organisms whose defenses have been destroyed, enormous oedema where these skeletal bodies fill themselves with water then empty them in incredible diarrheas. At the morning visit, the dormitories smell like dead bodies.[51]

In 1896 the head doctor at Ville-Évrard had noted that physical stagnation rendered internees incurable and eliminated nearly any prospect of their re-socialization. On a questionnaire he filled out upon his arrival at Ville-Évrard in 1939, Artaud stated that his goals during his institutionalization were 'to work, to busy my hands rather than my mind, and to occupy my mind with everyday things'.[52] Although some internees were allowed to work outside of Ville-Évrard, Artaud was largely physically inactive. Socially withdrawn, he spent a good deal of his time writing letters to old friends, beseeching them to bring him food or drugs or to procure his release; and, of course, there were endless letters written about the evil designs of the Initiates, some addressed to those he identified as Initiates! Artaud's misguided communications were a mark of his desperation as he searched for some connection with the outside world, some means for breaking out of the isolation and lack of meaningful human contact.[53] Until the start of the war Artaud received regular visits from friends and his mother; according to Blin, a regular visitor, he refused however to recognize Euphrasie during the first year at Ville-Évrard. The war soon changed all that. Aside from the occasional appearance of Blin or some other former associate, biweekly visits by Euphrasie – every Thursday and Sunday – were his only contacts with the world outside of Ville-Évrard; often as not, though, these visits consisted of mother and son, on a bench in the courtyard, sitting largely in silence, Artaud smoking countless cigarettes, their horizon defined and confined by the walls and wire fencing of Ville-Évrard.

Towards the end of 1941, he adopted the new persona Antonin Nalpas, his mother's family name, explaining, in a letter he would write from the asylum in Rodez,

> Antonin Artaud died from pain and grief at Ville-Évrard during the month of August 1939 and his body exited Ville-Évrard during the length of a white night like those of which Dostoevsky spoke and which take up the space of several leap days but are not included in the calendar of this world – however true it is today.[54]

Was Artaud intentionally developing a connection between his own 'death' and the start of the war a month later? Was he ruminating, like the unnamed narrator in Dostoevsky's 'White Nights', on the unfulfilled love, loneliness and unfamiliar hues his world had taken? Or, if for Dostoevsky, 'white nights' symbolized 'a state of rapture' in an otherwise dark existence – the long hours of sunlight during the St Petersburg summer – could Artaud have seen it as despair and an ecstatic reference to his imagined rebirth?[55] Lacking emotional and nutritional support, was the selection of his mother's name a regression to his infancy when his mother caressed and nursed him?[56]

Above all, Artaud craved food. In his letters to his mother (uncharacteristically addressing her by her first name), he claimed that 'it is absolutely false that Paris lacks for food' and made unreasonable demands for, among other things, olives, waffles, cheese, spiced breads, sweets, mushrooms, chocolate, butter, jams, nuts, fruits – dried and fresh – and vegetables; the reality of Artaud's hunger collided with the reality of wartime France. When he first arrived in Ville-Évrard, Artaud weighed 65.5 kilograms (144 lb); by July 1940 – just after the fall of France – his weight had dropped to 60 kilograms (132 lb); on 7 December 1940, this

Artaud at the Rodez
asylum, *c.* 1943–6.

had fallen to 55 kilograms (121 lb). Given Euphrasie's age and the
wartime conditions, her unswerving commitment to satisfy her
son's requests – queuing for his rations, spending what little she had
at the black market, and journeying to Ville-Évrard – were almost
Herculean; in all likelihood, they enabled Artaud to survive Ville-
Évrard where so many other internees died.[57]

Euphrasie's overall objective was her son's recovery of his senses
and reintegration into society; in her desperation, she even brought
a vial of consecrated water from Lourdes to sprinkle on her son.
However, if anything, Artaud's malady appeared to be worsening.
Sometime in 1942 Euphrasie learned that electroconvulsive therapy
might ameliorate her son's condition; as it turned out, one of the
therapy's leading practitioners, Dr Rondepierre, was at Ville-Évrard
(there is no evidence of it being tried on Artaud during his stay there,
however). The only other option for Euphrasie – a *maison de santé*
– was well beyond her financial means. Desperate for a solution,
Euphrasie contacted Robert Desnos and Paul Éluard, both of whom

had been members of the Surrealist movement with Artaud; during the war, both had been active in the resistance to Nazi occupation and its puppet government in Vichy. Dr Gaston Ferdière, the head psychiatrist at the asylum in Rodez, located in the Aveyron, was a poet and associate of the Surrealists (but after Artaud's departure).[58] Though reticent when approached by others about taking in Artaud, after being contacted by Desnos in late November or early December 1942 Ferdière readily agreed to treat Artaud in Rodez.[59]

On 11 December the wheels of Artaud's removal to Rodez were put in motion after a doctor at Ville-Évrard signed his certificate of transference. Logistically, however, there was still a problem: Ville-Évrard was in the Nazi-occupied zone and Rodez in the Nazi puppet state known as 'Free France'. Arrangements were made to transfer Artaud to the Chezal-Benoît hospital located in the Cher, a department within the ambiguous line of demarcation between the Occupied and Free zones. Ferdière had been medical director there (before being fired by the Vichy government for his trade unionist beliefs) but he maintained contacts in the region, while Desnos, through a sympathetic functionary at the department prefecture, facilitated Artaud's temporary removal to the hospital. On 21 January 1943, Desnos visited Artaud at Ville-Évrard and wrote to Ferdière of his observations:

> I went to Ville-Évrard on Thursday; Artaud was due to leave the next day, Friday 22. I found him completely delirious, speaking like Saint Jerome and no longer wanting to leave because it would separate him from the magical forces that work for him. I last saw him five years ago, and this has been a spectacle as painful as his elation and madness. I persuaded his mother not to take into account his speeches and to let him leave, as I am sure that he will be better with us. But he appears well ensconced in these fantasies and hard to cure . . . Artaud will no doubt consider me to be a persecutor![60]

Artaud arrived at Chezal-Benoît on 22 January, wearing the same clothes as when he arrived in Le Havre in 1937, though, at 53.5 kilograms (118 lbs), more emaciated. He had only three personal

effects – a passport, a penknife and a nail file – all his papers and
other possessions having been lost, stolen or discarded over the
years. After nearly three weeks at Chezal-Benoît, at 10 pm on 10
February, Artaud was transferred to Rodez.[61] Desnos, whose efforts
on behalf of Artaud likely saved the latter, travelled a crueller path:
an activist in the Resistance (procuring false identity papers for Jews
and other victims of fascism), Desnos was arrested on 22 February
1944 and succumbed to typhus on 8 May 1945 at the Theresienstadt
concentration camp.

Dr Ferdière's tenure in Rodez began nearly thirty months prior
to Artaud's arrival. Under Ferdière's directorship much had changed
in Rodez. Comprised of neglected and dilapidated buildings, it was
slated to close. Faced with an inbred culture of insouciance among
the staff in Rodez, Ferdière was determined to set things right. Only
one staff member had a degree; the others were simply caretakers,
and many of them were alcoholics, incompetent or disinterested
in the responsibilities to which they had been entrusted. During
the month prior to Ferdière's arrival in July 1941, malnutrition
had claimed the lives of sixty patients. After sacking employees
whose irresponsibility had contributed to the awful conditions,
Ferdière took a more direct role in the daily functioning of the
hospital. Under Ferdière's direction, Rodez also provided asylum
to individuals pursued by the Nazis or the Vichy régime, including
Surrealist artist Frédéric Delanglade.

Ferdière's chief objective was to follow a treatment plan that
reawakened Artaud's creativity. Years bereft of social contact
and stimulation had reduced Artaud's existence to a luxuriant
imaginary world where his persecution by the medical profession
and the police was a 'state secret'.[62] Whether he had irretrievably
lost all touch with reality or was conscious of his transformation
but unable to control it, Artaud's rejection of his name,
concoction of an alternative biography and ecstatic, unrelenting
re-engagement with Christian fanaticism completed his retreat
from his pre-institutionalized self. In a letter dated 12 July 1943,
Artaud wrote that even if his body (as Antonin Nalpas) had only
been on earth for three years, 'I have in the body the absolute and
exact psychological memory, fully and inalienably exact, of six

years of tortures, lack of understandings, renunciations, spells and confinements.'[63]

Artaud could no longer exist under the conditions at the asylums. Resurrected as Nalpas, he became a caricature of himself, defined by his alter ego as something he was not: 'in the case of Antonin Artaud, it is neither an issue of literature nor of theatre, but of *religion*, and this is on account of his religious ideas, for his religious and mystical attitude, that Antonin Artaud UNTIL HIS DEATH has been hunted by the French masses.'[64] A new soul now inhabited the body of Artaud, and his name was of little importance. In identifying his parents as Joseph and Mary, Artaud awaited an approaching millenarian transformation; Christ had taken up residency in his body.

The war heavily influenced Artaud's visions, whether in Christ's resurrection in Artaud's body or in his reference to his deceased sister Germaine as a modern-day Joan of Arc, a heroine divinely summoned to repel the foreign invader from French soil.[65] As he slid deeper and deeper into grandiose religiosity, his chronic history of sexual frustrations neatly dovetailed into his purification of Christianity; his metamorphosis into Nalpas was an immaculate conception:

> This Religion desires total chastity not only for the Priest but for all men worthy of this name and preaches total separation of the genders and the *resolute* elimination of all sexuality. All that is sexual and not chaste, outside of marriage AND WITHIN marriage, is condemned, and human reproduction is not justified by filthy copulation.[66]

Dr Jacques Latrémolière was Ferdière's 25-year-old assistant. A devout Catholic, Latrémolière believed Artaud's religiosity was no more than a toxic combination of his megalomania, incomprehensibility and egoism, thus lacking sincerity. Rather than engage Artaud's idiosyncratic interpretation, Latrémolière endeavoured to correct his understanding of Catholicism; for example, he concluded that Artaud's views on sex and love were motivated by his impotence and attempt 'to emasculate others [and] lead them to his own dimension'.[67] Latrémolière also considered that Artaud might have been a closeted homosexual. Yet he also viewed Artaud's spiritual protestations as a manipulative subterfuge for his principal objective: the procurement of heroin. In one of his first letters to Latrémolière, Artaud argued that if the young doctor refused him the heroin necessary to cleanse his body of the 'sperm and excrement' of the liaison that produced him, it would be proof that Latrémolière was still tainted by 'original sin'.[68]

In his assessment of Artaud, Latrémolière straddled precariously between his own religious convictions and his professional responsibilities. One year after Artaud's arrival in Rodez, Latrémolière successfully defended his doctoral thesis, 'Accidents and Incidents Observed in the Course of 1,200 Electroshocks'. Having administered around 1,000 electroshocks in three years, Latrémolière's thesis reduced the frightening stories associated with the treatment to mere aberrations in an otherwise effective therapy; he substantiated the mental health profession's sincere belief that it was an efficacious alternative to the prior practice of confining internees until they withered away from their severe psychological disorders.

Awakened on the morning of 20 June 1943, Artaud was told not to eat breakfast because 'he was going to have, during the afternoon, a treatment.' Ferdière did not discuss the procedure in advance with Artaud: 'it would be cruel to make him await the electroshock.'[69] Two nurses strapped Artaud to a bed, loosened or removed his clothes, placed a rubber hose between the rows of his teeth (to prevent him from breaking them or biting or swallowing his tongue) and fastened two electrodes to the frontal regions of his head. The first jolt of electricity would cause his body to stiffen, then convulse, his teeth clenched on the rubber hose, his eyes rolling in the back of his head. He would lapse into a coma for fifteen minutes after which he would awaken completely disoriented, remaining in that state for several hours; once he recovered his memory, depression set in. During his nineteen months in Rodez, Artaud received 58 electroshock treatments, spread over six series; slightly more than half of those occurred over a five-month span that began with the first session.

The second electroshock series resulted in a fracture of the ninth vertebra. The doctors asserted that after two months' bed rest and the administration of painkillers, Artaud suffered no lasting pain or discomfort, but two years after the treatment, Artaud wrote to Paulhan, 'I don't know if there is damage to my spinal column because the base of my back always feels horribly bad and to get out of bed each morning, I have to struggle a few minutes to lift my back from the pillow.'[70] As he awaited the third series of electroshocks in late October 1943, Artaud recalled the accident to Ferdière: 'The electroshock therapy has caused me to suffer terribly, and I beg you to spare me another suffering.'[71] In spite of Artaud's pleadings, thirteen more electroshock treatments were administered between 25 October and 22 November 1943.

After those first three series of 28 electroconvulsive therapies, there was a six-month reprieve. Latrémolière wrote in his thesis that, though there was a diminution in Artaud's 'bizarre and theatrical reactions during his hallucinations', his delirium persisted and required another round of electroshocks. Changes in Artaud's behaviour encouraged Latrémolière and Ferdière to think that the treatment was bearing fruit: in addition to an increase in weight to 66 kilograms (146 lb), by September he had abandoned his 'Nalpas' identity and was again signing his name 'Antonin Artaud'. On 17 September 1943, he wrote to his mother for the first time in months:

> You have been inspired by God in suggesting that I come to Rodez because the environment is completely different and the atmosphere *of affection* and human support I have found has inspired a healthy crisis which, without doubt, has shaken me but, in the end, has returned me to myself and has now given me back my healthy understanding of everything.[72]

Artaud was beginning to communicate with old friends such as Paulhan, Barrault, Blin, Anne Manson, André Gide and Anie Besnard. For the first time in six years, he was writing essays. Actually, five weeks after Artaud arrived in Rodez, before the first electroshock, Ferdière asked him to write a commentary on a poem by Pierre de Ronsard, 'The Devil's Hymn'. Three decades later, Ferdière called Artaud's vocabulary 'transcendent', opining that

Artaud 'is the victim of his terminological richness'. Ferdière's goal was to encourage Artaud to rediscover his creative impulses.[73]

Artaud's prodigious writings in Rodez were largely populated with incoherent ramblings on familiar topics: religion, sexuality, drugs and persecution by demons.[74] Beginning with the essay on Ronsard, Artaud peppered his Rodez writings with phrases or passages written in glossolalia. Often identified with charismatic religious movements in which congregants are suddenly speaking an ethereal language, a tongue they never learned, glossolalia, according to some Christians, was 'inspired by the Spirit'; at the advent of psychiatry, glossolalia signified 'the subliminal consciousness', a language buried within the recesses of the conscience.[75] In his present state of spiritualism, glossolalia was Artaud's 'received language', a confirmation of his divine stature; as a Surrealist, however, it was a language from his subconscious, removed from hegemonic social and cultural forces.

Artaud's mental state improved and, in coordination with Father Julian, a priest in Rodez who knew English, he translated several works, including Lewis Carroll's *Through the Looking Glass* and writings by Poe, Byron, Shelley and Keats. Under the tutelage of Delanglade, Artaud took up drawing more seriously than ever before. In 1939 at Ville-Évrard, he had composed 'gris-gris', figures 'ravaged by fits of asthma, torments and the hiccups',[76] punctuated with inflammatory verbiage: 'and the figures therefore that I made were curses – that I burned with a match after having meticulously drawn them' (employing the Tarahumaran idea of purification through fire or burning). When he commenced drawing in Rodez, Artaud abandoned 'gris-gris': 'And I changed in understanding that I was interned, poisoned and subjugated for being a magician.'[77] Initially drawing at the invitation of Ferdière for therapeutic purposes, Artaud embraced the medium, seeing it as more than merely a cathartic exercise: it was a liberation of his thoughts from the strictures of verbal expression.

Visual expression enabled Artaud to forge a new communicative medium – 'some gestures, a verb, a grammar, an arithmetic, a whole Kabbalah' – to reveal 'magic' ancient sources and beliefs that 'are still alive and unaltered'.[78] Alone, magic was a panacea for this '"troublesome schism", this rupture between things and words, ideas and signs, this separation between culture and life', the petrification of everything touched by the West.[79] Artaud did not consider his drawings to be mere drawings, but 'documents'; however, if predicated solely on what the eye perceives, they defy interpretation. 'I want to say that we have a leucoma [white opacity in the cornea] on the eye, given that our present ocular vision is *deformed*, repressed, oppressed, reverted and suffocated by certain misappropriations because of our skull, as by the architecture of our soul . . .'.[80]

For Artaud, his drawings were an extension of his revolt against sensory and intellectual perceptions that have been preordained and preconditioned by hegemonic forces. In 1947 Artaud provided what was probably (for him, at least) his clearest statement on the meaning behind the mélange of chaotic images in his drawings:

> The goal of all drawn and coloured figures was to exorcize the curse, a corporeal rant against the moral necessities of spatial form, perspective, value, equilibrium and dimension, and through this ranting protest, a condemnation of the psychological world encrusted like a crab on the physical world that it incubates or succubates in claiming to have formed it.[81]

Artaud's friends and family rallied around him, sending him money, parcels, news and encouragement; he became more focused and creative. Optimism had to be tempered, as Artaud still wrote of demons, curses, doubles, curious imaginings (for example, that Breton, allied to the fascist *Action Française*, had been machine-gunned to death by the police in Le Havre) and his incessant need for opiates and cocaine. In response to a return of his hallucinations, a fresh round of twelve electroconvulsive therapies – his fourth series – took place between 23 May and 16 June 1944. Cognizant of the authority they had over him, Artaud's letters to Ferdière and Latrémolière were deferential, if not obsequious. But he also pleaded with them to terminate the treatments and wrote to his mother, on 4 July 1944, that the treatments 'rendered me incapable of writing for a month because I no longer know where

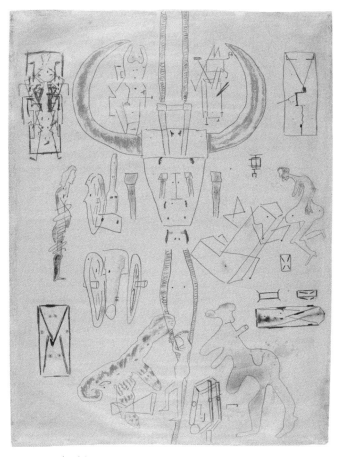

Le Minotaure, sketch by Artaud.

I was nor who I was, and this is a suffering that could have been avoided'.[82] After his penultimate series of ten sessions (25 August to 15 September), Artaud wrote a long letter to Latrémolière, complaining that, far from helping him work, the treatments debilitated him: 'it has made of me an absentee who is aware of his absence and, for weeks, can see himself in pursuit of his being, as a dead person alongside a living who is no longer him.'[83]

Les Illusions d'âme, sketch.

Beginning in April 1945, Artaud began to move away from the religious ecstaticism that, for the past eight years, had been at the core of nearly everything he wrote. On 7 September, he wrote to Henri Parisot, a publisher once associated with the Surrealists, whose celebrated 'L'Âge d'or' collection included Artaud's *Voyage to the Land of the Tarahumara,* alongside works by Herman Melville and Franz Kafka. Artaud asked Parisot to ignore a letter written at a time when

I had the imbecility to say I converted to Jesus Christ, even though I have always abhorred Christ, and this conversion has only been the result of a horrendous spell that made me forget my true nature and has forced me here in Rodez to swallow under colour of communion a dreadful number of hosts intended to keep me for the longest time possible, eternally, if possible, in a being who is not me.[84]

Exorcizing religion's hold on him and rejecting the spiritual for the corporeal were the principal objectives in Artaud's quest to regain control of his being:

This so-called Passion of the Sunday, I threw the communion, the Eucharist, god and his Christ from the windows and decided to be me – that's to say simply Antonin Artaud, a sceptical irreligious by nature and by soul who has nothing but hatred of god and his religions, whether of Christ, Jehovah or Brahma, without omitting the naturalist rituals of the lamas.[85]

From Artaud's new perspective, to assert their mastery over the body, all religions claimed to be within the spirit; religion was the driving force behind the demonization of opiates, and he blamed the English for working in the interests of all religions in burning the Chinese opium fields: 'This is to prevent men from ever returning to an old pre-genital notion of the being that all the sects and religions have buried.'[86]

Gradually regaining greater clarity of thought (notwithstanding the streams of consciousness in his Rodez *cahiers*), Artaud wanted to rediscover the world outside the walls of asylums.

You have not only helped me to live; you have *invited me to live* while I wither.

In other words, to go, to come, to exit, to see people and things. It is not good to remain perpetually in oneself, in the imaginary, as I have done for six years because I no longer have any friends around me. F. Delanglade had an excellent idea that I go with him to Rodez twice a week. In my present stage, it's

best for me to reconnect with the things that internment has
made me forget.[87]

Artaud made that request of Ferdière on 5 February 1944. Fearful
that in Nazi-occupied Rodez Artaud could be compromised by his
propensity for erratic behaviour, Ferdière, nonetheless, permitted
him to go into Rodez with Delanglade to visit with Denys-Paul
Bouloc, a young poet and member of the Resistance. Spending
time in cafés, conversing with fellow artists, Artaud's life, for the
first time in seven years, took on an air of normalcy. By August
1945 he was allowed to leave the asylum and circulate in the town
unescorted.

Along with writer, poet and playwright André de Richaud,
newly arrived at Rodez, Ferdière permitted Artaud an eight-day
stay in Espalion, a picturesque town in the Aveyron, around 20–30
kilometres (12–19 miles) from Rodez. Ferdière worried that Artaud
would contact friends in Paris for narcotics; after all, during his
authorized visits to Rodez, Artaud scoured pharmacies in search
of opium (Ferdière suggested the pharmacists give him medicine
that had small doses of codeine). However, Ferdière also saw this
as a trial run for Artaud; if things went well, the stay in Espalion
could be extended to two months (Artaud believed he would be
fully released if he behaved himself during the eight-day trial).
In retrospect, allowing such liberty to an alcoholic and a drug
addict was a recipe for disaster; the two-week period lived up to
expectations. In a drunken stupor, Richaud struck his head on a
washstand while Artaud fruitlessly ran the gamut of pharmacies in
search of laudanum, writing to friends and family in Paris to send
him drugs. In both the town and at the hotel, Artaud's penchant
for bizarre behaviour – throaty renditions of Mexican songs,
exaggerated extemporaneous theatrical performances, declamations
about his treatments in asylums and demands to be sent to Tibet
for pure, uncut opium that alone could cure him – generated
complaints to Ferdière. After slightly more than three weeks,
Artaud was brought back to Rodez.[88]

Beginning in September 1945, Artaud's friends, likely
traumatized by their first glimpse of him in years, found a target

La Pendue, sketch created in January 1945.

for their despair in Ferdière. They lobbied the doctor for Artaud's
liberation or transference. Though he entertained the idea of
moving Artaud to a private clinic near Paris, Ferdière did not
believe Artaud was ready to leave a more controlled environment.
However, faced with the demands of Artaud's friends, Ferdière felt
he had little choice. He delayed things a bit by insisting that Artaud
be housed at a clinic that could closely monitor him and that he

have the financial resources to pay for his stay at a private clinic in Ivry-sur-Seine, just south of the Périphérique that encircles and confines Paris.

Artaud hoped his author's royalties from the recently published *Voyage to the Land of the Tarahumara* and *Letters from Rodez* would enable him to support his stay at the clinic; however, by law, the rights were sent directly to the Rodez hospital to pay for Artaud's treatments. Consequently, Henri and Colette Thomas, Arthur Adamov and Marthe Robert organized an art auction and a reading of Artaud's works to be held at the Théâtre Sarah Bernhardt (now the Théâtre de la ville). Ferdière notified Adamov that he would be bringing Artaud to Paris on 26 May; Adamov, however, did not want Artaud in Paris for the homage, writing to Ferdière that it would be 'odious and unimaginable' to subject him to the scrutiny and 'general curiosity of people all over the world.'[89]

Nonetheless, on 25 May Ferdière accompanied Artaud and two other internees destined for the Sainte-Anne Hospital on a night train to Paris. Coiffed with a beret and smoking endless cigarettes, Artaud may not have known the meaning of the journey. When the train arrived the next morning at the Gare d'Austerlitz, several of Artaud's friends were waiting (Jean Dubuffet, Marthe Robert and Colette and Henri Thomas). Ferdière said goodbye to Artaud and left with the other two patients; he and Artaud would never meet face-to-face again.[90] Artaud's sister Marie-Ange later claimed that those who pushed for Artaud's release acted temerariously in seeking his freedom; even if his condition had improved, he was still a drug addict. 'They succeeded in getting his freedom. From then on, the poet was lost.'[91]

Artaud's receipt of electroconvulsive therapy is both the most readily identifiable experience from his years of institutionalization and the most controversial. It is uncontestable that, after the treatments, Artaud became more productive, his thoughts less scattered; yet it is equally true that, throughout his life, a fine line separated Artaud's creativity from his frenetic behaviour and quixotic ideas. For Artaud, the line simply did not exist; paradoxically, his intensity, his penchant for the mystical and magical, and his revolt against social conventions were the very definition of both his creative impulses and his madness. Artaud's extremism increasingly transformed his life into performance art, as his actions ultimately fell on the wrong side of a socially and culturally constructed sanity–insanity divide. Shuffling through a succession of asylums, Artaud's mere presence in that setting seemed to confirm the need for either his confinement or his normalization, but not the engagement of a 'madman'. In the judgement of mental health professionals, whether would-be Surrealists like Ferdière, who found him too surreal, or ultra-Catholics like Latrémolière, who found his convictions too unorthodox, Artaud's performance of life had transmogrified into a malady, and, in their estimations, a malady had to be treated, not engaged, not normalized.

8

Restoration

The banlieue of Ivry-sur-Seine lies just south of the Boulevard
Périphérique, the ring road that surrounds Paris; to its north is
Paris's 13th arrondissement, to its east the River Seine. Established
in 1828, Ivry-sur-Seine housed a psychiatric nursing home, a 'model'
institution (according to its prospectus of 1911) that prided itself on
a humane approach to mental health.[1] Beginning on 26 May 1946,
Antonin Artaud spent his final 648 days in this dimension at the
nursing home in Ivry-sur-Seine. The attention provided him by the
nursing home staff, friends and family, together with his mobility
and access to Paris, substantially ameliorated Artaud's condition,
leading him to produce two of his most profound and memorable
literary works. However, his continued quest for narcotics and
cocaine, declining physical health and premonition of his own
demise, added a sad coda to Artaud's rediscovery of community,
happiness and creative productivity.

Though Artaud sold the rights to a couple of his works, the
proceeds were insufficient to meet Ferdière's condition that he
have the means to support his stay at Ivry-sur-Seine. Consequently,
the newly organized 'Committee of Friends of Antonin Artaud'
arranged an homage to Artaud for 7 June 1946 at the Théâtre
Sarah Bernhardt, featuring readings of Artaud's works by many
individuals who, in one way or another, passed through his life,
including Barrault, Blin, Breton, Dullin, Jouvet, Adamov and
Colette Thomas. As much as anything, the evening was proof of
Paris's resilience and cultural restoration; Artaud and Breton on
the stage again harkened back to Surrealism's outrages, proof that
the previous decade's veil of darkness had been lifted. Artaud,

Antonin Artaud in 1947, shortly before his death.

however, would not appear on the stage. On 16 May Adamov wrote to Ferdière in Rodez, requesting Artaud's transference to Paris be delayed, fearing that Artaud would consider the event an embarrassing charity; even more alarming to Adamov was his sense that Artaud's appearance at the event would end in humiliation, reducing him to an exhibition for the gawkers in attendance, an 'odious and unimaginable' circumstance.[2] Ferdière, however, advised the Committee that if Artaud remained in Rodez, the French state might place an encumberance on the proceeds from the event to pay for his internment; consequently, Artaud spent the evening, according to Marthe Robert, loitering alone near place du Châtelet, barred from the event in his honour.[3]

Breton commenced the evening declaring Artaud 'splendid and dark', the equal of Rimbaud, Novalis and Achim von Arnim; a succession of readers, none of whom, save Colette Thomas, had committed his piece to memory, followed.[4] According to Jacques Prevel's recollections, Thomas recited as in a trance: 'She worked with Artaud. This is Artaud who spoke . . . This voice trembling and vibrating, fantastic. The voice of Artaud, the passion of Artaud, the exaltation of Artaud, the fury and the violence of Artaud.'[5] In spite of the success of the evening's performances – whether interpreting or reflecting on the importance of Artaud's works – the event's receipts totalled just under 50,000 francs, not even enough for two months at Ivry-sur-Seine.[6]

The reading was followed by an auction six days later at Pierre Loeb's Galerie Pierre (rue des Beaux-Arts) of manuscripts provided by, but not limited to, Georges Bataille, Simone de Beauvoir, Aimé Césaire, René Char, Georges Duhamel, Paul Éluard, Léon-Paul Fargue, André Gide, James Joyce, Michel Leiris, François Mauriac, Henri Michaux, Jean Paulhan, Jean-Paul Sartre, Gertrude Stein, Henri Thomas and Tristan Tzara. Paintings and sculptures on offer were produced by an equally impressive list: Jean Arp, Balthus, Georges Braque, Marc Chagall, Jean Dubuffet, Marcel Duchamp, Alberto Giacometti, Valentine Hugo, Jean Hugo, Fernand Léger, Dora Maar, Albert Marquet, André Masson, Francis Picabia, Pablo Picasso, Jacques Villon and Ossip Zadkine. The following day, Loeb turned over nearly

775,000 francs to Dubuffet, one of the auction organizers; sales of the donated pieces would continue over the next year.

When it formed in anticipation of Artaud's release from Rodez, the Committee of Friends of Antonin Artaud intended to administer Artaud's finances, whether derived from events like the homage and auction or rights to and royalties from his writings and art. Though the money legally belonged to Artaud, the Committee acted as trustees, paying for Artaud's upkeep in Ivry-sur-Seine.[7] Artaud received 10,000 francs in pocket money each month (approximately the minimum monthly salary at the time); after nine years of institutionalization, though, Artaud had few possessions and was unable to calibrate his desires with his means. During the first few months, Dubuffet (who handled the Committee's finances) regularly acceded to Artaud's requests for supplements; sometimes this amounted to more than 30,000 francs per month. Dubuffet feared Artaud's generosity was being exploited by those Artaud described as 'the pack of all the so-called needy of the letters or the arts'. The ever-present demons in his life also drained his resources. During a three-week stay at Sainte-Maxime (near Saint-Tropez) from mid-September to early October with Marthe Robert (and, for part of the time, Paule Thévenin and Colette Thomas), Artaud's charges ballooned after he graffitied the walls, drapes and linens in an attempt to exorcize his demons. Since his arrival in Paris, his expenses had totalled 150,000 francs; after Artaud's first year back, Dubuffet quit as the Committee's financial controller, having paid out 388,000 francs. Still Artaud complained to Paulhan of being treated

> as if I were some kind of prodigal son or crackpot who is unable to take care of himself. You have known me for nearly 25 years; you know that I have always *worked* . . . that I have always earned my own way without being a burden to anyone. I ask you therefore purely and simply to provide *to me* once again all the funds that have been collected for my benefit.[8]

Over time, Artaud gained more control over his royalties, becoming less dependent for his pocket money on the Committee. Regardless of whether Artaud was responsible enough to handle his finances (the nagging fear being that he would use whatever cash he had to buy cocaine or opiates), he viewed the Committee's control over his money as yet another instance of his lack of agency, an extension of Ferdière's control over his mind.

Physically, psychically and mentally, Artaud straddled many worlds – his native Midi, the Aegean and Mediterranean worlds of his forebears and the non-Western world before its cultural contamination by the West. However, above all, Paris was the centre of Artaud's universe. For nine years Artaud was shut out of Paris; during most of that time, Paris barely resembled itself. Now, in 1946, simultaneously with Paris's re-emergence from the nightmare of fascism, Artaud returned to the city – the capital and the artist both free from the strictures that had restrained them. Both had changed; the epicentre of Paris's cultural life had migrated a little north from Montparnasse to the Latin Quarter; then again, when Artaud first arrived in Paris in 1920, Montmartre, far on the other side of the Seine, claimed that title. Artaud adapted. Where his pre-asylum haunts had been in Montparnasse – Le Dôme and La Coupole – he now gravitated towards Brasserie Lipp, Café de Flore and Les Deux Magots.

Artaud had aged considerably; emaciated, rendered toothless by electroconvulsive therapy, his face drawn and haggard, he looked much older than his fifty years. His one-time fastidiousness over his physical appearance was now resigned to indifference: his hair fell to his shoulders, his dirty second-hand clothes full of holes and cigarette burns. Yet, like Paris, though ravaged by its Occupation, Artaud prevailed, dignified, alive and real. Paule Thévenin wrote of her first encounter with Artaud:

> When I knocked on Antonin Artaud's door, I felt that I was about to penetrate into another world. All I needed to hear, just one time, was this simple word: 'Enter!' The word was charged of a very special sense. It was pronounced with so much clarity, the two syllables unfastened with a complete precision, giving the impression of having left the place where one found oneself entering an 'otherworldliness'. I entered. I saw a man who wrote,

upright, a notebook resting above the fireplace. He turned his head and looked at me. Although he was of average height, the manner in which he turned his head, brushing back his long hair, the radiance of his look, the intense blueness of his eyes, gave him a commanding presence. In spite of his excessive skinniness, the ravages inscribed on his face by ten years of privations (he no longer had any teeth), there was in him something regal. Before now, I have hesitated to use this word, but this is the only one that appears just . . .[9]

Unlike the asylums, Ivry-sur-Seine was a nursing home; Dr Achille Delmas, its director since 1912, took a more indulgent approach to Artaud's treatment. Three days after arriving, Artaud wrote to Paulhan: 'I am pleased with Dr Delmas because, unlike the other doctors, he does not look to teach me something about myself nor to impose something on me – treatment or medicine – but to understand who I was and what I was looking for.'[10] Among the 'other doctors' to whom Artaud referred were Ferdière and Latrémolière. Although Artaud's letters to the Rodez doctors were deferential to a fault, in his notebooks, letters and essays, he unleashed a torrent of hostility at his treatment in Rodez; typical was a notebook entry from spring 1945: 'Gaston Ferdière loves my coma too much because he knows that during all my comas he has always taken something from me.'[11]

In contrast to electroconvulsive therapy, prohibition of opiates and confinement, Delmas provided Artaud with a key to the clinic's entrance gates; maintaining that long-time drug addicts, like Artaud, never detoxify but, if deprived, run greater risks in hunting for drugs, Delmas provided Artaud with daily doses of laudanum and chloral hydrate syrup.[12] The doses prescribed by Delmas were not enough. Though Artaud had gone through a forced detoxification and physical withdrawal during his nine years in asylums, he remained emotionally and mentally hooked; even while re-establishing his mental equilibrium in Rodez, his obsession with cocaine, heroin and laudanum never diminished. Artaud had a conflicted relationship with drugs; when his supply ran out, he often scoured the black market and pharmacies as far away as

Artaud's room at the Ivry-sur-Seine nursing home.

Strasbourg (where, in the post-war period, narcotics were still in large supply),[13] yet as Jacques Prevel noted, on 25 May 1947 Artaud wrote on his notebook in big letters 'FINISH THE HEROIN. *I don't want to live intoxicated*.'[14] And, as he had done with Barrault in the 1930s, Artaud continued to counsel his friends against using opiates.

Artaud initially occupied a modern room in the newest pavilion at Ivry-sur-Seine, one with central heating and running water. While walking the expansive grounds of the nursing home, he saw amid a floral-carpeted field, some distance from where he was staying, an uninhabited eighteenth-century pavilion. Taken by the isolated beauty of the spot and its remoteness from other residents of the nursing home, Artaud requested permission from Delmas to move into it. Reluctant at first to move Artaud into a space that lacked the amenities of the modern building, Delmas ultimately agreed. Artaud's domicile for the remaining seventeen months of his life was a two-room apartment with French doors overlooking a garden. Jugs of warm water and food were brought to him every day, with wood for his fireplace in the winter. Here, at last, was a space that screamed the freedom and autonomy he had missed for nearly a decade and that, in its remoteness from other patients, distanced him from the world of internment. No longer were his thoughts and ideas – no matter how abstruse – going to be the source of his persecution. The spot was idyllic; in Artaud's imaginings, it was a cosmos that invited him into a select group. In June 1947 Artaud wrote in 'Cahier 307':

> Here is a place full . . . of fabulous memories. The park of Ivry where Gérard de Nerval walked in front of the revolutionary town hall of 1788 and kept as a town hall by Jean Louis Marat [Jean-Paul Marat], doctor. He [Nerval] walked there before hanging himself. And you can still feel this under the high forests of the old park, just as petrified, the evening solemn and funereal under the moon . . .[15]

In Artaud's mind, this personal nirvana connected him with his literary soulmate, Gérard de Nerval, and one of his most celebrated cinematic roles, the revolutionary Jean-Paul Marat. Though neither Nerval nor Marat had lived, nor probably set foot, in Ivry-sur-Seine (though there is a rue Marat there), to Artaud this was hallowed ground; no literary figure echoed more in his conscience than did Nerval. Within days of his arrival in Ivry-sur-Seine, Artaud wrote to Breton:

> As you said to me yesterday, Gérard de Nerval . . . made allusion in his works to states of supernaturalist reverie. And you related my history to his, saying, 'All this is very Nervalian.' I responded to you that for me, Gérard de Nerval had not dreamed, but *lived*, really *lived* the states he speaks of and which for me are part of reality . . .[16]

Between the schisms engendered by his unpredictable and sometimes unfathomable behaviour, his isolation in asylums, the deaths of several friends (via natural causes, mysterious circumstances and Nazi violence) and the turmoil of the Nazi occupation, only a handful of Artaud's pre-asylum friends – Blin, Barrault and Paulhan – remained close to him. Breton's participation in the homage notwithstanding, an uneasy relationship, dating to

Artaud's ejection from the Surrealists, persisted between the two with a definitive break not far away.

Jacques Prevel first met Artaud on 27 May 1946, the day after Artaud's arrival at Ivry-sur-Seine. From that point, until Prevel, exhausted, suffered a haemoptysis on 11 August 1947, he was Artaud's constant companion, sometimes procuring opiates and laudanum and running errands for him, sometimes just sitting with him for hours. As a poet, Prevel made little money during his lifetime; Albert Camus paid for his initial hospital treatments. Prevel passed away from tuberculosis exactly five years to the day after he first met Artaud; his journal of his time with Artaud and the poems Artaud inspired in him garnered Prevel posthumous notoriety.

Other than Prevel, Artaud's most constant companions during his final years were several young women. Despite his stated aversion to sexuality, Artaud relished the company of young, attractive women. In Rodez, Artaud referred to his *filles de coeur*, an orbit that included his grandmothers, Yvonne Allendy, Anie Besnard, Cécile Schramme and Ana Corbin.[17] After arriving at Ivry-sur-Seine, Marthe Robert and Colette Thomas were included as *filles de coeur*. After meeting Artaud in the mid-1930s, Marthe Robert became one of his close confidants; Colette Thomas became acquainted with Artaud through her husband, Henri, a regular visitor during Artaud's final months in Rodez. During his stay at Espalion (a couple of months prior to his transference to Ivry-sur-Seine), Artaud explained to Colette his personal struggles, his refusal to conform and his need to form a 'little army who exist and live, for example, like a group of chouans or a revolt of ancient slaves'[18] in helping Artaud 'change existence, to get [him] away from this existence.'[19]

In late April 1947 Artaud told Prevel that he was 'passionately in love with Colette Thomas and Marthe Robert'.[20] Love to Artaud, however, was neither strictly platonic nor carnal: with both women, he forged a relationship that was romantic and seductive, but completely asexual; its ambiguity seemingly confused everyone, save Artaud. Thomas, in particular, occupied a special role in Artaud's universe, one that was simultaneously tender and unsettling. Beautiful (as Artaud had once been), temperamentally volatile and a former mental health internee, Thomas was, in Artaud's imagination, his female complement; and, as revealed at the homage to Artaud, Colette had the unique ability to channel Artaud and, in turn, to inspire him. He expected her to be celibate: 'You recall what I told you the other evening about Sodom and Gomorrah. Too many people manipulate your capacity for love while the love that should nourish and reassure you corrodes you and turns your hair white.'[21] Colette, for her part, wrote paeans of love to Artaud: 'You are not crazy; you are brilliant. I will not nurse you, I will love you. I love you, Antonin Artaud.'[22] Artaud, however, rejected carnal love in favour of an ethereal love that would never be consummated:

This is to say to you that to give into the eroticism of pure love
is to fuck my heart
to me Antonin Artaud
at the shithouses
of nothingness
The truth Colette Thomas is that I am an *invalid*
desecrated of life
of blood and of the forces of which
everyone
except him [me] has profited.[23]

Passionate, albeit celibate, the relationship between Colette and Artaud disturbed Colette's husband, Henri; Artaud monopolized Colette's time, energy and affection. Henri would later say that his wife and Prevel were victims of Artaud's machinations and his need to control the world around him by sucking fragile and vulnerable individuals into his universe.[24] With that said, Colette's own letters characterized herself and Artaud as fellow travellers in an alien world that could only process their alterity as madness. In Colette's *Testament de la fille morte* (Testament of a Dead Girl), published six years after Artaud's death, the latter's voice seemingly screams from the text: 'To love, this is to hate others; to make love, this is to betray them.'[25]

In Ivry-sur-Seine, Artaud continued with the fantastic stories he concocted in Rodez. While Artaud continued to write of his persecution and victimization, in Ivry-sur-Seine, his ideas and theories were more grounded, less exalted by his weird obsession with scripture. For knowing 'there is no spirit, but a body', Artaud morphed into a tormented, sacrificed and crucified prophet.[26] But Artaud no longer conceived of himself as Christ: 'I am me, Artaud, the crucified of Golgotha, who was not crucified as Christ but as an atheist and born enemy of Jesus Christ. Being born of himself and not like Jesus Christ from god.'[27]

Artaud claimed that all the persecutions he suffered – real or imagined (including his claim to have been stabbed in Montmartre in 1928) – were to prevent him from being a god. 'Now I know from where they come, because to prevent me from being god each evening, 100 thousand vampires, etc, pay me the honour of a visit, and it is because my body is *good* that it is always so carefully visited.'[28] However, the vampires and demons plaguing Artaud's life were no longer supernatural forces, but the societally powerful who were determined to undermine Artaud:

> and if Artaud complains
> well this is because he is delirious, as for him
> quickly, a little electroshock to cure him of his belief in spirits;
> but all the same Antonin Artaud does not believe in spirits, but
> he has always believed in men who have never done anything to
> support their ignoble life other than to take away the life in him[29]

Though consummately megalomaniacal, Artaud's words were also a cry of desperation from 'a petit bourgeois from Marseille'; tormented by, and victimized because of, his vision into the soul, he had entered into the rarified world of his literary heroes – Baudelaire, Nerval, Poe and Lautréamont. He had not so much likened himself to a god, as an unremittingly intolerant society, in persecuting him – in his 'long Calvary, which took him from one mental institution to another'[30] – had both demonized and deified him, assuring his literary immortality.

After Rodez, Artaud fixed his attention more and more on the body as a battleground between the self and exterior forces. Since his letters to Édouard Toulouse in the early 1920s, Artaud remained deeply alienated from knowledge derived from rational thought. Artaud was less a harbinger of fascism's rejection of reason than part of a queue of post-Enlightenment artists who disputed the inherent superiority of mind over sentiment; his quest for experiential authenticity rejected thought as an accompaniment to sensation.[31] For Artaud – and this is consistent with most of his ideas – thought is more socially, politically, culturally and economically conditioned; when the mind intervenes in understanding sensation, the sensorial experience is lost.

Relentlessly riveted on the physical pain he endured at other asylums, Artaud wrote contemptuously of the body as a vulnerable vessel, its orifices leaving it prey to penetration from external sources. Beginning with his diagnosis of meningitis, his body had been the source of much grief throughout his life, yet he attributed the corporeal agony he suffered to his mind, blaming it for opening the body to contaminations and contaminating influences. For example, he commenced his poem 'Artaud le Momo' with the following lines:

The anchored mind
screwed into me
by the psycho-lustful
thrust
of heaven
is the one that imagines
all temptation
all desire
all inhibition[32]

Artaud's later prose coherently and cohesively expressed his losing battle to exercise absolute control over his person and identity. Artaud never relinquished his distrust of language, seeing it either as a product of thought or as a progenitor of thought; either way, language and conscience were constructs over which no individual exercised agency.

The body was not only prey to the authority of external forces; its internal functioning was also subject to the organs within it.

The only means for restoring the body's autonomy was 'to remake [man's] anatomy':

> We must make up our minds to strip him bare, to scrub him of this animalcule that itches him mortally
>
> god,
> and with god
> his organs
>
> So bind me if you want,
> but there is nothing more useless than an organ
>
> When you will have made him a body without organs,
> then you will have liberated him from all his automatic reflexes
> and restored him to his true freedom.
>
> Then you will have taught him to dance wrong way round
> as in the frenzy of the dance halls
> and this wrong way round will be his real place.[33]

Just as thought obscured the pure functioning of the mind, so too the organs inhibited free flows within the body. Persistently persecuted for dancing 'the wrong way round', Artaud's conception of a 'body without organs' was perhaps his road map back to a primal experience and liberation from all the forces that obstructed and predetermined the functioning of his mind . . . and body.

During the last seventeen months of his life, Artaud's artistic focus shifted to visual renderings of friends, while his prose became more trenchant. Notwithstanding the physical toll it took on Artaud, the change might have resulted from electroconvulsive therapy's efficaciousness. Alternatively, Artaud's liberation from confinement, treatment and the craziness of asylums, coupled with his long-desired reintegration into society, might have stimulated his creative rebirth; having adapted his behaviour to whatever circumstances in which he was placed, Artaud was now restored through his return to Paris. Finally, given Artaud's premonition of his impending demise, his writings might have taken on a greater urgency to leave something deep for posterity, while portraits of his friends became expressions of love towards all those with whom he was connected, lasting commemorations of those whose friendships restored him in his final months.

Coincident with the opening of the exhibition 'Vincent van Gogh' on 24 January 1947 at Paris's Musée de l'Orangerie, the magazine *Arts* published two articles on Van Gogh, one on his life, and another on his madness; the latter included extracts from a recently published collection of psychiatric studies entitled *Du démon de Van Gogh*. Pierre Loeb gave Artaud the article, expecting that, as an artist similarly institutionalized, Artaud would be better positioned than psychiatrists to understand, and empathize with, Van Gogh's experiences. Loeb accurately gauged the parallels Artaud would draw between the two artists' life stories. On 2 February, accompanied by Paule Thévenin, Artaud attended the exhibition for the first time; over the course of February, he made several return trips with Loeb and his sister (photographer Denise Colomb), and with Marthe Robert and Roger Blin, dashing through the exhibition at breakneck speed, but preserving an astonishingly precise recollection of each piece.[34]

According to Loeb, after Artaud's first viewing,

> He arrived at mine that day overwhelmed, in a state of extreme elation. Out of the blue, I said to him, 'Artaud, why don't you write a book on van Gogh?' 'Very good idea, he responded to me, I am going to do that right away.' He then climbed up to the first floor, sat down in front of the table and rapidly and nervously wrote in a school notebook, without nearly any cross-outs, without 'regret', in two afternoons, the wonderful text known as the immortal *Van Gogh, le suicidé de la société* [Van Gogh, the Man Suicided by Society].[35]

Rather than 'two afternoons', Artaud wrote fragments of the text throughout February while Loeb entered into negotiations with the publisher, K. On 28 February Artaud signed a contract for the book, which was published in 1947. In January 1948 it was awarded the Sainte-Beuve Literary Prize.

As Loeb suspected, Artaud identified with Van Gogh's torments and victimization; in other ways, he was a different creature. Van Gogh by most accounts was able to maintain stable correspondences; Artaud was incapable of writing coherently, his delirium spilling over into his letters.[36] Yet Artaud connected with Van Gogh's story. While his treatise on Van Gogh is largely riveted on an analysis of his art, it also functions as both a *cri de coeur* and a meditation on the tension between the rational (medicine) and the irrational (art).

In Van Gogh's relationship with Dr Paul Gachet, Artaud saw parallels to his own experiences with mental health professionals working on behalf of larger social and cultural forces: 'There is in every mentally insane person a misunderstood genius, whose idea, sparkling in his head, gives fright, and who can only find an exit from the strangulations that life has prepared for him in delirium.'[37] Van Gogh's art was like 'bursts of Greek fire, atomic bombs' directed at the 'larval conformism of the Second Empire bourgeoisie'. Though Artaud was a little historically off in situating Van Gogh within the cultural milieu of the Second Empire (1852–70), the Second Empire marked the definitive rise of the bourgeoisie and the norms against which Van Gogh rebelled. 'Because this is not some conformity of customs that Van Gogh attacks, but the institutions themselves . . . Even more on the social level, institutions are disintegrating and medicine seems like a useless and stale cadaver, which declares Van Gogh crazy.'[38] Artaud wrote of his own experiences, singling out 'Dr L.', in particular, who 'decrees a working conscience delirious, while on the other hand strangling it with [his] ignoble sexuality' (though Dr Latrémolière claimed to be 'Dr L.', it was, in actuality, Jacques Lacan).[39] Artaud suggestively asked, 'What is a genuine madman?'

This is a man who has preferred to become crazy, in the socially accepted sense of the word, rather than forfeit a superior idea of human honour.

This is how society has strangled in its asylums all those it has wanted to be rid of or to protect itself against, for refusing to become accomplices in some great nastiness.

Because a madman is also a man whom society does not want to hear and who it wants to prevent from broadcasting intolerable truths.[40]

Rather than being institutionalized for madness, it was after Van Gogh 'succeeded and discovered what he was and who he was' that society 'suicided' him.[41] Van Gogh's offence – and Artaud's – was to envision nature differently from its conventional realization, to reach a level of genius that refused to be harnessed.

As Artaud had persistently asserted, all geniuses are prey to the machinations of evil spirits or demons. However, the evil spirits that penetrated the souls of Van Gogh, Nerval, Baudelaire, Poe and Lautréamont were not the supernatural forces of Artaud's prior delusions, but the bourgeoisie and the cultural regime upon which bourgeois hegemony is based.[42] Writing to Maurice Nadeau of Camus' *Combat*, Artaud explained that as the quintessential bourgeois revolution, the French Revolution challenged religion; what it established, however, was indistinct from religiosity:

I have already said, the bourgeoisie and god are one and the same thing; the same one and identical spirit . . . this inbred bourgeois spirit is a spirit of *religious* hatred against all that is poetic.

If bourgeois religiosity, the miserable conservatism that destroyed Baudelaire, Edgar Poe and most recently even Lenin in Russia, persists

it will not be through masses, consecrations, chrisms, absolutions, processions, litanies, mantras, profundities or matins (but from unbridled sexuality).[43]

To Artaud, the bourgeoisie's pursuit of material gratification was an extension of its unrelenting quest for carnal pleasure. Through materiality and sexuality, and in its empty pursuit of possessions, corporeal comfort and tasteless stimulation, the bourgeoisie had devalued aesthetic and ethereal fulfilment: 'Van Gogh did not die from a state of delirium, but from being a corporeal field of the problem, one that humanity's sinful spirit has struggled with since the beginning of time. The predominance of the flesh over the spirit, or of the body over the flesh, or of the spirit over both.'[44] In the end, psychiatry, a product of bourgeois society's fixation on the rational – a field that 'provoked and brought mania into existence for its own self-justification' – first branded Van Gogh, then drove him to suicide.[45]

Between 4 and 20 July 1947, Pierre Loeb staged an exhibition of Artaud's artwork: 'Portraits and Drawings'. Artaud had been drawing since his youth at Marseille and took up painting and charcoal sketching while under Dr Dardel's care.[46] During the 1920s, some of his earliest writings focused on artistic expression:

> The subject, and also the object, is of little importance. What is of importance is the expression, not the expression of the object but of a certain ideal of the artist, of a certain degree of humanity through the colours and the features.
>
> Why does the painter distort? Because the subject is nothing in itself but the result, all the subject implies, all which can be said of life stormy and wild, anguished or calming through the subject.[47]

Except for some sketches of set designs for *The Clergyman and the Seashell* and for some of his stage works (for example, *The Cenci*), Artaud pretty much stopped drawing between 1924 and his internment at Ville-Évrard, when he produced his 'gris-gris'. It was not until Rodez that, under the tutelage of Delanglade, Artaud equated his charcoal and gouache drawings with his literary compositions; he even expressed to Paulhan his hope that, through the sale of his books and his art, he could earn a living from his creative output.[48]

Outside of a self-portrait and a couple of renderings of individuals who had passed through his life (for example, Sonia Mossé after he learned she had perished in a Nazi gas chamber), Artaud rarely produced portraits prior to his release from Rodez. The first portraits he composed after his return to Paris were faithful renderings to please his friends and establish his artistic ability. However, his style soon changed and the human faces of friends and acquaintances became 'the battlefield for a frenzied struggle between the forces of life and death'.[49] As Artaud wrote in an essay to accompany the 4–20 July 1947 exhibition at Galerie Pierre:

Artaud, photographed by Denise Colomb, editing his *Cahiers de Rodez*, 1946 or 1947.

The human face is an empty force, a field of death.
The human face bears, in fact, a kind of perpetual death on its face
which it is up to the painter to precisely recover
in giving it back its own features . . .
this is why, in the portraits I have drawn,

Untitled drawing, 1948. Among Artaud's last drawings were those of overlapping anonymous faces, though, possibly, his *filles de cœur*.

I have avoided above all not to forget the nose, the mouth, the eyes, the ears or the hair, but in the face that speaks to me I have tried to tell
the secret
of an old human history, which qualified as death in the minds of Ingres and Holbein.[50]

Self-portrait. Perhaps Artaud's final self-portrait, which he dated December 1948.

Paule Thévenin recalled Artaud's technique during a sitting in
November–December 1946:

> He had seated me across from him, but didn't force me into
> immobility. At moments, he was completely absorbed by his
> work, sweeping his pencil over the paper or, suddenly stopping
> his movement, jabbing it hard into the paper or then again

squeezing his thumb against the page to give more nuance to the intensity of the blackened parts shadowing the forehead, the cheeks, the chin. He would lift his head from time to time, looking at me with his vivid blue eyes whose eyelids he wrinkled to better discern the detail he was trying to isolate and wanted to bring to the fore. But he could also hum or joke, without however relaxing his attention . . . It went on for several days. The result was surprising, magnificent, but terrifying. Antonin Artaud looked at me, looked again at his drawing, then again at me at last, declaring, 'I have given you the face of an old empire of barbarian times.' . . . I have the impression that Antonin Artaud had shown an extraordinary prescience in it, and that his drawing revealed in advance the face that life was going to give me.[51]

Thévenin, Artaud's constant companion during his final months, believed he correlated his visual artistry with the 'theatre of cruelty': art's purpose is neither to portray nor affirm the desirable and agreeable, but to awaken the audience to life's ravages, brutality and violence.[52] Artaud's numerous self-portraits are personal meditations on the pain and ugliness that are handmaidens of life's beauty: a face scarred and blemished, set off by eyes that are at once weary and alert; a face reflective both of life's torments and, deep within, its vibrancy. On one of his last self-portraits, composed in December 1947, Artaud wrote the date December 1948, 'as if ', Thévenin wrote, 'he had signed it already dead'. While the picture is a mélange of images, the focal point is a self-portrait at the top of the page. 'This is myself on the road from the Indies 5,000 years ago', Artaud explained to Thévenin, while the head on his right shoulder is 'the head that weighs on me'.[53]

In 1947 Artaud produced two important poetic works – *Le Retour d'Artaud, le Mômo* and *Ci-gît précédé de la culture indienne* – scatological expositions on two matters that most reviled Artaud: the human body and parent–child relationships. In *Artaud, le Mômo*, Artaud reduced the body to *barbaque* – literally, third-rate meat – highlighting its vulnerability to forces that eat away at it; Artaud was likely considering the fragility of his own body, weakened both by forces within and beyond his control, susceptible to insidious temptations, its relentless quest for stimulation – whether in the form of nourishment or sexual titillation – rendering it a slave to material gratification.[54] Artaud could have nothing but contempt for the body, in general, and for his own body, in particular; it was an 'intrusive' materialization of what he was not, and the locus of so much of his torment.[55]

Both pieces return to the theme of creation, focusing on Artaud's steadfast assertion that he, alone, was responsible for who he is and who he became. In *Ci-gît*, literally 'Here lies', Artaud contemplated his impending mortality, while he equally meditated on his own non-existence in this dimension. Though he acknowledged in *Ci-gît* being borne of 'mad meat and crazy sperm . . . the one whom being and nothingness made, just as one pees',[56] it was inconceivable that who he was and who he became could have resulted from something as abominable and contemptible as a body; the existence of the vessel that corporeally housed Artaud merely coincided with his emergence from the womb, but his life resulted from his acquisition of consciousness: 'But haven't I entered / *this fucked-up, wanker life* / in the 50 years since I have been born.'[57] He alone was responsible for his thoughts, and his thoughts and ideas defined him, emphatically denying any role to divine intervention in his consciousness:

I hate and despise as a coward every being who only wants to feel the benefit of existing and does not want to have worked to exist
I hate and despise as a coward every being who accepts having been made and does not want to be remade
That's to say those who accept the idea of a god creator at the origins of his being and his thought . . .
I don't accept that I have not made my body myself and I hate and despise as a coward every being who ascents to exist without previously remaking himself.
I hate and despise as a coward every being who does not recognize that life is only given him so that he can remake and reconstitute his body and his entire organism.[58]

In January 1947 Paule Thévenin organized Artaud's first public performance in more than a decade at the Théâtre du Vieux-Colombier, where, in 1922, Artaud had made his stage debut. As advertised, Artaud would read three of his more recent poems, including *Artaud, le Mômo*. Drawing partly from those hoping to be entertained by a 'famous lunatic', but also from Paris's artistic community (including Paulhan, Gide, Camus and Breton), the Vieux-Colombier was at its 300-person capacity on 13 January:

> When Artaud took to the stage, a man in the back row began to laugh and mock, and Artaud said calmly, 'The person who wants to make fun of me can wait for me outside. His place is not here.' And the silence prevailed until the end.

Thomas Maeder interviewed around twenty attendees of the performance; none agreed as to what occurred, causing one spectator to remark that Artaud's performance was 'so stupefying, so devoid of a relationship with simple words and acts, that we are like in a trance, and the memory of it remains completely personal'.[59]

For three hours, Artaud nervously recited poems and recounted his experiences, beginning with his voyage to Mexico and ending with his electroconvulsive therapy (excoriating Dr Ferdière for good measure). According to Prevel, Artaud was terrified, his reading 'choppy, jerky, incomprehensible'.[60] Fumbling with his papers, incapable (for the most part) of maintaining his train of thought, Artaud was devastated by his performance. Every word of his text had a unique and special resonance with him, but was lost, he sensed, on the audience; his agonized delivery of the text, his broken cadence, was a volcanic eruption of the bile, emotions and pain at the core of his being. Having lived inside his own headspace for years, the words' often-unfamiliar symbolism and violence, though clear to him, defied translation in a language and manner accessible to others. In the end, he did not speak, his silences, he later said, communicating better than words.[61] To that audience, seeing 'his thin and ravaged face . . . his raging hands . . . his hoarse voice, clipped by tragic sobs and stammers', Artaud was a compelling and moving figure: 'we felt carried away in a dangerous zone, and reflected by this black sun, won by this "universalized explosion" of a body in prey of the flames of the spirit.'[62] The writer Sarane Alexandrian, then a nineteen-year-old student, saw Artaud before the perform-ance, alone, impatiently reviewing his text, 'a man who had horrible tragedies, and who existed to speak in a manner to disturb the clear conscience of humanity. Not for an instant did I have the conviction that I was dealing with a psychotic.' The performance, Alexandrian noted, was 'the revelation of a great poet revolted against all the invisible forces of the Cosmos, and I hardly slept that night.'[63] Shortly after Artaud's death, Gide, in *Le Combat*, recounted,

> Artaud triumphed, held at bay the mocking, the disrespectful nonsense; he dominated . . . Never before had he appeared more admirable. From his material being, only the expressive remained . . . Leaving this memorable performance, the public was silent. What could one say? . . . There was a sense of shame in returning to a world where comfort is the result of compromises.[64]

Artaud, however, saw the evening differently. What could an audience 'full of men and women of the world clothed in sumptuous fabrics' possibly understand about the 'universal vampirism of a people on one man?'[65] In several letters, Artaud wrote of his intention to reveal 'the spells' placed on him by society and how nine years of physical and verbal abuse were to keep him from exposing 'this immense underground organization of manoeuvres and actions that are a perpetual conspiracy against the conscience of all and about which no one ever says anything because it is forbidden'.[66] However, he sensed that some in the audience simply mistook the emotions that overtook him for hammy acting.

Breton saw the reading as no more than a moment of theatricality, lacking substance. He chastised Artaud for allowing his new 'friends' to callously exhibit and subject him to the ridicule and stupefaction of 'an audience of strangers, curiosity seekers, voyeurs and sadists'.[67] Though Breton was genuinely saddened by the spectacle, in Artaud's estimation, Breton would never understand him. In five lengthy letters to Breton, Artaud admitted that the 'time to gather people in a theatre, *even* to tell them some truths has passed, and for society and its public, there is no other language than bombs, machine guns, barricades and all that would follow'.[68]

Within weeks of the Vieux-Colombier performance, Artaud received, and rejected, an invitation from Breton to participate in the 'International Exposition of Surrealism 1947'. Unwilling to let go of Breton's assessment of the Vieux-Colombier performance, Artaud affirmed that, regardless of what anyone thought of the evening, he had not been co-opted. By implication, he contrasted his principled stance with that of the Surrealists, accusing them, in holding a Surrealist exhibition at 'a capitalist gallery', of bourgeois Marxism:

> André Breton, you have known me for 30 years; I don't want to write for a catalogue that will be read by snobs, made for snobs, rich art lovers, in a gallery where you'll never see workers or the people because they work during the day.[69]

Nearly two weeks later, Artaud clarified to Breton that he was not targeting Breton, but 'the gallery, the bank and the entire system of institutions that temporarily arrange things for you, awaiting the day to strangle you for good'. Artaud concluded with a warning to Breton that the same people who encourage him to '[m]ake revolutionary art', threaten to kill him 'if he brings revolution into everyday life' (or, in the case of Artaud, institutionalized and subjected to electroconvulsive therapy).[70] This would be Artaud's last letter to Breton.

After telling Breton that the Vieux-Colombier would be his last stage performance, Artaud found an alternative medium to reach a mass audience: radio. This would extend his message beyond those who had the means and time to go to theatrical performances and art openings. In November 1947 Fernand Pouey, director of literary and dramatic programming for French radio, approached Artaud about creating a work for the show *La Voix des poètes* (The Voice of Poets). In addition to a couple of already-written texts, Artaud composed a new essay, *Pour en finir avec le jugement de dieu* (To Have Been Done with the Judgement of God), for the broadcast. Artaud's last essay was his most prescient, a cautionary tale of American industrial capitalism– militarism and nature's subversion. America, for Artaud, is

Simulating acupuncture by plunging a pencil in his back, Artaud, here, is seated on a bench at rue de la mairie, Ivry-sur-Seine with his friend Minouche Pastier awaiting the number 125 bus, 1946–7.

Close-up of Artaud seated on a bench at rue de la mairie, Ivry-sur-Seine, plunging a pencil into his back.

where all the fake manufactured products will reign
all the ignoble synthetic ersatz
where beautiful, true nature has no role
and must give way once and for all and shamefully to all the
triumphant substitute products

[American workers, with nothing to produce, will become soldiers]
to defend this senseless processing against all the competition
which would not fail to rise up on all sides . . .
Because we have more than one enemy
which lies in wait for us, my son,
us the born capitalists
and among these enemies
is Stalin's Russia
which is not lacking in armed men either.[71]

While Artaud's ruminations on America's growing global authority and the dangers of a military–industrial complex represented a new direction for him, Artaud also wove together a few familiar threads into the fabric of *Pour en finir*. Words are no more than flatulence,

> invented to define things
> which exist
> or don't exist
> in face of
> the pressing urgency
> of a need:
> that of abolishing the idea,
> the idea and its myth
> and to enthrone in its place
> the thundering manifestation
> of this explosive necessity:
> to expand the body of my internal night,
> of the internal nothingness
> of my self [72]

In his conclusion, Artaud argued:

> but what are called microbes
> is god
> and do you know with what the Americans and the Russians make their atoms?
> They make them with the microbes of god . . .
> I'm not crazy
> I tell you that microbes have at last been reinvented to impose a new idea of god. [73]

God was still the malevolent force of his recent writings, but now also a concept; a malleable concept subject to appropriation by malignant forces in whose quest for omnipotence nature becomes the prime casualty.

Artaud wanted – and was given – complete control over the production; he gave precise instructions to his actors – Blin,

Thévenin and María Casares (a Spanish-born actress who starred with Barrault in *Les Enfants du paradis*) – and rejected Blin's offer to procure the services of France's best radio producer (to maintain creative control, Artaud wanted the worst). Various percussion instruments served as improvisational accompaniment to the texts. Recorded between 22 and 29 November, the broadcast was set for Monday 2 February 1948 at 10.45 pm, an hour sufficiently late not to offend the sensibilities of some listeners. However, the day before the airing, Vladimir Porché, the director of Radio-Diffusion, listened to the recording; citing the violence of the language and the obscenities, he pulled the plug on its broadcast.

Outraged that his pledge to give Artaud complete artistic freedom had been countermanded, Pouey, on 5 February, convened a fifty-member jury comprised of literary, auditory and visual artists (and, for good measure, a Dominican priest);[74] after listening to the broadcast, it would determine whether or not the broadcast had artistic merit. Included on the jury was a veritable stroll through Artaud's past – Jouvet, Éluard, Raymond Queneau, Barrault, Vitrac, Paulhan and Cocteau. The jury heard the entire forty-minute broadcast as Artaud's voice, punctuated by drums and gongs, transcended this dimension; hauntingly modulating between pain and anger, his screams and screeches were the desperate warnings of a man out of time, melding his own personal sufferings to those about to be visited on the world. Although the jury voted unanimously in favour of the broadcast, several journalists later stated that if they believed there was a chance Porché would cede to the vote, they might have voted the other way. As predicted, Porché, citing his responsibility not to offend the larger public, would not be swayed.[75]

The press was divided. *Combat* defended the work's artistic merit: 'The crudeness of language for which he has been rebuked disappears in the current of this inspired voice, which appears to fall from heaven,' while the conservative *Le Figaro* wondered whether 'the vulgar wording and violent ideas' would only scandalize or provide prurient entertainment for most listeners.[76] The broadcast finally aired on French radio, 25 years later in 1973.

Artaud wrote to Porché of his disappointment, stating that it would be virtually impossible to scandalize with words a public 'in an atmosphere so beyond existence'. In response to an editorial by René Guilly (author of the *Combat* piece) that Porché's alarm was misguided because 'this public is composed of imbeciles' with little interest in Artaud, Artaud wrote that his respect for the public was higher than Guilly's opinion of it; *Pour en finir* was recorded for the honourable working people and not the 'secretly enriched [capitalists] who go to mass every Sunday and want, above all, respect for rituals and the law'.[77]

At Artaud's urging, Pouey organized, on 23 February, a reading in an old movie theatre on rue Washington of the texts; for Artaud this was an opportunity for an invited audience of the working people in his life – his barber and the shopkeepers he knew – to hear the forbidden material. Exactly ten days later, Artaud passed away.

In October 1947 Delmas had died, and Artaud expressed a desire to return to his native Midi. He was not well. Delmas' successor was not as tolerant of Artaud's drug usage, and, when Artaud's friends could not get opiates or cocaine, he resorted to debilitating cocktails of paregoric elixir and chloral hydrate. On 6 February 1948, through Thévenin's intervention, Dr Henri Mondor at the Saltpêtrière Hospital took X-rays of Artaud; he concluded that Artaud must remain in bed and, rather than restricting his opium usage, he should be given an unlimited supply. In reality, Mondor had concluded, and revealed to Thévenin, that Artaud was suffering from anal cancer, which, owing to its spread, had become inoperable.[78] Unaware of his true condition, Artaud wrote to Paulhan of being able, at long last, to go to Antibes with Thévenin to spend what remained of his life in peace; he fixed 15 March, the date until which he was paid up at Ivry-sur-Seine, for his departure.

Artaud may have had a premonition of his demise. During the last weeks of February, he told Thévenin he no longer had anything to say and nothing more to write. On 3 March he ate lunch at Thévenin's residence and gave her power of attorney, allowing her to negotiate with Éditions Gallimard for the publication of his complete works, hold the author's rights and to reap any financial rewards. That evening, 'for the first time in his life, he sent 1,000 francs to his mother.' As the cancer spread, and Artaud's pain increased, so too did his usage of chloral hydrate. On 2 March he had told his sister that he must be careful not to exceed the requisite dosage. Often awakening in pain during the middle of the night, Artaud would take a dose to fall back to sleep; however, he rarely kept track of his dosages on those nights when he awoke multiple times. When he went to sleep on 3 March, his bottle of chloral hydrate was nearly full; a note on his mirror reminded him to put on a fresh shirt for a meeting with Pierre Loeb the following day. On the morning of 4 March, the gardener at Ivry-sur-Seine entered Artaud's room to bring him his breakfast. Artaud was seated at the foot of his bed, grasping a slipper, the empty bottle of chloral hydrate on the floor, nearby. Antonin Artaud had passed away.[79]

Survivors

Shortly after Artaud's death, Jean Paulhan arranged for a death mask to be moulded. According to writer–artist André Voisin, in the presence of Adamov, Blin and others,

> a caster . . . took an imprint of the death mask. Artaud was spread out on his bed, holding a little bouquet of violets; this was very beautiful. When I arrived, the casting had already begun. I watched the action. Adamov left, I believe: he could not bear, how would I say it, the 'mechanized' manner of the caster who performed his work like a plasterer, in peace and quiet. And it's true that there was something unbearable about this operation. For my part, I found the silence, this calm that reigned over the room very pleasant. As the casting neared its end, the caster raised the mask, and Artaud was covered in an amber-coloured paraffin wax, like an old warrior, like all the characters of a royal theatre who had never been written but towards whom he gravitated. After this, the caster dressed his hair, and as it was still damp, it formed a larger perimeter, a veritable crown of hair around his face. I remember saying to Roger Blin, 'We need to leave him like this.' Evidently, this was not possible, and the caster redid it normally. But I maintain the memory of a fabulous legionnaire of the impractical; this was like a soldier of an indispensable poem, of a song of the world. He had gone to

the end of this road, and then he was there, peaceful, as a fighter who has finished his fight.[80]

The mask was later cast in bronze and became part of Paule Thévenin's collection; she had a second one produced and gave it to Jacques Derrida.[81]

As it turned out, the death mask was not the only part of Artaud's patrimony over which Thévenin took custodianship. According to Serge Malausséna, before the Artaud–Malausséna family was notified, members of Artaud's literary entourage, including Thévenin, arrived and carted away all of his writings and artwork.[82] From the perspective of Artaud's friends, this was necessary to prevent Artaud's family – his mother, his sister and his brother – from excising material they deemed objectionable from future publication of Artaud's works; in particular, their concerns were focused on the gulf separating the family's religious sensibilities from Artaud's rejection of religion, and on protecting the prodigal son from the family he left behind. What's more, Artaud had given Thévenin control over the posthumous publication of his works by Gallimard.

One might be excused from thinking that this arrangement with Thévenin, made just before his death, had settled the matter; however, as it was not a legally executed document, the Artaud–Malausséna family held the legal rights to Artaud's works. Simple legalities aside, the family also contended, and proved through correspondences, that Artaud never abandoned his family; he remained caring and close to them until the end. Yet it would be an oversimplification to suggest that the Artaud family spoke with one voice; in fact, the planets in the post-Artaud story never aligned in coherent galaxies; instead, their orbits sometimes shot off in unexpected directions. The controversy surrounding the publication of the first volume of Artaud's collected works is testament to that: when it first appeared in 1956, it was missing two important texts – Artaud's addresses to the Pope and to the Dalai Lama from 1925. Artaud's brother, Fernand, eleven years his junior and fanatically Catholic, had demanded the removal of texts he considered blasphemous; on the other hand, Marie-Ange Malausséna, Artaud's

Death mask of
Antonin Artaud.

sister (and Serge's mother), wanted to maintain the integrity of
Antonin Artaud's writings. In 1970 Gallimard republished volume
one, this time including the two texts.

With Fernand's death in 1989, Serge and his sister, Ghyslaine,
controlled the rights to Artaud's works. By 1990 Gallimard had
published 25 volumes of Artaud's collected works; it appeared
promising that all volumes would appear in the future. However, the
prospective publication of volume 26 ended the cordiality among
the Artaud–Malausséna family, Gallimard and Thévenin. Serge and
Ghyslaine objected to the manner in which Thévenin edited and
transcribed *Histoire vécue d'Artaud-Mômo*, a text Artaud had read at
the Vieux-Colombier performance. A French civil court adjudicated
the matter and in July 1994 ruled in favour of Gallimard. Even before
the ruling, Thévenin's death in November 1993 set the stage for an
eventual rapprochement between the family and Gallimard; since
Artaud's passing, her enmity towards the family, its perception of
her outsized role in Artaud's life and her subjective transcriptions
of Artaud's texts had all but ensured a climate of mistrust. By 2000
Gallimard and Serge had reconciled their remaining differences,
and Gallimard printed several new collections of Artaud's writings

and artwork, including a massive compendium of Artaud's literary and visual creative output – *Artaud: Oeuvres*. Produced under the direction of Évelyne Grossman, professor of French literature at Université Paris VII, this volume arranged Artaud's works chronologically, allowing readers to appreciate 'often startling continuities and contiguities'.[83]

Though Gallimard directly acknowledged the indispensable role played by Thévenin in the publication of Artaud's works, several cultural and scholarly luminaries – including Hélène Cixous, Julia Kristeva, Roland Dumas, Ariane Mnouchkine and Bernard Noël – viewed the publication of *Artaud: Oeuvres* as a betrayal of Thévenin. In a collectively drafted open letter, they objected to Thévenin's marginalization and Gallimard's ingratitude towards her; for his part, Derrida specifically placed the blame on Serge and his toxic relationship with Thévenin.[84] Naturally, even after his passing, Artaud's story could not end tidily.

The control Artaud struggled to exercise – over his body, his language, his beliefs and his consciousness – eluded his 'survivors'. Family, friends, scholars, artists, aficionados and neophytes – for whom adulation of Artaud became a *profession de foi* (declaration of faith) – have all but ensured that the enigma that was Artaud in this dimension remains the enigma of posterity, a mysterious visage captured in a death mask that continues to exude life through lifelessness.

Return

Though his uncle had been dead for 27 years, in 1975 Serge was determined to honour one of his deceased grandmother's deepest wishes: the reburial of his uncle in the family crypt at Saint-Pierre Cemetery in Marseille.[85] Artaud's funeral in the Paris suburb of Ivry-sur-Seine exposed the long-simmering conflict between his friends and family. The family wanted a Catholic burial; his friends threatened to disrupt the service if it was presided over by a priest. But in 1975 much had changed, and Serge decided it was time to transfer Artaud's remains. The cemetery at Ivry-sur-Seine exhumed the body, but the family, lacking the financial means to have it professionally moved, transported it themselves. On 18 April three passengers – Serge's mother, Marie-Ange; his father, Georges; and his sister, Ghyslaine – trundled into Serge's Renault R16. Because a casket was too much cargo for Serge's car – and because, after nearly thirty years, what remained of the decedent were bones – the cemetery transferred the remains into a small pinewood box, roughly 90 centimetres (35 in.) long, 35 cm (14 in.) high and 35 centimetres (14 in.) deep (in other words, a box for bones). This would fit perfectly in the Renault R16's trunk. The weather was spring-like, but the drive was long – nearly 800 kilometres (500 miles). Arriving in the Midi after the cemetery had closed, the Malausséna family stayed in Aubagne, a small town around 20 kilometres (12 miles) from Marseille. Fearful that thieves might break into the trunk and take the box of bones – of value to the family, but not necessarily to opportunistic thieves – the family took turns standing vigil over the Renault R16 and its irreplaceable cargo. The following morning, 19 April 1975, under a beautiful *méridional* spring sky, the family vault was opened and the pinewood box of bones deposited within it; with that, the peregrinations of Antonin Artaud came to an end, his final journey a fitting coda to a frenetic life.

Epilogue:
Posterity

After his corporeal passage from this dimension, Antonin Artaud's stature within artistic communities grew as reference point, direct influence and index on the 'coolness/hipness' meter. Permit me to explain: whereas some artists have at least partially imbibed and employed Artaud's theories and praxis in their works, for others, with only a superficial connection to Artaud, his name has become a defining mantra for inclusion within a particular canon or establishing *outré* credentials. Artaud might have been flattered to leave such a lasting impact on culture; but on the other hand, he might have freaked out that his life had been reduced to insanity and drug addiction, while the corpus of his complex work was often badly misappropriated and trivialized.

Cultural theorists, including Jean Baudrillard, Jacques Derrida, Michel Foucault, Julia Kristeva and Gilles Deleuze, have dipped their toes in Artaudian waters. In *La Folie et déraison: Histoire de la folie à l'âge classique* (History of Madness), Foucault wrote of the 'tragic consciousness of madness' of Artaud, questioning society's view of madness as 'the naked truth of man, only to place it in a pale, neutralized space, where it was almost entirely cancelled out[.] Why had it accepted the words of Nerval and Artaud, and recognized itself in their words but not in them?'[1] Sylvère Lotringer, founder of the journal *Semiotext(e)* and godfather of 'No Wave' (the mid- to late 1970s New York punk film scene), has immersed himself in Artaud, conducting interviews with several people who featured in Artaud's life, even speculating whether Artaud was, experientially at least, Jewish.[2]

Gratified though Artaud might have been to know that his life and works inspired some of the leading cultural theorists, he might have been more pleased by the extent to which he has informed artistic production. Artists working in the visual arts, theatre, film and music have either looked to Artaud for inspiration or drawn on his theories for their own creativity.

In the visual arts, the American artist Nancy Spero, expatriated to France between 1959 and 1964, encountered Artaud after seeing his poems reprinted in the literary journal *Tel Quel*, and, upon returning to America, incorporated Artaud's texts into the painting entitled *Artaud Paintings* (1969–70), and the 38 scrolls in her *Codex Artaud* (1970–71). Reacting to the violence around her – the Vietnam War, violence against women (though she was aware of Artaud's misogyny) – Spero channelled Artaud's rage: his explosions against the veneer of banality shielding language's constrictions and his contempt for bourgeois suffocation of unexpurgated artistic expression. 'I said, That's it, this complaint of Artaud's is the direct way to go from the violence of the war to the violence of the exposed self.'[3] Spero's 'paintings do not illustrate but rather resonate *alongside* Artaud's text, forcing his words to speak with her voice'; and yet she recognized that, though her appropriation of his words stays true to his sense of dislocation, Artaud would have hated how she shifted the implications drawn from his words.[4]

As should be expected, Artaud's most enduring influence has been in theatre. Spero's disillusionment with the narrowness of the visual arts echoed in a cohort of avant-garde theatre practitioners in the 1960s, triangulated between France, the United States and the United Kingdom; just as that of Spero had, their paths to a radically alternative form of expression led to Artaud. With his staging of *As I Lay Dying* in 1935, Jean-Louis Barrault first imbibed Artaud's idea of 'total theatre'; synergistically combining lighting, set design and other media, Barrault's production transformed theatre into a three-dimensional poetic space dialectically challenging its audience's preconceptions and assumptions. Named the director of the prestigious L'Odéon-Théâtre de l'Europe in 1959 (and removed from the position after turning over the theatre to students during the 1968 demonstrations), Barrault became something of a doyen to many Anglophone expatriates of theatre's avant-garde.

Questions persist, however, as to whether avant-garde theatre in the 1960s was the direct offspring of Artaud or the result of an 'immaculate conception'.[5] It would be hard to find an avant-garde theatre director or theatre company from the 1960s that did not claim to be Artaud's progeny, including Jerzy Grotowski, Judith Malina, Julian Beck's Living Theatre (which also offered a course in Artaudian acting) and Chicago's Open Theatre.[6] In some cases, they discovered Artaud *a posteriori* to the formulation of their own ideas; in others, their connections to Artaud were more tenuous than they – or their commentators – would like, often predicated on very selective readings and applications of Artaud to their practices. In other words, some avant-garde theatre practitioners sought to confirm their originality by distancing themselves from Artaud, while others consciously enrobed themselves in his visceral mentorship. Grotowski wrote of Artaudian chaos as

> authentic . . . holy, for they enabled others to reach self-knowledge.
>
> Among his successors, the chaos is in no sense holy, nor sufficiently determined: it has no reason for existing save to conceal something unfinished, to hide an infirmity. Artaud gave this chaos expression, which is quite another matter.[7]

Perhaps no theatre director has acknowledged a more direct debt to Artaud than Peter Brook. Referring to Brook, Grotowski wrote,

> when an eminent creator with an achieved style and personality . . . turns to Artaud, it's not to hide his own weaknesses, or to ape the man. It just happens that at a given point of his development, he finds himself in agreement with Artaud, feels the need of a confrontation, *tests* Artaud and retains whatever stands up to this test. He remains himself.[8]

In 1964 Brook and Charles Marowitz launched 'The Theatre of Cruelty', a theatrical group within the Royal Shakespeare Company committed to 'a language of actions, a language of sounds – a language of word-as-part-of-movement, of word-as-lie, word-as-parody, of word-as-rubbish, of word-as-contradiction, of word-shock or word-cry'.[9] For Brook, Artaudian theatre was theatre as 'holy space':

> He wanted a theatre that would be a hallowed place: he wanted the theatre served by a handful of dedicated actors and directors who would create out of their own natures an unending suc-cession of violent stage images, bringing about such powerful immediate explosions of human matter that no one would ever again revert to a theatre of anecdote and talk. He wanted the theatre to contain all that normally is reserved for crime and war. He wanted an audience that would drop all its defences, that would allow itself to be perforated, shocked, startled and raped, so that at the same time it would be filled with a powerful new charge.[10]

However, for Brook, 'Artaud applied is Artaud betrayed', since any application of Artaud could only be partial; applying Artaud's theatrical prescriptions to the actors is easier than to the lives of random spectators who enter a theatre.[11] Brook's first attempt at Artaudian staging was a series of short sketches performed for an audience of reviewers and theatre professionals. Starting with a short sketch Barrault related to Brook of Artaud's chaotic audition for Charles Dullin, the next two were three-minute run-throughs of Artaud's *Le Jet de sang* (The Spurt of Blood). The audience was decidedly unimpressed.[12]

This, though, was simply a starting point for Brook. His direction of Peter Weiss's *The Persecution and Assassination of Marat as Performed by the Inmates of the Asylum of Charenton under the Direction of the Marquis de Sade* (*Marat/Sade*) for the Royal Shakespeare Company at London's Aldwych Theatre in 1964 was more sophisticated and successful in actualizing many of Artaud's ideas. German productions of *Marat/Sade* in 1964 – in both the Federal Republic of Germany and the German Democratic Republic – remained faithful to Weiss's scripted play.

For the British version, however, Brook grounded his actors in an Artaudian sensibility, tapping into their primal state by screening for them an ethnographic film by Jean Rouch.[13]

Interviewed a few years after the play had garnered Tony Awards for Brook and for him, Weiss acknowledged that Artaud speaks more to directors than to playwrights:

> I didn't think of Artaud when I wrote *Marat/Sade*, which grew out of its own material and had to be played a certain way in the atmosphere that the material created. However, Peter Brook was thinking of Artaud before he produced *Marat/Sade*, and he used Artaudian techniques. This is a director's method, and for a writer, it's secondary.[14]

Artaud's influence on theatre praxis was not always so directly obvious. Fernando Arrabal, Alejandro Jodorowsky and Roland Topor's Panic Movement (or, Anti-movement) might have been consciously inspired by Artaud, as it used 'absurd ritual and demented violence' to create 'panic' in the audience.[15] In the 1990s the postmodern vocabulary and disturbingly confrontational productions of Reza Abdoh, the Iranian-born, Los Angeles-based director and playwright, drew, from none other than Marowitz, comparisons with Artaud. Some of Abdoh's own statements can be interpreted as spurred by an Artaudian sensibility. In an interview, Abdoh stated:

> Language is a ready-made tool of communication. It's a set of shared symbols, a form of repression. So, not to understand everything or not share all the symbols is perfectly ok for me; in fact, it helps my work because the work becomes more a puzzle rather than something that's easily digestible . . . I don't want to just sort of bow gracefully to traditions. I take traditions and I break them. That's my whole philosophical and aesthetic engagement. I have to subvert the forms that I'm using and learning from. It's not a museum piece. It's alive. It's about now, it's about contemporary culture.[16]

Before passing away aged 32 in 1995, Abdoh did not comment directly on the Artaud connection; but, in understanding theatre as a space that challenges, rather than affirms, our basic assumptions and doing so by instilling physical and emotional pain in his audience, Abdoh, as Arrabal had before him, drew logical parallels to 'The Theatre of Cruelty'.

Occasionally, Artaud's works are still produced. The directions taken by avant-garde theatre may have drained stagings of a play like *Les Cenci* of its shock value, but Artaud's words, applied to a new context, can resonate with immediacy and urgency. In 2004, as America waged war in Iraq and Afghanistan, theatre director Peter Sellars staged *To Have Been Done with the Judgement of God*. Performed in San Francisco and Los Angeles, the production featured a single actor in the role of General Stufflebeem, standing behind a lectern, manically reciting Artaud's text (as translated by Sellars), with images of war projected behind him.

Having been influenced by Eastern cultural references, Artaud's ideas on the body, on theatre as interactive experience, and on the subversion of social and cultural conventions inspired the Japanese dance theorist and choreographer Hijikata Tatsumi and the Japanese dance form known as Butoh in the 1960s. Drawing from second-hand knowledge of Artaud's Heliogabalus and a 1965 Japanese translation of *The Theatre and its Double*, Hijikata both transgressed gender and sexual boundaries and pushed corporeal expression to extremes. Like Artaud, Hijikata challenged the primacy of verbal communication, proposing, instead, a 'language of the body' as a more primal, less mediated means of expression.[17]

Although *The Seashell and the Clergyman* pre-dated Luis Buñuel's *Un Chien andalou*, the latter is credited with ushering in Surrealist film-making and has clearly had a more enduring influence on film. With that said, Alejandro Jodorowsky affirmed being inspired by Artaud's 'The Conquest of Mexico' when he conceptualized the conquest of Mexico with toads and chameleons dressed as Conquistadors and Aztecs in his film *The Holy Mountain* (1973).[18]

As with Artaud, punk leaves us shards from which to construct a mosaic of it, the emerging image dependent on the tiles used. Class conflict so ubiquitous in British punk was largely absent from American punk's cultural angst (notwithstanding the Dils' 'Class War' and 'I Hate the Rich').[19] For some, punk is a child of the Situationist movement; in turn, the Situationists claim filiation with Artaud. On the other hand, Sex Pistol and PIL (Public Image Ltd) frontman Johnny Lydon has unequivocally and consistently rejected punk's genealogical connections to any French cultural movements, including Surrealism or Situationism. In breeding interpretative chaos, punk simply remains faithful to its spirit of anarchy, defiant to the end of any nice, tidy packaging. What is undeniable is that punk challenged the prevailing bourgeois zeitgeist, often through absurdity, often through direct confrontation – a sonic and violent burst of energy, a scream from the deepest bowels of consciousness, aurally and visually assaulting cognitive norms, imploring its audience to break out of its habitual passivity. Taking all this together, punk might contain Artaud's DNA without necessarily being Artaud's offspring. Then again, punk could be an adoptive progeny of Artaud.

In 1984 an article in *Magazine littéraire* posed a rhetorical question: 'If Artaud lived today, would he be a rocker?' Acknowledging the absurdity of the question, the author went on to say that rock's aural assault on the senses best embodies the spirit of *The Theatre and its Double*.[20] While the thread connecting Artaud to the punk ethos is largely circumstantial, many of the progenitors of punk from the mid- to late 1970s made direct reference to Artaud, including Richard Hell, co-founder of the band Television before launching Richard Hell and the Voidoids. The sixth and last issue of *Genesis: Grasp*, the literary journal that Hell edited between 1968 and 1971, featured side-by-side pictures of Arthur Rimbaud and Artaud (Hell later stated he modelled his haircut on their hairstyles). The choice was hardly gratuitous. The manifesto Hell penned for the first issue of *Genesis: Grasp* read,

Of course, there is no art, only life. In the practical sense that nothing a living being can produce or imagine can transcend his being alive. But, art is entirely impractical, and transcendence is exactly what it attempts.[21]

In his manifesto, Hell encapsulated the founding ethos of punk: to create the kind of joyful and desperate noise, at once destructive and creative in its quest 'to "transcend" the loathed world of bourgeois rationality in order to discover a nameless, indefinable "outside" that had as its driving force an urge toward disorder'.[22]

Patti Smith, often credited as punk's priestess, discovered Artaud while in her late teens through the images in the City Lights' *Artaud Anthology*, 'falling in love with the face of the writer'.[23] Drawn to Artaud's art and words, Smith found a parallel with her own sense of being:

> It's very hard for certain people to accept that they have a gift, a calling independent of demons and things, and I think that if they can't accept that, it destroys them. I think that is the kind of man Artaud was. He just couldn't accept his own inner beauty and he did everything to deface it, disguise it, thwart it. I've been like that in my own way. He was a constant source of comfort, justification, for how I was. I used him continuously to justify my act, my performances, my way of being, and I felt, especially when I got a lot of criticism for what I was doing – I was taking things too far, I was pushing the envelope in a destructive way – I always felt I had him above me to draw from.[24]

The British post-punk band Bauhaus entitled a track 'Antonin Artaud' on its album *Burning from the Inside* from 1983. Beginning with the opening line 'The young man held a gun to the head of god', the lyrics draw on well-known details from Artaud's life ('put the audience in action', 'scratch pictures on asylum walls', 'limbs in cramps contorted' and 'the theatre and its double') while the closing line ('those Indians wank on his bones') obscurely references Artaud's claim of seeing some Tarahumara masturbating as he entered the Copper Canyon.

In the 1980s several French music fanzines, including *Hello Happy Taxpayers* (Bordeaux), *Destructor, Fog, Fogzine* and *Upanishads/Le Morbaque* (Marseille) featured articles on Artaud, appropriating him but, at the same time, reducing him to 'a rebel in a society in the throes of crisis, the madman of the Sierra Tarahumara, the plague-stricken of the Theatre of Cruelty'. For the fanzines and the musicians they covered, Artaud showed that 'their protest has a history, that it is part of a movement that includes prominent figures; on the other hand, they want to affirm their creative freedom'.[25]

In life, Antonin Artaud was paradoxical; in death, he remains enigmatic. His prescriptions for performance were neither readily accessible nor realizable, his objectives more achievable than the means he sketched for reaching them. Elevated to the status of cultural icon for his rebellion against the manipulations and contrivances of bourgeois cultural norms, Artaud has sometimes been bastardized, sometimes reduced to a cliché and, it has been argued, sometimes undeservedly deified. Though posterity might have left exactitude on the side of the road as it chauffeured Artaud from madman to visionary, as he has come to incarnate the danger, torment, subversion, confrontation and pain that are the very essence and highest ideals of art, the true spirit of Artaud materializes. In the postscript to the written text of *Pour en finir avec le jugement de Dieu* (To Have Done with the Judgement of God), Artaud wrote,

> Who am I?
> Where do I come from?
> I am Antonin Artaud
> and I say it
> as I know to say it
> right now
> you will see my existing body
> fall apart
> and pick itself up
> in 10,000 aspects
> well known
> a new body
> in which you will never be able to forget me again.[26]

In the end, Artaud is present: in the Artaud of our dreams, the Artaud we construct and the screaming body we fill with organs. An ellipsis.

References

General note: all translations of French texts, including Artaud's *Oeuvres complètes*, are by the author, unless otherwise stated.

Introduction

1 Jean Baudrillard, *The Conspiracy of Art*, ed. Sylvère Lotringer (Cambridge, MA, 2005), pp. 217, 221.
2 Antonin Artaud, 'Le Mexique et l'esprit primitif: María Izquierdo', *Messages révolutionnaires* (Paris, 1971), p. 157; Terry Geis, 'The Voyaging Reality: María Izquierdo, Antonin Artaud, Mexico and Paris', *Papers of Surrealism*, 4 (2005), p. 3.

1 Youth

1 Charles Péguy, *L'Argent* (Paris, 1913), p. 10.
2 Richard D. Sonn, *Anarchism and Cultural Politics in Fin-de-siècle France* (Lincoln, NE, 1989), p. 4.
3 Howard G. Lay, '"Beau geste!" (On the Readability of Terrorism)', *Yale French Studies*, 101 (2001), p. 80.
4 Jill Fell, *Alfred Jarry* (London, 2010), chap. 5.
5 Robert Wohl, *The Generation of 1914* (Cambridge, MA, 1979), p. 216.
6 Antonin Artaud, *Oeuvres complètes* (hereafter OC), vol. XXIV (Paris, 1988), p. 151.
7 Artaud, *OC*, vol. XX (Paris, 1984), p. 239.
8 Artaud, *OC*, vol. XIV* (Paris, 1978), p. 86.
9 Richard Gondrand, *La Tragédie de l'Asie Mineure et l'anéantissement de Smyrne: 1914–1922* (Marseille, 1935), p. 11.
10 Jonathan Pollock, 'Marseille et la langue marseillaise dans la dernière écriture d'Antonin Artaud', in *Antonin Artaud: Écrivain du Sud*, ed. Thierry Galibert (Aix-en-Provence, 2002), p. 40.
11 Thomas Maeder, *Antonin Artaud*, trans. Janine Delpech (Paris, 1978), p. 23.
12 Camille Dumoulié, *Antonin Artaud* (Paris, 1996), p. 7.

13 Artaud, *oc*, vol. I (Paris, 1970), pp. 14–15.

14 A feminist and art critic, Yvonne Allendy was also the wife of René Allendy, founder of the Group of Philosophic and Scientific Studies at the Sorbonne. Yvonne was a close friend of Artaud and, as we will see, she and her husband were among the first and most-sustained patrons of Artaud's theatrical ventures.

15 Antonin Artaud, *Oeuvres*, ed. Évelyne Grossman (Paris, 2004), p. 1441.

16 Denis Bertholet, *Le Bourgeois dans tous ses états* (Paris, 1987), pp. 90–91.

17 Florence de Mèredieu, *C'était Antonin Artaud* (Paris, 2006), p. 45.

18 Norbert Bandier, 'Artaud et la révolution surréaliste', in *Artaud en revues*, ed. Olivier Penot-Lacassagne (Lausanne, 2005), p. 47.

19 Maeder, *Antonin Artaud*, pp. 27–8; Mèredieu, *C'était*, p. 114.

20 However, in 1923, a year before Antoine's death, Artaud dedicated the publication of his first collection of poems, *Tric trac du ciel*, to his parents.

21 Antonin Artaud, *Messages révolutionnaires* (Paris, 1971), p. 12.

22 Ibid., pp. 17–18.

23 Naomi Greene, *Antonin Artaud: Poet Without Words* (New York, 1970), p. 16.

24 Marie-Ange Malausséna, 'Antonin Artaud', *La Revue théâtrale. Internationale revue du théâtre*, VIII/23 (1953), pp. 40–41.

25 Ibid., p. 46.

26 The grandfather of the French theologian and philosopher Jean Guitton averred, 'Christian and properly Catholic parents could not . . . place their children in the establishments of an atheist state when they could do otherwise.' See Adeline Daumard, *Les Bourgeois et la bourgeoisie en France depuis 1815* (Saint-Amand, 1987), p. 217.

27 Évelyne Grossman, *Artaud: 'L'Aliéné authentique'* (Tours, 2003), pp. 73–5.

28 Mèredieu, *C'était*, p. 83.

29 Maeder, *Antonin Artaud*, p. 31.

30 Mèredieu, *C'était*, p. 86.

31 Ibid., p. 90.

32 Gregory M. Thomas, *Treating the Trauma of the Great War: Soldiers, Civilians, and Psychiatry in France, 1914–1940* (Baton Rouge, LA, 2009), p. 68.

33 Mèredieu, *C'était*, p. 99.

34 Ibid., p. 85.

35 Ibid., pp. 84–5.

36 Artaud, *oc*, vol. XXVI (Paris, 1994), p. 73.

37 Artaud, *oc*, vol. X (Paris, 1974), pp. 13–14.

38 Maeder, *Antonin Artaud*, p. 33.

2 Paris

1 Gregory M. Thomas, 'Open Psychiatric Services in Interwar France', *History of Psychiatry*, xv/2 (June 2004), p. 133.

2 Bernard Baillaud and Martyn Cornick, 'Jean Paulhan's Influences: The Review *Demain*', *Yale French Studies*, 106 (2005), p. 14.

3 Florence de Mèredieu, *C'était Antonin Artaud* (Paris, 2006), p. 126.

4 Michel Foucault, *History of Madness*, trans. Jonathan Murphy and Jean Khalfa (London, 2009), p. 511.

5 Michel Huteau, *Psychologie, psychiatrie et société sous la Troisième République: La Biocratie d'Édouard Toulouse (1865–1947)* (Paris, 2003), p. 180.

6 Ibid., p. 38.

7 Ibid., p. 50.

8 Antonin Artaud, *Oeuvres complètes* (hereafter *oc*), vol. I (Paris, 1970), pp. 242–3.

9 For baccalaureate see ibid., pp. 235–6; for art criticism see Artaud, *oc*, vol. II (Paris, 1961), pp. 197–200.

10 Ibid., pp. 195–6.

11 Sally Debra Charnow, *Theatre, Politics, and Markets in Fin-de-Siècle Paris: Staging Modernity* (New York, 2005), pp. 5–6.

12 Harold Hobson, *French Theatre since 1830* (London, 1978), chap. 5.

13 Erin Williams Hyman, 'Theatrical Terror: Attentats and Symbolist Spectacle', *The Comparatist*, xxIx (May 2005), p. 114.

14 Frederick Brown, *Theater and Revolution: The Culture of the French Stage* (New York, 1989), p. 203.

15 Bernard Baillaud, 'Édouard Toulouse, Antonin Artaud et *la revue Demain*', in *Artaud en revues*, ed. Olivier Penot-Lacassagne (Lausanne, 2005), p. 192.

16 Artaud, *oc*, vol. vIII (Paris, 1980), p. 174.

17 Thomas Maeder, *Antonin Artaud* (Paris, 1978), p. 42.

18 Artaud, *oc*, vol. II, p. 153; Maeder, *Antonin Artaud*, p. 43.

19 Brown, *Theater and Revolution*, pp. 284–303.

20 Artaud, *oc*, vol. III (Paris, 1978), p. 96.

21 Artaud, *oc*, vol. II, p. 153.

22 František Deák, 'Antonin Artaud and Charles Dullin: Artaud's Apprenticeship in Theatre', *Educational Theatre Journal*, xxIx/3 (1977), p. 346.

23 Ibid., p. 353.

24 Artaud, *oc*, vol. III, p. 94. Max Jacob was featured in Pablo Picasso's

Three Musicians (1921). He died in 1944, two weeks after being sent to the Drancy concentration camp, where he was awaiting deportation to one of the German death camps.

25 Deák, 'Antonin Artaud', p. 351.

26 Maeder, *Antonin Artaud*, p. 46.

27 Dana S. Hale, *Races on Display: French Representations of Colonized Peoples, 1886–1940* (Bloomington, IN, 2008), pp. 146–53.

28 Mèredieu, *C'était*, p. 161.

29 Antonin Artaud, *Lettres à Génica Athanasiou* (Paris, 1969), p. 25.

30 Ibid., p. 30.

31 Ibid., pp. 41–2.

32 Artaud, *OC*, vol. VIII, p. 319.

33 Artaud, *OC*, vol. II, p. 219.

34 Pierre Chaleix, 'Avant le surréalisme. Artaud chez le Dr Toulouse. Interview recueillie par Pierre Chaleix', *La Tour de feu*, 63–4 (1959), pp. 55–60.

35 Artaud, *OC*, vol. VIII, p. 319.

36 Maeder, *Antonin Artaud*, p. 50.

37 Alain and Odette Virmaux, 'Le Crapouillot (1922): Quatre textes retrouvés sur des hommes de théâtre: Dullin, Signoret, Pitoëff, Sarmant', in *Artaud en revues*, pp. 31–9.

38 Maeder, *Antonin Artaud*, p. 51.

39 Ibid., p. 55.

40 Artaud, *OC*, vol. VIII, p. 177.

41 Artaud, *OC*, vol. III, p. 103.

42 Ibid., pp. 104, 105.

43 Virmaux, 'Le Crapouillot', p. 37.

44 Jean-Louis Brau, *Antonin Artaud* (Paris, 1971), p. 47.

45 Artaud, *OC*, vol. I** (Paris, 1976), p. 93.

46 Artaud, *Lettres à Génica*, p. 342, fn. 2.

47 Norbert Bandier, 'Artaud et la révolution surréaliste', in *Artaud en revues*, p. 49.

48 Artaud, *Lettres à Génica*, p. 46.

49 In 1927 Artaud published the letters under the title *Correspondence avec Jacques Rivière*.

50 Artaud, *OC*, vol. I, pp. 31–3.

51 Ibid., pp. 34–40.

52 Ibid., pp. 41–6.

53 Ibid., p. 51.

54 Ibid., p. 57.

55 Renaud de Portzamparc, *La Folie d'Artaud* (Paris, 2011), p. 26.
56 Artaud, *Lettres à Génica*, p. 89.
57 Ibid., p. 110.
58 Ibid., pp. 115–16.
59 Ibid., p. 123.
60 Ibid., pp. 158–62.
61 Mark Polizzotti, *Revolution of the Mind: The Life of André Breton* (New York, 1995), p. 166.

3 Beyond

1   Mark Polizzotti, *Revolution of the Mind: The Life of André Breton* (New York, 1997), p. 15.
2   After Vaché's death, Breton served as his chronicler, idealizing Vaché's ideas and posthumous contributions to Surrealism. Ibid., p. 39.
3   Tyler Stovall, *Paris and the Spirit of 1919: Consumer Struggles, Transnationalism, and Revolution* (Cambridge, 2012), p. 4.
4   Polizzotti, *Revolution*, pp. 176, 209.
5   Ibid., p. 96.
6   Antonin Artaud, *Oeuvres complètes* (hereafter *oc*), vol. I** (Paris, 1976), p. 112.
7   Artaud, *oc*, vol. I (Paris, 1970), pp. 50–51.
8   Thomas Maeder, *Antonin Artaud* (Paris, 1978), p. 77.
9   Florence de Mèredieu, *C'était Antonin Artaud* (Paris, 2006), p. 262.
10 Maeder, *Antonin Artaud*, p. 78.
11 Artaud, *oc*, vol. I, pp. 315–16.
12 Ibid., pp. 317–18.
13 Antonin Artaud, *Artaud: Oeuvres* (Paris, 2004), pp. 124–5.
14 Artaud, *oc*, vol. I, pp. 312–14.
15 Artaud, *oc*, vol. I**, pp. 29–30.
16 Ibid., p. 42.
17 Ibid., p. 43.
18 Ibid., pp. 38–9, 41.
19 Martine Antle, 'Surrealism and the Orient', *Yale French Studies*, 109 (2006), p. 4.
20 Naomi Greene, *Antonin Artaud: Poet Without Words* (New York, 1970), p. 108.
21 Artaud, *oc*, vol. I**, pp. 43–4.
22 Greene, *Antonin Artaud*, pp. 106–7.

23 Ibid., p. 81.
24 Polizzotti, *Revolution*, pp. 229–30.
25 Antonin Artaud, *Lettres à Génica Athanasiou* (Paris, 1969), p. 182.
26 Greene, *Antonin Artaud*, p. 23.
27 Camille Dumoulié, *Antonin Artaud* (Paris, 1996), p. 20.
28 Polizzotti, *Revolution*, p. 237.
29 Ibid., p. 251.
30 Artaud, *oc*, vol. 1**, p. 67.
31 Ibid., p. 71.
32 Ibid., p. 59.
33 Ibid., p. 61.
34 Ibid., pp. 73–4.
35 Ibid., p. 72.
36 Artaud, *oc*, vol. 1**, pp. 72–3.
37 Artaud, *oc*, vol. 1, pp. 124–5.
38 Ibid., pp. 126–7.
39 Ibid., p. 128.
40 John C. Stout, *Antonin Artaud's Alternate Genealogies: Self-portraits and Family Romances* (Waterloo, ON, 1996), p. 11.
41 Ibid., p. 34.
42 Artaud, *oc*, vol. 1, pp. 68–71.
43 Stout, *Antonin Artaud's*, p. 5.
44 Artaud, *oc*, vol. 1, p. 165.
45 Serge Margel, *Aliénation: Antonin Artaud: Les Généalogies hybrides* (Paris, 2008), pp. 28–9.
46 Évelyn Grossman, *Artaud, 'L'Aliéne authentique'* (Tours, 2003), p. 36.
47 Antonin Artaud, *Cahiers d'Ivry: Février 1947–Mars 1948* (Paris, 2011), vol. II, p. 1661.
48 Ibid., p. 74.

4 Performance

1 Martyn Cornick, 'Jean Paulhan and the "Nouvelle revue française": Literature, Politics, and the Power of Creative Editorship', *Yale French Studies*, 106 (2004), p. 39.
2 Bernard Baillaud and Martyn Cornick, 'Jean Paulhan's Influences: The Review *Demain*', *Yale French Studies*, 106 (2004); Cornick, 'Jean Paulhan and the "Nouvelle revue française"', p. 38.
3 Jean-Louis Brau, *Antonin Artaud* (Paris, 1971), p. 81.

4   Antonin Artaud, *Oeuvres complètes* (hereafter *oc*), vol. 1** (Paris, 1976), pp. 273–4.

5   Relationships among the Paris avant-garde could be relatively fluid during the middle years of the 1920s. Although he was never a Surrealist, Robert Aron was – and remained – a communist. Surrealists, including Vitrac, disrupted a lecture he presented on 'literature and the average Frenchmen' at the Vieux-Colombier on 29 May 1925 with shouts of 'Down with France!' It was at that point that Aron felt 'the taste of theatre' and became determined to start a theatre that would exemplify the 'real life of surreality'; see Odette and Alain Virmaux, *Artaud vivant* (Paris, 1980), pp. 179–80. René Allendy was a noted psychoanalyst, interested in astrology and homeopathy. Among his other patients were Surrealist poet René Crevel and Anaïs Nin, who wrote extensively of Allendy in her diaries, describing him variously as looking like a Russian peasant, having 'the eyes of a crystal-gazer' and being 'proud and sure of himself'. Allendy also warned Nin against being part of the Henry and June Miller 'milieu'; see Anaïs Nin, *The Diary of Anaïs Nin* (Orlando, FL, 1994), vol. I, p. 131. According to Nin, in 1933 Maurice Sachs, author of *Decade of Illusion* and *Witches' Sabbath*, described Yvonne Allendy as having the 'beautiful face of a revolutionary of '89, serious, confident, good, intelligent. Her eyes are superb', ibid., p. 139.

6   Antonin Artaud, *oc*, vol. II (Paris, 1961), p. 12.

7   Ibid., p. 16.

8   Ibid., p. 18.

9   Ibid., p. 22.

10 Ibid., p. 25. Between 1931 and 1932, Breton definitively split from the French Communist Party over the latter's dogmatism, rigidity and ultimate irreconcilability with the premises behind Surrealism.

11 Alain and Odette Virmaux, *Artaud: Un Bilan critique* (Paris, 1979), p. 29.

12 Ronald Hayman, *Artaud and After* (Oxford, 1977), p. 69.

13 Mark Polizzotti, *Revolution of the Mind: The Life of André Breton* (New York, 1997), pp. 292–3.

14 Florence de Mèredieu, *C'était Antonin Artaud* (Paris, 2006), p. 367.

15 Artaud, *oc*, vol. III (Paris, 1978), p. 309.

16 Virmaux, *Artaud: Un Bilan critique*, p. 31.

17 Artaud, *oc*, vol. III, p. 134.

18 Virmaux, *Artaud vivant*, p. 59; Mèredieu, *C'était*, p. 250.

19 Roy Armes, *French Cinema* (New York, 1985), p. 52.

20 Thomas Maeder, *Antonin Artaud* (Paris, 1978), p. 73.

21 Alan Williams, *Republic of Images: A History of French Filmmaking* (Cambridge, MA, 1992), p. 86; Pierre Lherminier, *Annales du cinéma français: Les Voies du silence, 1895–1929* (Paris, 2012), p. 530.

22 Lherminier, *Annales*, p. 694.

23 Artaud, *OC*, vol. III, pp. 63–4.

24 Ibid., pp. 115–16.

25 Virmaux, *Artaud vivant*, p. 223.

26 Artaud, *OC*, vol. III, pp. 129–30. Jean Epstein directed the film in 1927, but with Jean Debucourt in the role of Usher.

27 Antonin Artaud, *Lettres à Génica Athanasiou* (Paris, 1969), p. 187.

28 According to Lherminier, France's President Gaston Doumergue was absent; his presence at a film celebrating the Empire might have compromised the French Republic; see Lherminier, *Annales*, p. 922. However, Mèredieu places Doumergue at the premiere; see Mèredieu, *C'était*, p. 344.

29 Artaud, *OC*, vol. III, p. 305.

30 *Le Cinéopse* (1 September 1926).

31 *Mon Ciné* (21 July 1927).

32 Mèredieu, *C'était*, p. 299.

33 Ros Murray, *Antonin Artaud: The Scum of the Soul* (Basingstoke, 2014), p. 112.

34 Ibid., p. 113.

35 Artaud, *Lettres à Génica*, pp. 274, 370 fn. 4.

36 Artaud, *OC*, vol. III, p. 306.

37 *Gringoire* (9 November 1928).

38 *Lettres françaises* (13 March 1952).

39 Nin, *Diary of Anaïs Nin*, vol. I, p. 350.

40 Mèredieu, *C'était*, p. 380.

41 Artaud, *OC*, vol. I**, pp. 142–3.

42 Artaud, *OC*, vol. III, pp. 9–10.

43 Mèredieu, *C'était*, pp. 344–5.

44 Maeder, *Antonin Artaud*, p. 108.

45 Artaud, *OC*, vol. III, p. 120.

46 Ibid., p. 123.

47 Ibid., pp. 128–9.

48 See Lee Jamieson, 'The Lost Prophet of Cinema: The Film Theory of Antonin Artaud', *Senses of Cinema*, XLIV (August 2007), available at http://sensesofcinema.com, accessed 16 July 2014.

49 For example, Dulac claimed that Artaud was not even at the screening. On the other hand, nearly every account places Artaud at the screening.

50 Alexandra Pecker claimed that she attended the screening with Artaud and their mothers and that, outside of shouting 'Enough! Enough!' (at whom, she could not say), Artaud did not react; see Alain and Odette Virmaux, *Antonin Artaud: Qui êtes-vous?* (Lyon, 1986), pp. 133–4.

51 Artaud, *oc*, vol. III, p. 325.

52 Virmaux, *Artaud vivant*, pp. 237–42.

53 Jamieson, 'The Lost Profit of Cinema'.

54 Artaud, *oc*, vol. III, pp. 18–20, 332 fn. 10.

55 Artaud, *Lettres à Genica*, pp. 276–9.

56 Ibid., pp. 295–7.

57 Artaud, *oc*, vol. VII (Paris, 1982), p. 316. It should be noted, however, that Madame Sacco's predictions were almost comically off. For example, she predicted that Breton and Simone would not divorce (they divorced in 1929), that he would lead a political party and that after spending twenty years in China, he would return rich and famous (Breton never visited China and never led a political party); see Polizzotti, *Revolution*, p. 244.

58 Artaud, *oc*, vol. VII, pp. 317–18.

59 Ibid., p. 330.

60 Pecker refused to release the letters she exchanged with Artaud nor to deposit them in an archive. What we know of the relationship has come from Alain and Odette Virmaux's interview with 'an anonymous friend of Antonin Artaud'; based on the answers, it is reasonably certain that the interviewee was Pecker. See Virmaux, *Artaud: Qui êtes-vous?*, pp. 127–43.

61 Ibid., p. 130.

62 Mèredieu, *C'était*, p. 348.

5 Cruelty

1 Antonin Artaud, *Oeuvres complètes* (hereafter *oc*), vol. III (Paris, 1978), pp. 143–4.

2 Ibid., p. 307.

3 Ibid., pp. 144–5.

4 In 1920s France, advertising was considered to be more of an art form than a commercial venture. Victoria de Grazia, *Irresistible Empire: America's Advance through 20th Century Europe* (Cambridge, MA, 2005), p. 229.

5 As one of the founders of the Psychoanalytic Society of Paris, René

Allendy promoted the value of dreams, even as a device in advertising; see Florénce de Mèredieu, *C'était Antonin Artaud* (Paris, 2006), p. 395.

6 Artaud, *OC*, vol. III, p. 151.

7 Mèredieu, *C'était*, p. 399.

8 Artaud, *OC*, vol. III, p. 147.

9 Ibid., p. 158.

10 In the quote used, see 'I sense that my soul is dead'– here Artaud used the word *noyau* (technically, 'stone' or 'nucleus'), but in the context of what he is writing, he is referring to his 'soul'. Artaud abbreviated laudanum. See Antonin Artaud, *OC*, vol. I** (Paris, 1976), pp. 144–7.

11 Ibid., pp. 148–51.

12 Artaud, *OC*, vol. III, p. 146.

13 Artaud, *OC*, vol. I**, pp. 152–3, 282.

14 Started by Robert Denoël and American Bernard Steele, Éditions Denoël et Steele published what could best be described as an eclectic galaxy of authors that included several Surrealists, René Allendy, Jean Genet, Sigmund Freud, Louis-Ferdinand Céline, Franklin Roosevelt and Adolf Hitler.

15 Antonin Artaud, *OC*, vol. I (Paris, 1970), pp. 150–51.

16 Artaud, *OC*, vol. III, pp. 160–62.

17 Artaud, *OC*, vol. I**, pp. 154–5.

18 Antonin Artaud, *OC*, vol. II (Paris, 1961), pp. 33–4.

19 Artaud, *OC*, vol. III, p. 174.

20 Artaud, *OC*, vol. II, pp. 37–48.

21 Artaud, *OC*, vol. III, pp. 167–8.

22 Ibid., pp. 185, 191.

23 Ibid., p. 177.

24 Alain and Odette Virmaux, *Antonin Artaud: Qui êtes-vous?* (Lyon, 1986), p. 134.

25 Artaud, *OC*, vol. II, pp. 175–7.

26 Odette and Alain Virmaux, *Artaud vivant* (Paris, 1980), pp. 61–2.

27 Mèredieu, *C'était*, pp. 419–21. The director G. W. Pabst had previously directed a 'psychoanalytic film' with the help of Hanns Sachs produced by the German film company UFA. Sachs and Allendy shared a common interest in dreams and their cinematic representation.

28 Artaud, *OC*, vol. III, pp. 257–62.

29 Ibid., pp. 426–7.

30 Antonin Artaud, *OC*, vol. VI (Paris, 1982), p. 13.

31 Ibid., p. 324.

32 Donna V. Jones, 'The Prison House of Modernism: Colonial Spaces

and Construction of the Primitive at the 1931 Colonial Exposition', *Modernism/modernity*, XIV/1 (January 2007), pp. 55–69.

33 Dana S. Hale, *Races on Display: French Representations of Colonized Peoples, 1896–1940* (Bloomington, IN, 2008), p. 167.

34 Jack J. Spector, *Surrealist Art and Writing, 1919–1939* (Cambridge, 1997), p. 154.

35 Though the Balinese performance was a mix of dance and theatre, and both aspects of it resonated with Artaud, the term 'Balinese theatre' will be used here.

36 Nicola Savarese, '1931: Antonin Artaud Sees 'Balinese Theatre' at the Paris Colonial Exposition', *Drama Review*, XXXXV/3 (Fall 2001), p. 67.

37 Artaud, *OC*, vol. III, pp. 217–18.

38 Antonin Artaud, *Antonin Artaud: Selected Writings*, ed. Susan Sontag (Berkeley, CA, 1976), p. 208.

39 Artaud, *OC*, vol. IV (Paris, 1964), p. 357 fn. 2. As will be discussed further on, this essay became the fourth chapter in Artaud's classic work *The Theatre and its Double*, which was published in 1938. Artaud had made some editing changes between his original essay for the *NRF* and the version that appeared in *The Theatre and its Double*. The quotations in this section come from his original essay, as they are most representative of his thinking at the time.

40 Ibid., p. 65.

41 Ibid., pp. 73–4.

42 Ibid., p. 74.

43 Ibid., p. 76.

44 Savarese, '1931', pp. 71–2.

45 Ibid., p. 68.

46 Artaud, *OC*, vol. IV, pp. 64–5.

47 Martine Antle, 'Surrealism and the Orient', *Yale French Studies*, 109 (2006), p. 5.

48 Artaud, *OC*, vol. I, pp. 340–43.

49 Artaud, *OC*, vol. I**, p. 180.

50 Naomi Greene, *Antonin Artaud: Poet Without Words* (New York, 1970), p. 113.

51 Artaud, *OC*, vol. III, p. 283.

52 Ibid., p. 247.

53 Artaud, *OC*, vol. IV, pp. 165–8.

54 Artaud, *OC*, vol. III, p. 268.

55 Ibid., pp. 196–7, 201.

56 Artaud, *OC*, vol. IV, p. 40.

57 Ibid., p. 45.
58 Ibid., p. 54.
59 Artaud originally intended to call it the Théâtre de la NRF, but changed the name when both Paulhan and Gaston Gallimard objected to it; see Ronald Hayman, *Artaud and After* (Oxford, 1977), p. 82.
60 Artaud, *OC*, vol. IV, pp. 120–21.
61 Ibid., p. 130.
62 Ibid., p. 118.
63 Ibid., pp. 106–7.
64 Ibid., p. 115.
65 Martin Puchner, *Poetry of the Revolution: Marx, Manifestos, and the Avant-Gardes* (Princeton, NJ, and Oxford, 2006), p. 202.
66 In the original copy of the manifesto that he sent to Paulhan, Artaud claimed that André Gide would make the adaptation of the work. However, after writing to Gide for confirmation, Artaud was forced to write to Paulhan, telling him that in spite of sending Artaud three letters authorizing him to use his name, Gide no longer wanted his name used in the manifesto. See Antonin Artaud, *OC*, vol. V (Paris, 1979), pp. 104–6.
67 Artaud, *OC*, vol. IV, p. 119.
68 Anaïs Nin, *The Diary of Anaïs Nin* (Orlando, FL, 1994), vol. I, pp. 186–7.
69 Ibid., pp. 191–2.
70 Artaud, *OC*, vol. V (Paris, 1979), pp. 146–7.
71 Ibid., p. 150.
72 Nin, *Diary*, pp. 225–9.
73 Ibid., p. 229.
74 Camille Dumoulié, *Artaud, la vie* (Paris, 2003), pp. 64–6.
75 Artaud, *OC*, vol. IV, p. 34.
76 Ibid., p. 37.
77 Ibid., p. 38.
78 Hyman, *Artaud*, pp. 92–3.
79 Artaud, *OC*, vol. V, p. 181.
80 Ibid., pp. 228–9.
81 Mèredieu, *C'était*, p. 513. André Derain also painted Abdy's portrait between 1934 and 1938.
82 Ibid., pp. 515–16.
83 Virmaux, *Artaud: Qui êtes-vous?*, p. 154.
84 Thomas Maeder, *Antonin Artaud* (Paris, 1978), pp. 167–9. After providing Blin with a copy of the script and a box of coloured pencils, Artaud instructed Blin to 'Record all that I say . . . and record what I don't say.'

85 Ibid., p. 170.
86 Mèredieu, *C'était*, p. 523.
87 Artaud, *oc*, vol. v, p. 188.
88 Puchner, *Poetry*, p. 196.

6 Voyage

1   Jean-Louis Barrault, *Memories for Tomorrow* (New York, 1974), p. 68.
2   Barrault, *Memories*, p. 83.
3   Ronald Hayman, *Artaud and After* (Oxford, 1977), p. 100.
4   *Lettres de Antonin Artaud à Jean-Louis Barrault* (Paris, 1952), pp. 89–92.
5   Florence de Mèredieu, *C'était Antonin Artaud* (Paris, 2006), p. 527.
6   Jean-Louis Barrault, *Reflections on the Theatre* (London, 1951), p. 39.
7   Antonin Artaud, *Oeuvres complètes* (hereafter *oc*), vol. iv (Paris, 1964), pp. 168–71.
8   Barrault, *Memories*, p. 81.
9   Ibid., p. 82.
10 Artaud, *oc*, vol. viii (Paris, 1980), pp. 281–4.
11 Ibid., pp. 319–23.
12 Mèredieu, *C'était*, pp. 531–2.
13 Ibid., pp. 285–8.
14 Mèredieu, *C'était*, p. 543.
15 Sylvère Lotringer, *Fous d'Artaud* (Paris, 2003), p. 119.
16 Artaud, *oc*, vol. iv, pp. 146–53.
17 Artaud, *oc*, vol. viii, p. 290.
18 Ibid., pp. 293–5.
19 Artaud, *oc*, vol. v (Paris, 1979), p. 192.
20 Ibid., pp. 196–7.
21 Ibid., p. 197; Artaud, *oc*, vol. viii, p. 304.
22 Antonin Artaud, *Nouveaux écrits de Rodez* (Paris, 1977), p. 167.
23 Artaud, *oc*, vol. viii, p. 307.
24 Mèredieu, *C'était*, p. 557.
25 Artaud, *oc*, vol. viii, p. 247.
26 Ibid., p. 250.
27 Ibid., pp. 251–5.
28 Terri Geis, 'The Voyaging Reality: María Izquierdo and Antonin Artaud, Mexico and Paris', *Papers of Surrealism*, 4 (2005).
29 Ibid., pp. 1, 8.

30 Luis Cardoza y Aragón, 'Pourquoi le Mexique', *Europe: Revue littéraire mensuelle*, 667–8 (1984), p. 105.

31 Ibid., p. 101.

32 Ibid., p. 103.

33 Mèredieu, *C'était*, pp. 558–60.

34 Artaud, *OC*, vol. VIII, pp. 141–50.

35 Artaud, *OC*, vol. VIII, pp. 160–68. Drawing, perhaps, from his acquaintance with George Soulié de Morant (see Chapter Five), Artaud also spoke about the effectiveness of ancient Chinese healing in preventing cholera.

36 Ibid., pp. 192–6.

37 Artaud, *OC*, vol. V, pp. 202–3. The actual names of the deities are *rayénare* (Sun god) and *michá* (Moon god). William L. Merrill, *Rarámuri Souls: Knowledge and Social Process in Northern Mexico* (Washington, DC, 1988), p. 203, fn 5.

38 Mèredieu, *C'était*, pp. 568–9.

39 Artaud, *OC*, vol. VIII, pp. 314–15.

40 Maeder, *Antonin Artaud* (Paris, 1978), p. 184.

41 Ibid., pp. 183–4.

42 J.M.G. Le Clézio, 'Antonin Artaud: Le Rêve mexicain', *Europe: Revue littéraire mensuelle*, 667–8 (1984), p. 115.

43 Odette and Alain Virmaux, *Artaud vivant* (Paris, 1980), pp. 150–51.

44 Maeder, *Antonin Artaud*, p. 185.

45 Artaud, *OC*, vol. IX (Paris, 1979), pp. 40, 49.

46 Ibid., pp. 35–6.

47 Ibid., pp. 79–80.

48 Ibid., pp. 17–19.

49 Ibid., p. 68.

50 Ibid., pp. 91, 31.

51 Ibid.

52 Ibid., p. 42.

53 Ibid., p. 27.

54 Ibid., p. 81.

55 Ibid., p. 91.

56 Ibid., p. 49.

57 Ibid., p. 102.

58 Ibid., p. 30.

59 Mèredieu, *C'était*, p. 577.

7 262 602

1 Cécile Schrammer, *Souvenirs familiers sur Antonin Artaud* (Paris, 1980).
2 Antonin Artaud, *Oeuvres complètes* (hereafter *OC*), vol. VII (Paris, 1982), p. 155.
3 Ibid., pp. 160–61.
4 Ibid., pp. 161–2.
5 Ibid., pp. 166–8.
6 Thomas Maeder, *Antonin Artaud* (Paris, 1978), p. 195.
7 Ibid.
8 Artaud, *OC*, vol. VII (Paris, 1980), pp. 433–4.
9 Ibid., p. 173.
10 Ibid., pp. 175–7.
11 Ibid., p. 178.
12 Ibid., pp. 117–44.
13 Kimberly Jannarone, *Artaud and his Doubles* (Ann Arbor, MI, 2010).
14 Florence de Mèredieu, *C'était Antonin Artaud* (Paris, 2006), p. 600.
15 Artaud, *OC*, vol. VIII, p. 424. According to Dr Gaston Ferdière, who had already commenced electroshock therapy on Artaud in Rodez at the time of the inscription to Hitler, this was further evidence of Artaud's delirium. Gaston Ferdière, 'J'ai soigné Antonin Artaud,' *Le Tour de feu*, 63–4 (1959), pp. 31–2.
16 Artaud, *OC*, vol. VIII, p. 190.
17 Maeder, *Antonin Artaud*, pp. 197–8.
18 Mèredieu, *C'était*, pp. 607–8.
19 Artaud, *OC*, vol. VII, p. 202.
20 Ibid., p. 219.
21 Mèredieu, *C'était*, pp. 615–23.
22 Artaud, *OC*, vol. VII, pp. 226–7.
23 Artaud, *OC*, vol. V (Paris, 1979), p. 171.
24 Artaud, *OC*, vol. VII, p. 203.
25 Ibid., p. 209.
26 Maeder, *Antonin Artaud*, pp. 204–5.
27 Artaud, *OC*, vol. XI (Paris, 1974), p. 62.
28 Mèredieu, *C'était*, pp. 637–40.
29 Artaud, *OC*, vol. XI, pp. 62–3.
30 The law remained nearly intact until it was modified in 1990.
31 Maeder, *Antonin Artaud*, p. 309.
32 Mèredieu, *C'était*, p. 643.
33 Maeder, *Antonin Artaud*, p. 216.

34 Mèredieu, *C'était*, p. 667.
35 Ibid., p. 668.
36 Artaud, *oc*, vol. XI, pp. 211–12, 234, 245.
37 Mèredieu, *C'était*, p. 663.
38 Maeder, *Antonin Artaud*, p. 217.
39 Artaud, *oc*, vol. XIII (Paris, 1974), p. 16.
40 André Roumieux, *Artaud et l'asile 1* (Paris, 1996), p. 59.
41 Diagnosed with 'paranoid dementia' and with persecution complex,
    Claudel was transferred out of Ville-Évrard upon its evacuation at the
    start of the First World War and spent her remaining 29 years at an
    asylum in the Vaucluse, around 100 km (62 miles) north of Marseille.
42 Cited in Roumieux, *Artaud*, p. 68.
43 Maeder, *Antonin Artaud*, p. 221.
44 Mèredieu, *C'était*, pp. 677–9.
45 Maeder, *Antonin Artaud*, p. 223.
46 Antonin Artaud, *Lettres à Génica Athanasiou* (Paris, 1959), p. 307.
47 Quoted in Roumieux, *Artaud*, p. 73.
48 Quoted in Maeder, *Antonin Artaud*, pp. 225–6.
49 Max Lafont, *L'Extermination douce* (Latresne, 2000).
50 Quoted ibid., p. 39.
51 Ibid., p. 41.
52 Roumieux, *Artaud*, p. 69.
53 Mèredieu, *C'était*, pp. 730–33.
54 Antonin Artaud, *Nouveaux écrits de Rodez* (Paris, 1977), p. 28.
55 Konstantin Mochulsky, *Dostoevsky: His Life and Work*, trans. Michael A.
    Minihan (Princeton, NJ, 1971), p. 37.
56 Mèredieu, *C'était*, p. 740.
57 Maeder, *Antonin Artaud*, pp. 226–8.
58 Roumieux, *Artaud*, pp. 80–82.
59 Ibid., p. 121.
60 Ferdière, 'J'ai soigné', pp. 28–37.
61 Maeder, *Antonin Artaud*, pp. 230–31.
62 Roumieux, *Artaud*, p. 123.
63 Artaud, *Nouveaux écrits*, p. 44.
64 Ibid., p. 28.
65 Ibid., p. 45.
66 Ibid., p. 28.
67 Sylvère Lotringer, *Fous d'Artaud* (Paris, 2003), p. 136.
68 Artaud, *oc*, vol. X (Paris, 1974), p. 43.
69 Lotringer, *Fous*, p. 219.

70 Artaud, *oc*, vol. xi, p. 134.

71 Artaud, *Nouveaux écrits*, p. 73.

72 Artaud, *oc*, vol. x, p. 92.

73 Lotringer, *Fous*, pp. 213–14.

74 Ferdière claims that Paule Thévenin, Artaud's confidante, authored the preponderance of the writings from Rodez, acting, essentially, as Artaud's 'double'; see ibid., p. 215.

75 Anne Tomiche, 'Glossolalies: Du sacré au poétique', *Revue de littérature comparé*, cccv/1 (2003).

76 Antonin Artaud, *oc*, vol. xiv** (Paris, 1978), p. 148.

77 Antonin Artaud, *Oeuvres* (Paris, 2004), p. 1467.

78 For Kabbalah see ibid., p. 1513; Artaud, *oc*, vol. viii, p. 131.

79 Évelyne Grossman, 'Préfacée', *50 Dessins pour assassiner la magie* (Paris, 2004), p. 6.

80 Artaud, *oc*, vol. xxi (Paris, 1985), p. 266.

81 Artaud, *Oeuvres*, p. 962.

82 Artaud, *oc*, vol. x, p. 247.

83 Artaud, *Oeuvres*, p. 247.

84 Artaud, *oc*, vol. ix (Paris, 1979), p. 51.

85 Gérard Durozoi, *Artaud: L'Aliénation et la folie*. (Paris, 1972), p. 186.

86 Artaud, *oc*, vol. ix, pp. 181–2.

87 Artaud, *oc*, vol. x, p. 197.

88 Maeder, *Antonin Artaud*, pp. 250–56.

89 Roumieux, *Artaud*, p. 150.

90 Ibid., pp. 150–53.

91 Marie-Ange Malausséna, 'Notes bio-bibliographiques', *La Tour de feu*, 63–4 (1959), p. 82.

8 Restoration

1 The nursing home no longer exists, having been replaced some years ago by an extension of Ivry-sur-Seine's town hall and its additional car park.

2 André Roumieux, *Artaud et l'asile* (Paris, 1996), vol. i, p. 150.

3 Florence de Mèredieu, *C'était Antonin Artaud* (Paris, 2006), p. 888.

4 Ibid. p. 887.

5 Jacques Prevel, *En compagnie d'Antonin Artaud* (Paris, 1994), p. 58.

6 Thomas Maeder, *Antonin Artaud* (Paris, 1978), p. 267.

7 Legally required to register with the Prefecture of Police, the

Committee had failed to do so until 10 June 1947. During Artaud's lifetime, this was not a problem; however, conflict – on a variety of fronts – between the Committee and Artaud's family resulted in the latter claiming control over the funds after Artaud's death.

8 Maeder, *Antonin Artaud*, p. 275.

9 Ibid., p. 265.

10 *Antonin Artaud: Un Poète à Ivry, 1946–1948*, exh. cat., Parc Maurice Thorez, Ivry-sur-Seine (2008), p. 35.

11 Antonin Artaud, *Oeuvres complètes* (hereafter *OC*), vol. xv (Paris, 1981), pp. 162–3

12 Maeder, *Antonin Artaud*, p. 263.

13 Typical is the entry for 22 October 1946: 'Then the eternal question of laudanum. I promise tomorrow and I accept 100F. What was the alternative.' See Prevel, *En compagnie*, p. 110.

14 Ibid., p. 162.

15 Antonin Artaud, *Cahiers d'Ivry: Février 1947–Mars 1948, cahiers 233–309* (Paris, 2011), vol. I, p. 1115.

16 Artaud, *Artaud: Oeuvres* (Paris, 2004), p. 1311.

17 Ana Corbin remains a mystery; while Artaud referred to her as one of his *filles de coeur* there is no other mention of her, and it's likely that she was a fabrication.

18 The *chouans* was the name of a group of peasants in the west of France who rebelled against the revolutionary authorities during the French Revolution.

19 Artaud, *Artaud Oeuvres,* p. 1293.

20 Prevel, *En compagnie*, p. 154.

21 Artaud, *Oeuvres*, p. 1322.

22 Ibid., p. 1427.

23 Ibid., p. 1431.

24 F. de Mèredieu, *C'était, Antonin Artaud* (Paris, 2006), p. 872.

25 René (Colette Thomas), *Le Testament de la fille morte* (Paris, 1954), p. 51.

26 Artaud, *Oeuvres*, p. 1160.

27 Ibid., p. 1329.

28 Ibid., p. 1417.

29 Ibid., pp. 1418–19.

30 Naomi Greene, *Antonin Artaud: Poet Without Words* (New York, 1970), p. 160.

31 Kimberly Jannarone, *Artaud and his Doubles* (Ann Arbor, MI, 2010).

32 Artaud, *OC*, vol. XII (Paris, 1989), p. 13.

33 Artaud, *OC*, vol. XIII (Paris, 1974), p. 104.

34 Maeder, *Antonin Artaud*, pp. 280–81.

35 Mèredieu, *C'était*, p. 952.

36 Paul Denis, 'D'une folie l'autre', in *Van Gogh/Artaud: Le Suicidé de la société*, exh. cat., Musée d'Orsay, Paris (2014), p. 41.

37 Artaud, *oc*, vol. XIII, p. 32.

38 Ibid., pp. 14–15.

39 Ibid., p. 16.

40 Ibid., p. 17.

41 Ibid., p. 20.

42 Ibid., p. 30.

43 Artaud, *Oeuvres*, pp. 1623–5.

44 Artaud, *oc*, vol. XIII, p. 20.

45 Ibid., pp. 31–2.

46 Paule Thévenin, 'The Search for a Lost World', in Jacques Derrida and Paule Thévenin, *The Secret Art of Antonin Artaud* (Cambridge, MA, 1998), pp. 3–4.

47 Artaud, *oc*, vol. II (Paris, 1961), p. 203.

48 Artaud, *oc*, vol. XI (Paris, 1974), p. 20.

49 Thévenin, 'The Search', p. 6.

50 Artaud, *Oeuvres*, pp. 1534–5.

51 Thévenin, 'The Search', p. 31.

52 Ibid., p. 37.

53 Ibid., p. 38.

54 *Mômo* could refer to any number of things. In the parlance of Marseille, a *mômo* is a simpleton. However, *mômo* could also be a variation on *môme* (kid or brat), or perhaps it's a play on *momie* (mummy); for *barbaque* Artaud, *oc*, vol. XII, p. 29; for stimulation see Artaud, *Oeuvres*, p. 1487.

55 Ibid., pp. 1383–4.

56 Artaud, *oc*, vol. XII, p. 52.

57 Ibid., pp. 78, 92.

58 Artaud, *Oeuvres*, p. 1577.

59 Maeder, *Antonin Artaud*, p. 279.

60 Prevel, *En compagnie*, pp. 132–4.

61 Artaud, *Oeuvres*, p. 1198.

62 Ibid., p. 1190.

63 Ibid., p. 1192.

64 Ibid., p. 1191.

65 Ibid., p. 1193.

66 Ibid., p. 1204.

67 Mark Polizzotti, *Revolution of the Mind* (New York, 1997), p. 543.

68 Artaud, *Oeuvres*, p. 1208.

69 Ibid., p. 1227.

70 Ibid., p. 1229.

71 Ibid., pp. 1639–41.

72 Ibid., p. 1649.

73 Ibid., p. 1653.

74 Artaud would later write a letter to Laval (the priest) acknowledging Laval's defence of his right to individual expression, but excoriating him for celebrating mass 'which for me has the value of a veritable curse'. Ibid., p. 1674.

75 Maeder, pp. 283–5.

76 Ibid., p. 1665.

77 Ibid., pp. 1671–2.

78 Dr Ferdière would deny that Artaud had cancer, claiming that an X-ray taken in Rodez in 1943 had not revealed any trace of cancer and further asserting that opiate addiction can produce obstructions, which, on X-rays, can be mistaken for cancer. However, as Maeder noted, between the X-rays taken in Rodez and the ones in Paris, five years had passed, ample time for the cancer to develop.

79 Maeder, *Antonin Artaud*, pp. 287–9.

80 Odette and Alain Virmaux, *Artaud vivant* (Paris, 1980), pp. 82–3.

81 Florence de Mèredieu, *L'Affaire Artaud: Journal ethnographique* (Paris, 2009), p. 41.

82 According to Artaud's sister, Marie-Ange Malausséna, the family was not notified of his death until nine hours later. Marie-Ange Malausséna, 'Affaire Antonin Artaud: Ce qu'il faut savoir', *La Tour de feu ou la santé des poètes*, 63–4 (Paris, 1961), p. 38.

83 Olivier Penot-Lacassagne, '"La Juste place . . ."', in *Artaud en revues* (Lausanne, 2005), p. 195.

84 Penot-Lacassagne, '"La Juste"', p. 196.

85 This anecdote was personally related to me by Serge and Simone Malausséna.

Epilogue: Posterity

1 Michel Foucault, *History of Madness* (London, 2009), pp. 27, 541–2.

2 Sylvère Lotringer, 'Artaud juif', *Antonin Artaud: Figures et portraits vertigineux* (Ville Saint-Laurent, QC, 1995), pp. 173–89.

3   Margit Rowell and Sylvère Lotringer, 'A Conversation with Nancy
    Spero', in *Antonin Artaud: Works on Paper*, exh. cat., Museum of
    Modern Art, New York (1996), p. 137.

4   Lucy Bradnock, 'Lost in Translation? Nancy Spero/Antonin Artaud/
    Jacques Derrida', *Papers of Surrealism*, 3 (2005), p. 12.

5   Christopher Innes, *Avant-garde Theatre, 1892–1992* (New York, 1993),
    p. 61.

6   Arnold Aronson, *American Avant-garde Theatre: A History* (London,
    2000), p. 56.

7   Jerzy Grotowski, 'He Wasn't Entirely Himself ', in *Antonin Artaud:
    A Critical Reader*, ed. Edward Scheer (London, 2004), p. 63.

8   Grotowski, 'He Wasn't', pp. 59–60.

9   Peter Brook, *The Empty Space* (New York, 1996), p. 49.

10 Brook, *Empty*, p. 53.

11 Ibid., p. 54.

12 Innes, *Avant-garde*, pp. 125–6.

13 Ibid., p. 130.

14 Anne Beggs, 'Revisiting *Marat/Sade*: Philosophy in the Asylum,
    Asylum in the Theatre', *Modern Drama*, LVI/1 (2013), p. 62.

15 Allen Thiher, 'Fernando Arrabal and the New Theater of Obsession',
    Modern Drama, XIII/2 (1970), p. 174.

16 Aronson, *American Avant-garde Theatre*, p. 197.

17 Bruce Baird, *Hijikata Tatsumi and Butoh: Dancing in a Pool of Gray Grits*
    (New York, 2012), pp. 124–35.

18 'Interview with Alejandro Jodorowsky', in *Electric Sheep: A Deviant View
    of Cinema* (16 April 2007), www.electricsheepmagazine.co.uk.

19 Roger Sabin, ed., *Punk Rock: So What? The Cultural Legacy of Punk*
    (London, 1999), pp. 3–4; for a contrasting perspective, see Fabien Hein,
    Do-it-yourself: Auto-détermination et culture punk (Congé-sur-Orne,
    2012), p. 37.

20 Alain Clerc and Olivier Penot-Lacassagne, 'Artaud dans la presse
    alternative: L'Exemple des fanzines rock', in *Artaud en revues*, ed.
    Olivier Penot-Lacassagne (Lausanne, 2005), p. 177.

21 Daniel Kane, 'Richard Hell, Genesis: Grasp, and the Blank Generation:
    From Poetry to Punk in New York's Lower East Side', *Contemporary
    Literature*, LII/2 (2011), p. 341.

22 Ibid.

23 Margit Rowell, 'A Conversation with Patti Smith', in *Antonin Artaud:
    Works on Paper*, exh.cat., Museum of Modern Art, New York (1996),
    p. 141.

24 Ibid., p. 143.
25 Clerc and Penot-Lacassagne, 'Artaud dans la presse', pp. 187–8.
26 Antonin Artaud, *Artaud: Oeuvres* (Paris, 2004), p. 1663.

Select Bibliography

Many of Artaud's principal works appear in stand-alone volumes (for example, *The Theatre and its Double*, New York, 1958). The following are collections of his works.

Editions in French

50 Dessins pour assassiner la magie (Paris, 2004)
Antonin Artaud: Oeuvres complètes (Paris, 1956–94)
    Gallimard has published the authoritative annotated collection of Antonin Artaud's works, 28 volumes in all; the 26th volume (two of the numbers are divided in two parts) appeared in 1994. As exhaustive as this collection might appear to be – particularly after examining several nearly incomprehensible volumes devoted to his writings in Rodez – a complete reading of Artaud's works will require one to consult the following:
Antonin Artaud: Cahiers d'Ivry, 2 vols (Paris, 2011)
    These two volumes contain all of the poems, random thoughts and drawings Artaud recorded in more than 400 school notebooks from his period in Ivry-sur-Seine.
Artaud: Nouveaux écrits de Rodez (Paris, 1977)
    Letters written while Artaud was in Rodez, primarily to Dr Gaston Ferdière.
Artaud: Oeuvres (Paris, 2004)
    Under the editorship of Artaud-scholar Évelyne Grossman, Gallimard put out a single-volume of Artaud's writings; many of the works in this volume can be found in the *Oeuvres complètes*. However, this work also contains some pieces not found in the former, including many letters and other writings from later in his life.

Lettres à Génica Athanasiou (Paris, 1969)
    An epistolary chronicle of the relationship between Artaud and
    Athanasiou.
Lettres d'Antonin Artaud à Jean-Louis Barrault (Paris, 1952)

Translations (into English) of Artaud's works

Antonin Artaud: Collected Works, 4 vols, trans. Victor Corti (London,
    1968–74)
*Antonin Artaud: Selected Writings: Edited, and with an Introduction, by Susan
    Sontag,* trans. Helen Weaver (Berkeley, CA, 1976)
Artaud Anthology, ed. Jack Hirschman (San Francisco, CA, 1965)
Artaud on Theatre, ed. Claude Schumacher and Brian Singleton
    (London, 1989)
Watchfiends and Rack Screams: Works from the Final Period by Antonin Artaud,
    ed. and trans. Clayton Eshleman and Bernard Bador (Boston, MA, 1995)

Museum Catalogues

Antonin Artaud: Works on Paper, Museum of Modern Art (New York, 1996)
Fau, G., *Antonin Artaud*, Bibliothèque nationale de France (Paris, 2006)
Antonin Artaud: Un Poète à Ivry, 1946–1948, exh. cat. Parc Maurice Thorez,
    Ivry-sur-Seine (2008), p. 35.
Van Gogh/Artaud: La Suicidé de la société, Musée d'Orsay (Paris, 2014)

Recollections of Artaud (in French)

Lotringer, S., *Fous d'Artaud* (Paris, 2003)
La Tour de feu: Antonin Artaud ou la santé des poètes, 63–4 (1959)
La Tour de feu: De la contradiction au sommet ou pour en finir avec Artaud, 69
    (April 1961)
Prevel, J., *En compagnie d'Antonin Artaud* (Paris, 1974)
Schrammer, C., *Souvenirs familiers sur Antonin Artaud* (Paris, 1980)
Virmaux, A. and O., *Antonin Artaud: Qui êtes-vous?* (Lyon, 1986)
—, *Artaud vivant* (Paris, 1980)

Recollections of Artaud (in English)

Barrault, J.-L., *The Memoirs of Jean-Louis Barrault: Memories for Tomorrow* (New York, 1974)
—, *Reflections on the Theatre* (London, 1951)
Nin, A., *The Diary of Anaïs Nin*, 7 vols (New York, 1966–80)

Studies on Artaud (French)

Borie, M., *Antonin Artaud: Le Théâtre et le retour aux sources* (Paris, 1989)
Dumoulié, C., *Antonin Artaud* (Paris, 1996)
—, *Nietzsche et Artaud: Pour une éthique de la cruauté* (Paris, 1992)
Durozoi, G., *Artaud: L'Alienation et la folie* (Paris, 1972)
Europe: Revue littéraire mensuelle: Antonin Artaud, LXII/667–8 (November–December 1984)
Galibert, T., *Antonin Artaud, écrivain du Sud* (Aix-en-Provence, 2002)
Grossman, É., *Artaud, 'L'Aliéné authentique'* (Tours, 2003)
—, *Antonin Artaud: Un Insurgé du corps* (Paris, 2006)
Harel, S., *Antonin Artaud: Portraits et figures vertigineux* (Montreal, 1995)
Maeder, T., *Antonin Artaud* (Paris, 1978)
Margel, S., *Aliénation: Antonin Artaud: Les Généalogies hybrides* (Paris, 2008)
Mèredieu, F. de, *C'était Antonin Artaud* (Paris, 2006)
—, *L'Affaire Artaud: Journal ethnographique* (Paris, 2009)
Neyrat, F., *Instructions pour une prise d'armes: Artaud et l'envoûtement occidental* (Strasbourg, 2009)
Penot-Lacassagne, O., *Artaud en revues* (Lausanne, 2005)
—, *Vies et morts d'Antonin Artaud* (Saint-Cyr-sur-Loire, 2007)
de Portzamparc, R., *La Folie d'Artaud* (Paris, 2011)
Rogozinski, J., *Guérir la vie: La Passion d'Antonin Artaud* (Paris, 2011)
Roumieux, A., *Artaud et l'asile*, 2 vols (Paris, 1996)
Thévenin, P., *Antonin Artaud: Fin de l'ère chrétienne* (Paris, 2006)
Virmaux, A. and O., *Artaud: Un Bilan critique* (Paris, 1979)

Studies on Artaud (English)

Barber, S., *Antonin Artaud: Blows and Bombs* (London, 1993)
Bernel, A., *Artaud's Theatre of Cruelty* (New York, 1977)

Derrida, J., and P. Thévenin, *The Secret Art of Antonin Artaud* (Cambridge, MA, 1998)

Greene, N., *Antonin Artaud: Poet Without Words* (New York, 1970)

Hayman, R., *Artaud and After* (Oxford, 1977)

Jannarone, K., *Artaud and his Doubles* (Ann Arbor, MI, 2010)

Knapp, B. L., *Antonin Artaud: Man of Vision* (New York, 1969)

Murray, R., *Antonin Artaud: The Scum of the Soul* (Basingstoke, 2014)

Scheer, E., ed., *100 years of Cruelty: Essays on Artaud* (Sydney, 2002)

—, ed., *Antonin Artaud: A Critical Reader* (London, 2004)

Stout, J., *Antonin Artaud's Alternate Genealogies: Self-portraits and Family Romances* (Waterloo, ON, 1996)

Acknowledgements

In one way or another, Artaud has been a constant companion of mine over the past decade. Consequently, nearly everyone who knows me, in one form or another, and for better or for worse, shared in Artaud's presence. So many people deserve my gratitude, but in the interests of limiting this to those who were essential, I thank the following. The College of Liberal Arts at California State University, Long Beach, helped to defray financial expenses (for example, copyright costs) and provided me with a much-needed sabbatical to finish the manuscript. Vivian Constantinopoulos at Reaktion generously extended me both extra time and extra words. Several friends and colleagues read portions of the manuscript, and I would like to recognize Houri Berberian, Jeff Lawler, Richard Hawkins, Ali Igmen, Kyle Hamlett and Kjehl Johansen for the comments they provided. For more than a quarter of a century, Pascal Dupuy and Anne Gardiner have been two of my closest friends; in addition to their unfailing kindness and support, they also alerted me to sources that enriched the text. I feel very fortunate to have gotten to know and become friends with Serge and Simone Malausséna. They have been absolutely indispensable to the production of this book, sharing anecdotes, their extensive collection of family photos and their time. During the many phases of this book, Idéfix was a loyal and undemanding companion; I miss him. From the project's inception, my children – Andrew, Alison and Annèlise Shafer – read key parts of the text, provided insight and criticism, listened to endless stories and offered encouragement. Through the project, Annèlise took a particular interest in the Tarahumaras and, while earning her BFA in Theatre, gained an appreciation for Artaud. Andrew read the entire manuscript and brought the perspective, sagacity and insight of the theatre professional he is to several key parts. Alison and Grégory Moille graciously provided me with a place to stay in Paris, conscientiously cleared up my queries on Artaud's prose, and accompanied me on my long visits with Serge and Simone, getting to know them as well as I did. Above all, I wish to express my appreciation and love to my partner in life, Selma Selmanagić. More than anyone, Selma has experienced the ebbs and flows of this project, my frustrations and elations, my procrastinations and frenetic writing flows. Through it all, she encouraged me, gave me the needed push to finish this book, and bridged my personal ellipsis.

Photo Acknowledgements

The author and the publishers wish to express their thanks to the below sources of illustrative material and/or permission to reproduce it:

Photo © Centre Pompidou, MNAM-CCI, Dist. RMN-Grand Palais / Georges Meguerditchian / © ADAGP, Paris and DACS, London 2016: p. 169; Photo © Centre Pompidou, MNAM-CCI, Dist. RMN-Grand Palais / Georges Meguerditchian / © Eli Lotar: p. 102; Photo © Centre Pompidou, MNAM-CCI, Dist. RMN-Grand Palais / Philippe Migeat / © ADAGP, Paris and DACS, London, 2016: pp. 40, 49, 170, 173, 194, 195; Courtesy of Serge and Simone Malausséna: pp. 6, 9 left and right, 10, 15, 17, 19, 21, 22, 24, 30 (© ADAGP, Paris and DACS, London 2016), 32, 33 (© ADAGP, Paris and DACS, London, 2016), 55, 66, 68, 91 left and right, 105, 107, 122, 161, 177 (Photo Denise Colomb), 201 top and centre, 207; Photo © Ministère de la Culture – Médiathèque du Patrimoine, Dist. RMN-Grand Palais / Denise Colomb: p. 182; Photo © Ministère de la Culture – Médiathèque du Patrimoine, Dist. RMN-Grand Palais / René-Jacques / © RMN-Grand Palais – Gestion droit d'auteur: p. 193; Rex Shutterstock: pp. 86 (Everett), 121 (Roger-Viollet).